Media in Africa

A comprehensive and accessible introduction, this book examines a range of issues pertaining to theory, history and critiques of media in Africa.

Featuring contributions from global scholars, that represent both new and established voices on the African continent and the diaspora, this volume explores themes of decolonization, media freedom, media censorship, identity, representation, pluralism, media framing, political economy of the media with emphasis on ownership, market trends and transnational media operations in Africa. Contributors explore these and other topics across a variety of media tiers, types, genres and platforms. The book also features contributions from practicing journalists and media practitioners working in Africa, providing students with hands-on knowledge from the field. Chapters in this volume take an instructional approach with contributors engaging key concepts and related theories to explore the praxis of media in Africa through specific case studies.

An essential text for students of media, communication, journalism, and cultural studies who are studying media in Africa, as well as those studying global media.

Toks Dele Oyedemi is a communication and media scholar, who has taught at universities in South Africa and the United States of America. He engages critical studies of technology and digital culture, and media, culture, and identity. He is the co-editor of *Social Inequalities, Media and Communication: Theory and Roots* (2016) and *The Praxis of Social Inequalities in Media: A Global Perspective* (2016).

René A. Smith is an academic, facilitator and arts administrator. She has worked for a variety of media bodies in South Africa and as a gender and media trainer in other African countries. She has extensive academic and arts management experience, teaches and advises on media studies curricula, and is the co-editor of *Sociology: A South African Perspective*, 2nd Edition (2020).

Media in Africa

Issues and Critiques

Edited by Toks Dele Oyedemi and
René A. Smith

Routledge
Taylor & Francis Group

NEW YORK AND LONDON

Designed cover image: Bulgnn / Getty Images

First published 2024
by Routledge
605 Third Avenue, New York, NY 10158

and by Routledge
4 Park Square, Milton Park, Abingdon, Oxon, OX14 4RN

Routledge is an imprint of the Taylor & Francis Group, an informa business

Library of Congress Cataloging-in-Publication Data
Names: Oyedemi, Toks, editor. | Smith, René A,, 1976- editor.
Title: Media in Africa : issues and critiques / edited by Toks Dele Oyedemi and René A. Smith.
Description: New York, NY : Routledge, 2024. | Includes bibliographical references and index. | Identifiers: LCCN 2023037740 (print) | LCCN 2023037741 (ebook) | ISBN 9781032399256 (hardback) | ISBN 9781032392394 (paperback) | ISBN 9781003352907 (ebook)
Subjects: LCSH: Mass media--Africa. | Mass media--Social aspects--Africa.
Classification: LCC P92.A35 M434 2024 (print) | LCC P92.A35 (ebook) | DDC 302.23096--dc23/eng/20230815
LC record available at https://lccn.loc.gov/2023037740
LC ebook record available at https://lccn.loc.gov/2023037741

ISBN: 978-1-032-39925-6 (hbk)
ISBN: 978-1-032-39239-4 (pbk)
ISBN: 978-1-003-35290-7 (ebk)

DOI: 10.4324/9781003352907

Typeset in Sabon
by SPi Technologies India Pvt Ltd (Straive)

Contents

Contributors

Khadijat Adedeji-Olona lectures at the Department of Broadcasting, Faculty of Communication and Media Studies, Lagos State University, Nigeria. She is a qualitative data analyst, and certified professional trainer in ATLAS.ti and MAXQDA. Her research interest covers a range of interdisciplinary studies, including film, gender, media and cultural studies. Her latest publication "Dry: A Filmmaker's Perspective on Addressing Violence against Women and Girls", is published in Quarterly Review of Film and Video, https://doi.org/10.1080/10509208.2023.2254671.

Kealeboga Aiseng holds a PhD in African Languages and Linguistics from the University of the Witwatersrand. He is a journalism and media studies lecturer at Rhodes University, Makhanda. Aiseng's research interests are sociolinguistics, language policy, African popular culture, new media, and film studies. He has published articles in local and international journals. He also serves on numerous journal editorial boards.

Lee Artz (Ph. D., University of Iowa), a former machinist and union steelworker, is Professor of Media Studies and Director of the Center for Global Studies at Purdue University Northwest. Artz has published twelve books, including *Global Media Dialogues: Industry, Politics, and Culture* (2023), *Spectacle and Diversity: Transnational Media and Global* Culture (2022), and *The Pink Tide: Media Access and Political Power in Latin America* (2017). He has contributed dozens of book chapters and journal articles on global media, US popular culture, media practices, and social movements. He speaks regularly on social media, contemporary politics, and global popular culture.

Tendai Chari is an Associate Professor and a National Research Foundation (NRF) C3 Rated Researcher in the Department of English, Media Studies and Linguistics at the University of Venda, South Africa. He holds a PhD in Media Studies from Wits University. He has authored and co-authored more than 70 publications in the form of articles in internationally acclaimed peer reviewed journals, chapters in books and five co-edited books. His latest co-edited books are *Global Pandemics and Media Ethics; Issues and Perspectives* (Routledge, 2022) *Communication Rights in Africa: Emerging Issues and Perspectives* (Routledge 2023), and *Military, Politics and Democratisation in Southern Africa: The Quest for Political Transition* (Springer Nature, 2023).

Shitemi Khamadi is a Kenyan media development practitioner with over 13 years' experience. He has designed, implemented and evaluated projects in Kenya and Eastern Africa. His research interests are in information disorder, political communication, audiences, climate change reporting and refugees and migration. Shitemi holds two Masters Degrees, one in Digital Journalism from the Aga Khan University Graduate School of Media and Communication (GSMC), Nairobi and another in Peace and Conflict Management from Kenyatta University. His undergraduate Degree is in International Relations from the United States International University (USIU).

Tammy Rae Matthews is an assistant professor of digital and sports journalism at St. Bonaventure University's Jandoli School of Communication. She earned a Doctoral degree in media research and practice from the University of Colorado Boulder, a Masters in journalism and media communication from Colorado State University and a Bachelors in journalism from the University of Missouri-Columbia. Her nearly 20 years in major-market media included serving as special sections editor for the *Chicago Sun-Times*. Matthews researches global sport experiences, storytelling, language, oral histories, social media and journalism. Her dissertation explored LGBTIQ+ narratives in Namibian sport.

Rofhiwa Felicia Mukhudwana is an academic in the Department of Communication Sciences, at the University of South Africa (Unisa). Her areas of interest are international, political, and government communication and international relations. She holds a PhD in Communication Management. Rofhiwa is a reader of decolonial literature, blackness, neocolonial and neoliberal literature in understanding the coloniality of the global structure and global capitalism that is unequal and unjust. She is concerned with how the Anthropocene world is unfolding with issues of ecological injustice, energy injustice, the coloniality of the virocene and inequality of AI.

Sara Namusoga-Kaale is currently a lecturer in the Department of Journalism and Communication at Makerere University. Her work focusses on print and digital/multimedia journalism. Dr Namusoga-Kaale is currently researching multimedia storytelling for archiving COVID-19 experiences in Uganda, under the archives, memory and method from the Global South project. She is also exploring multimedia production and use for online teaching and learning.

George Nyabuga is an Associate Professor of media and journalism and Associate Dean at The Aga Khan University's Graduate School of Media and Communications. He taught at the University of Nairobi for more than 13 years before joining Aga Khan. Prof. Nyabuga has also taught journalism, and media and cultural studies at the University of Worcester, and international media and communication, and comparative politics at Coventry University both in the United Kingdom. He worked as a journalist and newspaper editor before joining academia.

Tokunbo Ojo is an Associate Professor in the Department of Communication & Media Studies, York University, Toronto, Canada. His teaching and research interests are in global media studies, development communication, journalism studies, African media studies, geopolitics of international communication and political communication. His current research projects include news media sustainability, political economy of African media industries, international news flows, Black Press in Canada, ICT4D, and China-Africa relations.

Lai Oso (1955–2023) was a Professor of Media and Communication at Lagos State University, Nigeria. He was the inaugural president of the Association of Communication Scholars & Professionals of Nigeria (ACSPN). He played significant roles in the development of media and communication education, research, and practice in the West African country. He was a notable scholar, an astute leader, an inspiring mentor, and a compassionate teacher. He served as consultant for national and multinational organisations and published in both local and international journals in the areas of political communication, journalism, public relations and development communication.

Ganiyat Tijani-Adenle lectures journalism at Lagos State University, Nigeria. She obtained her Ph.D. in Media, Gender and Communication from De Montfort University, Leicester, United Kingdom. She practiced as a news editor at Voice of Nigeria before joining the academia. Her research sits at an intersection of media, communication, and sociology. Her most recent publication is "Women FM (W.FM): The women-focused radio station amplifying the voices of Nigerian women" in Lindgren, M. and Loviglio, J. (eds), *The Routledge Companion to Radio and Podcast Studies* (2022).

Siyasanga Tyali is an NRF rated (2023–2028) Professor and Director: School of Arts at University of South Africa (UNISA). He previously served as Chair of Department (CoD) at the Department of Communication Science, UNISA. He holds a PhD from the University of the Witwatersrand, a Masters Degree (Media and Cultural Studies) from the University of KwaZulu- Natal and is a past recipient of the Ford Foundation International Fellow (2011/12). His past associations include the University of Fort Hare, University of KwaZulu- Natal, Rhodes University, the University of the Witwatersrand and Johns Hopkins University. His research interests are in media and cultural studies, broadcasting, African media systems, Black subject representation, political communication, health communication and the cultural archive.

1 Introduction

Media in Africa: Key issues

Toks Dele Oyedemi

The media are fundamental to the transformation, development, socio-cultural and economic contestations in Africa. To understand Africa, one needs a critical appraisal of the media as institutional, economic and cultural domains that shape and influence African identity, representations and being. This ontological situatedness of Africa with the media reinforces the critical role of the media in the historiography and cultural sculpting of Africa. From the colonial origin to current global digital order with its economic base, the media have become a dominant sphere of economic, social and political activities in Africa, and play essential roles in deepening democratic principles. There are some critical themes that need to be recentered in the scholarly analysis of the media in Africa today. Amongst many themes, we need to refocus on African media historiography, engage current debates about decolonization of the media in practice and scholarship, theorize the media in Africa, examine media in Africa within the global media sphere, assert media freedom in democracy, evaluate the digital turn in media, and critique the structure of media ownership within the current fragmented tiers of media structure. All these are essential because they shape how culture, identity, representation, participation, nationalism, diversity, and other socio-economic descriptors impact what it means to be African through the lens of its media.

African media historiography

To understand the nature of media in Africa, it is necessary to situate the current dispensation within the historical, cultural, political and economic trajectories that cumulatively color the character of African media systems today. The colonial origin of modern media in Africa is critical to the study of African media systems (Bourgault, 1995; Mano, 2010; Brennan, 2013). This colonial origin does not only shape the development of the media in Africa, but it also helps in configuring the nature of media practice and the academic studies of communication and the media. The first newspaper in

DOI: 10.4324/9781003352907-1

Africa was published in 1773 in Mauritius by the French, there is an account of a newspaper published in Egypt in 1797, the first English newspaper on the continent was published in Cape Town, South Africa in 1800, followed immediately by a publication in 1801 in Freetown, Sierra Leone. These earliest newspapers in Africa were controlled and published by colonial and settler Europeans concerned with colonial governance. Christian missionaries were also instrumental to the establishment of the press in Africa. For instance, *Iwe Irohin*, the first newspaper in Nigeria and considered to be the first indigenous language newspaper in Western Africa, was published in the Yoruba language in 1859 by the Church Missionary Society under the direction of the Anglican missionary Henry Townsend.

An analysis of the early press reveals the colonial control and religious ideology that shaped the media as an institution and platform of information for Africans. Their control and ideology would influence modern understandings of the role of media in Africa. The colonial beginning of African media is not limited to newspapers, it includes other forms of print and broadcasting. *The West Africa* was an early magazine published as part of the British empire building. It was published in 1917 in London with contributions from British colonial officials. The introduction of broadcasting also closely followed the colonial and empire administrative systems (Mano, 2010). The first radio broadcast was in South Africa in the 1920s developing to other regions of Africa by late 1920s and early 1930s. The British founded the Empire Service with the goal of broadcasting to the colonies. Nwulu et al. (2010) observe that when the first television station started in Africa, in Western Nigeria, the Western Nigeria government turned to British Overseas Re-diffusion Limited. This British company did not only provide the technical expertise needed for the new station, they equally controlled the news and programming divisions.

Arguments can be made, and probably sustained, that this colonial origin of African modern media is understandable considering the political imperialist and colonialist landscape of Africa at the time. Also, that these colonial beginnings brought technical skills and equipment to Africa for the establishment of nascent African media institutions. Underlying this history is how these beginnings shape the ideology of media in Africa, that permeates the structure, production, format, content and general system of media operations. Historical beginnings are not value-neutral, they instill traits that become entrenched in cultural practices. Let's take, for example, the British encouragement of local participation in media in the colonies in the form of local language publications and broadcasting as part of its colonial policy of indirect rule. On the other hand, the French operated a different model in its colonies. The French philosophy of colonization was assimilation, where French territories in Africa were considered as extensions of France. While the British encouraged publications and broadcasting in African languages to reach a broad audience, nearly all broadcasts in French colonies were in the French language. In line with the French direct rule colonial approach, radio broadcasting was centralized, French in orientation and delivery, with most content initially originating in France (Mano, 2010; Mytton n.d.).

The consequences of these different colonial approaches can be seen in the character of media today in English and French speaking Africa. Capitant and Frère (2011) argue there are two broad African media landscapes: the Anglophone Africa media landscape is characterized by the powerful media groups owning several titles, radio and television stations; however, media organizations in Francophone Africa have often remained single-owner corporations, relatively weakly structured and tend to use only one medium. They observed, further, that media content regulation also differs, Francophone legal system is interventionist, while Anglophone laws often leave content regulation to professional codes of ethics and media associations in the form of press councils and self-regulating monitoring bodies (see also Duplat, 2002). Also, the nature of state interventions in the media differs. While the state is relatively absent from the media sector in Anglophone Africa, apart from the public funding of media, the state intervenes on multiple levels in the organization of the sector in Francophone Africa (Capitant & Frère, 2011). The scholarship of media studies is also different with English-speaking Africa having a longer-established tradition than French-speaking Africa. Linking this to the colonial heritage, Capitant and Frère (2011, p. 8) argue:

> While at the end of the nineteenth century British colonies such as Nigeria and Kenya already had a "native" press that was dynamic, diverse, and sometimes even impertinent towards the colonial powers, the press in the French colonies at the same time, which was privately run by a few colonists, was barely uttering its first words. It was only in the 1950s, after the reforms brought about by the new constitution of the Fourth Republic in 1946 granted political, trade union, and press freedoms to the inhabitants of French colonies, that the private press was able to develop freely in these areas, while it still remained embryonic in territories dominated by the Belgians.

The resilience of the colonial origin of the media in Africa is seen in how the sector is structured, how the news is written, and in the professionalization of the media players that reflect two different African media landscapes as a legacy of the British and French colonial model of the media (Capitant & Frère, 2011).

African media historiography also becomes essential in understanding the historical trajectories of power and control of the media, which is insightful to current analysis of the political economy of the media in Africa. Take, for instance, that Cecil Rhodes bought the controlling interests in *Cape Argus*, one of the notable newspapers of the Cape Colony era of 1800s, and grew it into a major newspaper chain spreading from the Cape to current day Zimbabwe and Zambia (Mano, 2010). The Argus Group later bought up the Bantu Press, with its successful titles that were read by Black South Africans and removed all the Africans employed in the management of the press (BBC World Service, n.d.). This economic act had political undertones of channeling indigenous African political views about politics, whilst suppressing the growth of opposition press in southern and central Africa (Mano, 2010). The activist press of Africa today cannot be fully understood without the historical context of anti-colonial media during colonial Africa.

Critical scholarship of media in Africa thus requires engagement with how the historical trajectories of all forms of African media over the centuries intersect with political and cultural principles that shape current media practices in Africa.

Decolonizing the media

Another key theme relevant to the current study of African media is the resurgence of decolonization discourse, specifically as it relates to the practice and scholarship of media in Africa. Considering the colonial historiography of media in Africa, we should then ask "what are the legacies of these histories in the current nature, practice and structure of African media today?" This is a crucial question that requires that we examine the practice and scholarship of communication and media studies broadly in Africa today. There is increasing interest and push for a decolonized academe and the scholarship of communication and media studies (Waisbord & Mellado, 2014; Oyedemi, 2018, Chakravartty et al., 2018; Mohammed, 2021). The call for a decolonized communication and media studies is based on criticisms of the dominant elitist Western epistemological tradition asserting universal validity, neglecting indigenous and localized philosophical traditions from non-Western settings (Glück, 2018).

Chasi and Rodny-Gumede (2016) request that we rethink the scholarship of communication studies (including media studies), which remains mired in paradigmatic approaches that enshrine the Euro-American norm as the standard upon which communication theories are founded. Many educational systems in Africa, where scholarship of communication, journalism and media studies are offered, tend to reproduce Eurocentric curriculum that centers Euro-American ideologies in knowledge production, distribution, consumption and reproduction, which subsequently leads to internalization of these ideologies in Africa. How then do African communication scholars, and those marginalized in other regions and communities in the global South with interest in communication and media studies, conduct research and produce knowledge when histories and epistemologies severely privilege Western ideas (Chasi & Rodny-Gumede, 2016)?

Mugari (2021) argues a decolonized curriculum is supposed to reduce inequalities in knowledge production, and a decolonized study of media and journalism should decenter the curriculum from the hegemonic Western models. This would imply a shift from privileging Euro-normativity as a prism in the scholarship of the media. It will require questioning the academic infrastructure that elevates a "monologic canonization and universalization of Western perceptive on media and communication" (p. 3). Oyedemi (2018) argues for a *polycentric epistemic culture*, noting that a "decolonizing epistemic tradition takes a polycentric approach, where histories, innovations, myths, cultures, science and knowledge production from diverse cultures form academic scholarship within the dominance of local histories and realities" (p. 10). To decolonize media studies in Africa requires a re-examination of all we have taught and have been taught about media studies in the Global South that are racist, and have ascribed Euro-American dominance and white supremacy (Mohammed, 2012). It involves subverting racial inequalities and colonial legacies that permeate scholarly publications, citations and editorial positions (Chakravartty, et al., 2018). The task for African media scholars is to examine the texts use in classes, evaluate content of media curriculum, question theoretical assumptions, develop new theories, employ diversity of citations and reevaluate all aspects of research and teaching of media in Africa in a way that brings Africa to the center.

Decolonizing the media in Africa should go beyond the scholarship of communication and media, it must include assessing the practices in media institutions and industry. This will require a critical reexamination of the content of the media, and how the histories of African media and its colonial legacies shape current practice and structure of the media. It also involves questioning how the ownership structure of African media is configured – not only about foreign control and ownership pattern of African media, but equally to subvert the dominant capitalistic nature of the media industry.

Theorizing media in Africa

A critique of the current epistemologies of media studies in Africa is the Euro-American dominance of the conceptual and philosophical anchors of the discipline in Africa. Wasserman (2014, P. 781) asks, "does African media theory exist? What does it look like?". Wasserman, as an African media scholar, asking these questions provides not only a challenge for African media scholars, but a vital pondering of the need for the theorization of the media in Africa. For too long, students, researchers and instructors of media in Africa tend to mostly rely on functionalist or critical media theories from the global North in addressing local media problems in Africa. Mugari's (2021) study of doctoral theses in selected South African universities attests to this critique. The study shows there is a preference for media theories that have attained canonical status and dominance in the discipline, with doctoral theses referencing academic sources from journals edited by academics based in North America and Europe. Mugari (2021) then concludes that the knowledge that drives much of scholarship of media studies at South African universities is firmly Eurocentric. This then attests to the critique that the production of knowledge about the media has been crafted to scholarly internalization that philosophical thoughts about the media as developed in the North are dominant with universal validity (Wasserman, 2014).

Beyond geographical thinking about media theorization, there are changes in the media landscape that force us to rethink "established" theories about media. As Fourie (2014, p. 144) notes, "the media have become so big, so varied, so omnipresent that they can no longer be described meaningfully or comprehensively in terms of old theories and philosophies". Much of the media/mass communication theories grew out of specific era of Western industrialization, and communication scholars should think beyond many of these old theories of the media. If one accepts the charge that few African scholars in media studies theorize from within the continent, and that few scholars also ground their work in indigenous African epistemologies (Mohammed, 2021), then the task for students, instructors and media scholars in Africa is the need for productive theorizing of African media.

The critiques of conceptual, theoretical and philosophical anchors in the study of media in Africa are by now obvious: The theorization of communication and media studies in Africa tends to normalize the Euro-American scholarships as the standard in the development of media scholarship in Africa; that within Africa the knowledge of established Western theoretical canon of media studies by African scholars tend to be flaunted as an arrogant display of knowledge in the field; and the emerging theorizations from Africa (and the global South) are not only ignored in Euro-American media scholarship, but also within Africa. African scholars of the media need to embark on theory development based on local realities and cultures, where local academics can draw from indigenous realities toward epistemic theory development (Oyedemi, 2018). African scholars should question theoretically how the expansion and fragmentation of the media, emboldened by rapid digital innovations and artificial intelligence, are reshaping life and culture in Africa. Because the cultural is also economic and political, new theorization of the media in Africa should explore this intersection within local specificities, and because media practice in Africa is within different context of circumstances than those obtain in the global North, a mere importation of Euro-American theorical frameworks would be inappropriate (Wasserman, 2014).

Africa and the global media

Whilst local realities are important, the global is also relevant. The scholarship of media in Africa should engage the global nature of media today and the place of Africa. Innovations and developments in the media have led to a point where local media have become global. Media distribution is no longer hindered by space or time, and hence consumption of media content has increasingly become global. Scholarly inquiries about media in Africa need to question what this means for Africa, African media content creators, African media audience and the implications on the cultural and political landscapes in Africa. Historical analyses of global media and Africa have often explored the core-periphery structure of global media, where content from the core (Euro-America media) flood the media sphere of the periphery (the global South). Discourses about global media are often situated within broader frames of globalizations and internationalization. But critiques of globalization have repeatedly highlighted the skewed and unequal locations of power in the global order – where the more powerful states exploit the power inequality to their political and economic advantages, often to the disadvantage of the less powerful states. The pattern is also replicated in the cultural realms, where Euro-American cultural purveyors, through the media, often exploit cultural content from Africa in creating global blockbuster media content. The exploitation of African history, motifs, culture, wildlife, music and many cultural artifacts in global marketing of media stories have accrued immense economic profit for American movie studios, such as Disney.

Critiques of the imperialist nature of global media led to the charge of cultural imperialism that has dominated the scholarly critiques of global media for decades. The cultural hegemony of Euro-American media on the global media landscape is often critiqued as part of the configuration of globalization. Globalization and cultural hegemony are linked as a result of the Western dominance of the cultural, political and economic systems, supported by the hegemony of Western capitalism in the propagation of its cultural narratives globally. As a result, the mass media are essential tools in establishing an attractive Euro-American global leadership (Eko, 2003). Euro-American media have a dominant presence in Africa. In the news sector, there are CNN, BBC, Voice of America and many others. In fact, these media also provide platforms for Africans to communicate with each other in African languages (note examples of BBC News Pidgin, BBC Hausa, BBC Yoruba). These international media also have visible presence on the sport and entertainment sectors.

The cultural hegemony and cultural imperialism critiques of Western media presence in Africa is only one part of the analysis of Africa and the global media. On the other hand, while Western media have propagated Eurocentrism, through attractive and alluring images of European and American cultures, Africa and Africans experience symbolic annihilation in Western media. Stories about Africa and Africans are mostly absent on U.S. television, when present, Americans see negative representations of Africa than positive ones (Oyedemi, 2023). American TV has done African representation outright harm with narratives that present the African jungle, wildlife, and a natural state image that contrasts an Africa of Black servility and White sensuality. As Steeves (2008) also observes, African representation in the U.S. media reveals an erasure, but also the absence of Africans as creators and voices of their representation. Western media reproduce the colonial tropes of Africa as a "dark continent", accentuated with images and iconography of chaos, poverty, diseases, economic and political instability. These negative narratives and iconography are amplified with images of a starving child with a swollen belly and a displaced, forlorn mother in need of aid and assistance. Many Americans and those in the broader Western world and beyond, who have never visited Africa, may find it hard to believe that any good ever happens in Africa (Cupples & Glynn, 2013; Oyedemi, 2023).

Developments in global media now point to a positive prospect for African media as a result of the *Digital Turn* that is disrupting traditional media systems. The increasing access to the Internet and smartphones, and the impressive creativities of young Africans are leading to growth in African media content creation for global audiences. Africa's entertainment and media industry is showing a global presence that is attracting interest in African media. South Africa, Nigeria and Kenya seem to be currently leading this revolution. South Africa enjoys a relatively stable and established creative media industry, exemplified by its film, television and music industries. South Africa's Multichoice has been a very popular platform for digital television broadcasts in Africa, and the introduction of its streaming video on demand service, Showmax, reflects a growing transnational media platform in Africa. Nigeria, with its large population and tech-savvy youth, is "Africa's entertainment powerhouse, dominating in music, film, fashion and even visual arts" Mitchell (2023, p. 40). As a result, the global media industry is paying attention to the emerging media culture in Africa. There are now content creation deals and collaborations between African film makers, TV producers, global studios and the international streaming platforms. Netflix, Disney and other global media corporations are providing platforms for African producers to showcase their works, not only to the growing African audiences on these platforms, but to a global audience. Contrary to the erasure of African narratives on global traditional media networks, the streaming platforms, such as Netflix are carrying contents of African origin on their subscription domains.

At this nascent stage, the bulk of international investments in Africa content is largely in three countries: Nigeria, South Africa and Kenya. Netflix and other studios are crafting their investments in African media as a corrective act against how Hollywood has long portrayed Africa. Although while this may be relatively correct, there are business motivations for the interest in Africa. As subscription rates in North America and other regions may be stagnating, Africa is seen as an untapped market that should be explored (Roxborough, 2022). Other digital media and social media platforms, such as YouTube, Facebook, and Instagram, have also been instrumental in proving global visibility for African media content.

There are still many challenges. As the historiography of African media shows, the pattern of Western nations providing conduits for African media and communication that started during colonial era seems to persist, even in the digital era. Many African content creators, TV producers and film makers utilize platforms provided by foreign media corporations, which is largely dominated by American corporations. Aside from the dominance of American subscription video platforms, the global media platform for African digital content are predominantly American. In fact, the dominant platforms of social interactions and communications amongst Africans are largely American – YouTube, Facebook, WhatsApp, Netflix, Amazon, Instagram, Google, and Twitter dominate media and social interaction platforms in Africa. Increasingly, Chinese corporations are entering the African communication space, Chinese cellphone manufacturer, Transsion Holdings, is the largest smartphone vendor in Africa (Statista, 2023). Chinese corporations are investing in telecommunication infrastructure and venturing into partnerships with African media corporations. Another challenge in this era of digital turn is the current limited connectivity to the Internet in Africa. Although there has been rapid growth, Internet penetration in Africa, at 43.2% of the population, is still the lowest in the world. All these critical developments should inform our analysis of Africa and the global media.

Media freedom, plurality and democracy in Africa

Relevant to the study of media in Africa is the issue of media freedom, as the media play important roles in the functioning of democratic principles in society. The tenets of human rights, accountability, transparency and freedom of expression are important for achieving a responsible and just society that African states aspire. The concept of accountability is essential for governance; as Callamard (2010) notes, accountability relates to responsibility, duties and obligation. It reflects how a government is answerable to the people and how state power is applied in the democratic process of governance in order to uphold human rights of the citizens. As such, government officials are accountable to the people of a country to abide by the law and constitution, and to implement policies in the public interest. The democratic process is structured in a way to hold the state and public officials accountable through elections, local and international laws, and the tiers of government – such as the legislative/parliamentary structure and the judiciary. State accountability also requires a free and vibrant media that can freely and without fear, report, question, and denounce actions of the state and officials with public power (Callamard, 2010).

This process of monitoring accountability allows for the realization of transparency in governance. Transparency provides opportunity for public awareness of administrative and state decision-making process, it relates to the "right to know" and "public access to information" with the goal of keeping the state accountable whilst creating an atmosphere of public confidence in state apparatus. This can be achieved through the protection of freedom of expression as a basic human right (guaranteed in Article 19 of the Universal Declaration on Human Rights, and in state constitutional declarations). As Callamard (2010, p. 1215) notes:

> Freedom of expression, including the right to access and receive information, is a fundamental right, central to achieving all human rights, individual freedoms, and meaningful electoral democracies. It not only increases a society's knowledge and provides a sound basis for participation within a society but it can also secure checks on state accountability and thus help to prevent the corruption that thrives on secrecy and closed political environments.

Media freedom is central to freedom of expression, state accountability, transparency and the protection of human rights of the citizens. In Africa, there has been substantial growth in media plurality, many independent and community media outlets have come up and citizens have access to variety of media platforms. The liberalization of the airwaves has allowed private radio ownership, the independence of the press is increasing appreciated, which energizes the vibrancy of press freedom and democratic processes in Africa. The public are participating more in the media, especially on radio, voicing opinions and concerns about the state. The African Commission on Human and Peoples' Rights (the African Commission) adopted the Declaration of Principles of Freedom of Expression and Access to Information in Africa in 2019 in Banjul, Gambia. This Declaration affirms the principles of freedom of expression and access to information, which guarantees the right to receive information as well as the right to express and disseminate information.

Irrespective of the improvements in advancing media freedom in Africa, many challenges persist. Journalists complain about state high-handedness towards the media and the clamping down on media freedom in some African countries, especially during elections. Bafana (2022) writes about the conditions of journalists in Zimbabwe, how they often face criminal charges and are persecuted for exposing corruption and human rights abuses. Although the freedom of expression and the media is enshrined constitutionally, journalists have been arbitrarily arrested, jailed and entangled in court cases for doing their jobs. Serite (2018) writes from a personal experience to decry the condition of press freedom in Botswana. Claiming that journalists were being gagged and arrested, newspapers and radio stations were starved of government advertising revenue as punishment. In fact, Serite claims that Botswana in 2018 was a country where government-owned radio, television and newspaper are censored and did not have editorial independence. Plaut (2018) acknowledges the vibrancy of the media in South Africa, noting that the country enjoys a relatively free media with excellent and independent newspapers, but equally warns of what seems to be a gradual erosion of media freedom that mirrored the gradual loss of support for the governing party. He draws on editorial decision at the South African Broadcasting Corporation (SABC), the public broadcaster, for 'sunshine news' where news stories broadcast should be mostly positive with less focus on negative news and a ban on reporting violent civil protests. There are also instances of Internet shutdown in few African countries, especially during key political events, such as elections and protest actions.

It is essential that scholarly inquiries into media in Africa should spotlight the state of media freedom in Africa. Irrespective of achievements made about media plurality and freedom in Africa, many challenges abound. The mission is to defend the space in which independent media can freely operate, develop stronger constitutional and legal safeguards for the media, and to strengthen standards of media professionalism in Africa (Karikari, 2004).

Media in Africa: Issues and critiques

In the collection of essays in this volume, contributors explore various thematic concerns that are pertinent to the broad issues discussed above, but are equally situated within key areas of media studies. The eclectic contributions in this volume draw on specific cases foregrounded by relevant conceptual and theoretical frames to explore issues around decoloniality, transnationalism and market trends; media freedom, democratic participation and African media culture; and identity, representation and media in Africa.

Toks Dele Oyedemi opens the volume by offering a critical conceptual analysis of the imperialist nature of Western digital technology corporations in Africa. Drawing on postcolonialism and the understanding of coloniality as an on-going process of economic and cultural domination, Oyedemi examines the place of Africa in global digital capitalism. Supported by empirical evidences of data from the digital market structure and analysis of global communication corporations in Africa, he proposes a model of digital coloniality in Africa and recommends a decolonial thinking about technology in Africa. Lee Artz engages with transnationalism by addressing the media relations between diverse Nigerian video producers and the transnational media company, Naspers, which operates Africa Magic and other MultiChoice streaming sites across Africa. By unpacking critical theoretical concepts, such as capitalism, colonialism, cultural imperialism and transnationalism, Lee Artz explores the growth, cultural context and neoliberal transnationalism of Nollywood, the Nigeria film industry, and situates the operations of Napsers, a South African transnational media corporation within this analysis. The chapter explores how this South African TNMC relies on multiple transnational partners in Nigeria to co-produce profitable content distributed across the continent. The chapter ends with an argument for citizen media, different from the dominant commercial ideology that currently prevails. This sort of community centered media with direct citizen access to production would greatly improve human creativity and allow collective cooperation as a means not just for media and entertainment, but as a pathway to more democratic and culturally-diverse societies in Africa.

Tokunbo Ojo takes a political economic approach by examining the market structure of telecommunications industries. This chapter provides a case study analysis of Nigerian mobile wireless sector to illustrate the current ownership and market trends in the African telecommunication industries. Kealeboga Aiseng contributes to the debates on decolonization by examining how journalism education can be decolonized in South Africa from a sociolinguistic perspective. Aiseng reviews course descriptions of journalism curricula at three universities in South Africa and suggests possible ways to decolonize the curricula from sociolinguistics perspectives.

The section on media freedom, democratic participation and African media culture opens with Tendai Chari's examination of how some governments in Africa have resorted to Internet shutdowns of different guises to counter online free expression, citing different reasons for their actions. Using digital rights as a conceptual lens, and based on literature review, this chapter illuminates triggers of Internet shutdowns in Africa and the justifications provided by governments for implementing Internet shut-downs. The chapter locates access to the Internet within the broader realm of communication rights, whereby any disruptions or manipulation of the Internet is viewed as a violation of human rights. George Nyabuga and Shitemi Khamadi take a look at media censorship in East Africa during elections. They note that in the past decade, the three East African countries of Kenya, Tanzania and Uganda have had elections during which there have been serious concerns about media censorship and suppression. Media houses operated under constant fear of closure or censure and journalists were constantly harassed, detained or arrested. They argue in their chapter that political intolerance and clampdown on media freedom have affected the capacity of media to provide information and space vital to open and participatory political and democratic processes. The chapter further contends that media censorship during elections is a threat not only to media freedom but also freedom of expression, and democracy.

Siyasanga Tyali explores African media culture by examining what it means to have an African public sphere. He asserts that if we are to understand media platform within the discourse of decoloniality, their history as well as their current roles need to be understood and linked to the role of media institutions and communities of media content reception. This chapter fulfils this role by addressing the characteristics of an African community radio broadcaster in relation to its role of functioning as an African public sphere that is rooted in the discursive identities of an African community. Drawing on the case study of Vukani Community Radio (VCR) in South Africa as a micro or regional African public sphere platform, Tyali advances the discourse on African public sphere in relation to the African media culture. Khadijat Adedeji-Olona, Ganiyat Tijani-Adenle and Lai Oso explore the African media culture through a historical overview of the growth and development of the Nigerian film industry, with particular reference to the Southern extraction (Nollywood). Reflecting on the development of Nollywood, through six distinct evolutionary phases, this chapter discusses the challenges of filmmaking in each of the phases and the significant contributions of each era to the overall growth of the industry in the West African country.

The theme of identity and representation is also explored by contributors in this volume. Rofhiwa Felicia Mukhudwana tackles the politicizing of immigration in South Africa. Noting that immigration has taken center stage in election campaigning by various political parties. The adage that "South Africa belongs to all who live in it" has come into a challenge from civil movement groups, who have put the issue of immigration on the table suggesting that for South Africa to recover economically and socially, immigration must be managed. Mukhudwana argues that South Africa is caught between the decolonial turn of solidarity with the global South and facing the socio-economic challenges of open globalization. As much as the media is responsible for the representation and framing of the immigration issue, this role also falls on the prerogatives of politicians as rhetorical stakeholders in the political and public discourse that affect migration policy and its enactment. This chapter looks at the politicizing of immigration by two political parties in South Africa (The Economic Freedom Fighters and ActionSA).

Sara Namusoga-Kaale's chapter discusses how the Ugandan press frame the Ugandan national identity around the issue of homosexuality. Drawing on content analysis of two Ugandan newspapers' framing of homosexuality from 2007–2011, the chapter demonstrates that the two newspapers framed homosexuality as a cultural/religious issue and as a national issue. It emerged that this framing constructed Ugandan national identity as one that does not include being homosexual. This volume ends with contribution from Tammy Rae Matthews, who examines how African media present and discuss intersex athletes, noting that sport media could help formulate attitudes or judgments about intersex athletes. The chapter builds on the case of the summer Olympics Tokyo 2020, held in 2021 due to COVID-19, where World Athletics disqualified two Namibian track and field runners – Christine Mboma and Beatrice Masilingi – due to naturally high testosterone levels and banned them from running in the 400-meter to 1,600-meter races. Mathews explores how their story created a gateway for the media to deliberate about intersex athletes. Through engagement with themes that explore theories, critiques and the media industry in Africa, the chapters in this volume showcase some of the current issues and critiques in African media today.

References

Abuya, K. (2023). TECNO, Infinix and Itel remain unbeaten in Africa's market share. *Techcabal*, https://techcabal.com/2023/05/24/transsion-remains-unbeaten-in-africa/

Bafana, B. (2022). Muzzling the media in Zimbabwe. *New Internationalist*, 540, 48–50.

BBC Worldservice (n.d.) *The story of Africa*. www.bbc.co.uk/worldservice/specials/1624_story_of_africa/page16.shtml

Bourgault, L. M. (1995). *Mass Media in Sub-Saharan Africa*. Bloomington, Indiana: Indiana University Press.

Brennan, J. (2013). Communication and media in African history. In J. Parker & R. Reid (eds), *Oxford Handbook of Modern History*, pp. 492–510, https://doi.org/10.1093/oxfordhb/9780199572472.013.0026

Callamard, A. (2010). Accountability, transparency, and freedom of expression in Africa. *Social Research* 77(4), 1211–1240.

Capitant, S., & Frère, M. (2011). Africa media landscapes. *Afrique Contemporaine*, 240(4), 25–41. Translated from French by JPD Systems.

Chakravartty, P., Kuo, R., Grubb, V., & Mcllwain, C. (2018). #Communication So White. *Journal of Communication*, 68(2), 254–266.

Chasi, C., & Rodny-Gumede, Y. (2016). Smash-and-grab, truth and dare. *The International Communication Gazette*, 78(7), 694–700.

Cupples, J., & Glynn, K. (2013). Postdevelopment television? Cultural citizenship and the mediation of Africa in contemporary TV drama. *Annals of the Association of American Geographers*, 103(4), 1003–1021.

Duplat, D. (2002). *Liberté de la presse, responsabilité des médias: L'Afrique sur la voie de l'autorégulation*. Paris: GRET.

Eko, L. (2003). Globalization and the mass media in Africa. In L. Artz and Y. R. Kamalipour (eds), *The Globalization of Corporate Media Hegemony*. SUNY Press

Fourie, P. J. (2014). "New" paradigms, "new" theory and four priorities for South African mass communication and media research. *Critical Arts: South-North Cultural and Media Studies*, 24(2), 173–191.

Glück, A. (2018). De-Westernization and Decolonization in Media Studies. In *Oxford Research Encyclopedia of Communication*, https://doi.org/10.1093/acrefore/9780190228613.013.898

Internet World Stats (2023). World Internet usage and population statistics 2023 year estimates. www.internetworldstats.com/stats.htm

Karikari, K. (2004). Press freedom in Africa: Challenges and opportunities. *New Economy*, 184–186.

Mano, W. (2010). Africa: Media systems. In W. Donsbach (ed.), *The International Encyclopedia of Communication* (1st edn, pp. 1–8). John Wiley & Sons.

Mitchell, C. (2023, March). Africa's entertainment and media industry is at a crossroads. *African Business*, March 23, 40–43.

Mohammed, W. F. (2021). Decolonizing African media studies. *Howard Journal of Communications*, 32(2), 123–138.

Mugari, Z. E. (2021). The decolonial turn: Reference lists in PhD theses as markers of theoretical shift/stasis in media and journalism studies at selected South African universities. *London Review of Education*, 19(1), 1–16.

Mytton, G. (n.d.). *A brief history of radio broadcasting in Africa*. www.transculturalwriting.com/radiophonics/contents/usr/downloads/radiophonics/A_Brief_History.pdf

Nwulu, N., Adekanbi, A., Oranugo, T., & Adewale, Y. (2010). Television broadcasting in Africa: Pioneering milestones. *Second Region 8 IEEE Conference on the History of Communications*, Madrid, Spain, 2010, pp. 1–6, doi:10.1109/HISTELCON.2010.5735315

Oyedemi, T. (2018). (De)coloniality and South African academe, *Critical Studies in Education*, doi:10.1080/17508487.2018.1481123

Oyedemi, T. (2023). From symbolic obscurity to cultural visibility? African immigrants on U.S. television and the ambivalence of Nigerians on American sitcom. *International Journal of Communication*, 17, https://ijoc.org/index.php/ijoc/article/view/20500

Plaut, M. (2018). Media freedom in South Africa. *The Round Table*, 107(2), 151–162.

Roxborough, S. (2022, January 12). Why streamers are (finally) investing in Africa. *The Hollywood Reporter*, January 12, 2022, 48–49.

Serite, S. (2018). Challenges to media freedoms: Government channels and information flows in Botswana. *The Round Table*, 107(2), 225–227.

Statista (2023). Africa smartphone unit shipments' share from fourth quarter 2018 to fourth quarter 2022, by vendor. www.statista.com/statistics/1104732/africa-smartphone-shipments-share-by-quarter/

Steeves, L. (2008). Commodifying Africa on U.S. network reality television. *Communication, Culture & Critique*, 1(4), 416–446. doi:10.1111/j.1753-9137.2008.00033.x

Waisbord, S., & Mellado, C. (2014). De-westernizing communication studies: A reassessment. *Communication Theory*, 24, 361–372.

Wasserman, H. (2014). Media ethics theories in Africa. In R.S. Fortner & Fackler, P. M. (eds), *The Handbook of Media and Mass Communication Theory*. John Wiley & Sons.

Part I

Decoloniality, Transnationalism and Market Trends

2 Africa and Digital Coloniality

Toks Dele Oyedemi

Neoliberalism thrives in the workings of capitalism and the market structure of communication. Aided by globalization, free-market capitalism and global trade treaties, liberalization of the telecommunications sector has been touted as a market ideology that has transformed the global communication and technology market by opening up local markets to international capital. Attracting Foreign Direct Investment (FDI), job creation, expanding competition in the telecom sector and increasing public access to communication services are often touted as benefits of communications liberalization (Verikios & Zhang, 2004; ICC, 2007). Beyond this exaltation of neoliberal free-market regimes in communication, scholarly analysis of global communications calls for both an industry-market review and a critical analysis of the operations of global communications corporations.

A critical approach to global communications draws on the political economy of communication critique to reveal the imbalances in communication market structures. It questions ownership patterns, market operations of communication corporations, reveals concentrations of market power and the inequality in the market structure of communication industry. For the communication sector in many developing regions of the world, liberalization and international trade operations also reveal an imperialist pattern of control by technology conglomerates. This imperialist nature of global media corporations in the communication environment inspires a postcolonial turn in the theorization of global media.

Historically, works such as *Mass Communication and the American Empire* (1969) and *Communication and Cultural Domination* (1976) by Herbert Schiller have provided seminal critical analyses of the cultural impact of American broadcast media and telecommunications on the cultural sculpturing of both national and individual identities in the developing world. The emergence of a *Network Society* (Manuel Castells) spurred by the Internet and digital technology revolution has expanded the global, imperialist nature of American communications. Facebook, Google, YouTube, Twitter, WhatsApp and many other American-owned social

DOI: 10.4324/9781003352907-3

media platforms are the dominant media of today's digital society. Along-side the accelerated speed of technological innovations and increasing reliance on the Internet as dominant conduit for human communication is the realization that about half of the world's population are unconnected, mostly in the developing regions of the global South, such as Africa.

Africa is an attractive market for future technology. With a population of about 1.4 billion, it offers huge market potential for technology corporations. The African population is projected to grow exceptionally in the next decade, it is estimated that, by 2030, Africans will represent one-fifth of the world population (Geiger & Bamba, 2021). Africa is projected to account for more than half of global population growth, with the population of sub-Saharan Africa doubling between now and 2050. Africa has a large youth population and the youngest population in the world with 70% of sub-Saharan Africans under the age of 30 (United Nations, 2022). Although there is increasing access to digital technologies, there are challenges and limitations. Internet usage penetration is less than 50% of the African population (Internet World Stats, 2023), and there are challenges with access to broadband connection and digital tools. This creates opportunities for Western technology corporations to explore this market and the potential of the enormous growth of the African population. As the emerging growth in the potentials of Africa's digital economy has inspired keen interests of Western corporations to explore the continent, it has brought a critique of empire building, colonial thinking about the technology corporations' interests in Africa, and Africa's place in the current era of digital revolution.

Africa in the history of Western capitalism

Africa in the history of capitalism has always been a supplier of resources – human and mineral – that fueled innovations in global commerce. But while Africa as a market may be taking an interesting turn in the digital mobile phone industry, this has not changed the place of Africa as supplier of raw materials for global capitalist innovations. Africa as a supplier of natural resources for capitalist innovations in the current epoch of digital communication has a historical precedence dating back to colonial exploitation that fueled many innovations in the West. Take the case of innovations in automobile manufacturing in the 1920s and the desire for rubber in that process. During this period Americans owned 85% of the world's automobile and consumed 75% of the world's rubber, most of the USA's consumption of rubber, about 80%, went into manufacturing of automobile tires (Mitman & Erickson, 2010). However, the US only grew 1% of the world's rubber production, while Britain with its colonial and imperial network controlled about 77% of the world's rubber production largely due to the production in the colonies. The American Firestone Company started operating a rubber plantation in the West African country of Liberia in 1926, which by 1955 accounted for 70% of Liberia's total export revenues (ibid.).

The demand for African rubber brought about one of the genocidal occurrences in Africa. The menace of Belgian King Leopold II in the late 19th century Congo still remains one of the world's worst atrocities and a painful colonial history of capitalism and empire in Africa. When the worldwide demand for rubber boomed, Leopold exploited the Congo for this resource in an extremely violent manner. Villagers were set quotas of rubber to produce and armed police forces would collect the quotas. Villages that failed to meet the quota suffered immensely with hostages taken, villages looted and burnt, people being enslaved, many were killed, and women raped. To ensure that the armed police force didn't waste their bullets hunting for food, they were forced to produce the severed hands of the victims. The death toll of this period was put around 10 million of Congo's population, almost half of its population then (Hochschild, 1998; Stanley, 2012). The mining of natural resources of gold, diamond, copper, colton, bauxite, platinum and many others fueled colonial capitalist exploitation, and today Africa remains a huge mineral producer for global industries. The innovations in human communication with the technological revolution in information and communication have placed Africa prominently in this globalized capitalist structure. Africa has emerged as the next frontier to be colonized for its market potential and this requires a coloniality critique of Africa's place in global digital capitalism.

Digital coloniality, global communications and Africa

Understanding coloniality as an on-going process of economic and cultural domination provides a critical explication of digital capitalism. Coloniality describes how the relationship between the Western world and others continues to be of colonial domination, often shaped by capitalism and culture (Quijano, 2007). Engaging coloniality from the realm of culture has always been critical to the location and allocation of power. Culture as a tool of domination is emboldened by capital on one hand and by technology on the other, and communication, as an innate aspect of culture, has always been essential to colonial practices. Just as the innovations in telegraphy, telecommunications and broadcasting have been essential to colonialism and empire building, the Information Communication Technology (ICT) revolution, exemplified by the Internet and digital technologies, has become an essential backbone of a current form of coloniality – digital coloniality. Digital coloniality describes the imperial nature of technology corporations and marks a turn where the neoliberal free trade economic rationale of globalization aided the spatial expansion of technology corporations in the sourcing of raw materials, manufacturing and marketing of communication products and services. Digital coloniality is evident in three ways, through the pattern of exploitation, the colonization of communication spaces and in the spatial expansion of communication corporations.

Pattern of exploitation

A core aspect of the current digital revolution is in the pattern of exploitation exemplified in the mining of both natural and human resources from outside the home bases of the technology corporations. This involves the extraction of raw materials in the Global South, the exploitation of human labor in manufacturing of digital products and recently the mining of human's behavioral traces as data that are aggregated and commodified for capital, with a potential for political surveillance and control. Critical articulation of digital post-colonialism by Jandrić and Kuzmanić (2015) directs analysis towards geographical thinking in arguing that contemporary society has created digital worlds from two main components: the material spaces of the Internet and the non-material spaces of the World Wide Web. This thinking about physical space in relation to the virtual digital space raises the question about the dialectics of the digital, where the virtual has physical materiality. The virtual ethereal space is not possible without the materiality of wires, devices and raw mineral resources. Appropriating this geographical thinking to digital coloniality then draws attention to spaces where the physical raw materials of the digital world are mined.

Africa, Democratic Republic of Congo (DRC) specifically, remains a major source of materials for the manufacturing of technological devices. This has reenacted the geographic thinking about space and empire in this digital age. Just as the rubber from colonial Congo was necessary for automobile innovations, cobalt from the Democratic Republic of Congo has become essential for car batteries in new innovation in electric automobile. But broadly, Congo bears the brunt of innovations spurred by the ICT revolution. Tantalum, which is a heat resistance derivative of colton (columbite-tantalite), is a rare metal component that is essential in many modern electronic devices, such as mobile phones, tablets, laptops, DVD machine, iPod etc. In fact, it is argued that "nothing in our world today can survive without tantalum" (Sharife, 2008). About 80% of the world's Colton reserves are estimated to be in Africa, with 80% of this in the DRC (Grespin, 2010). It is unquestionable that the minerals of the Congo are essential to the digital revolution. Note also the global need for Cobalt, a mineral that is very important to the rechargeable lithium-ion batteries that power most of our modern technologies like smartphones and laptops made by companies such as Apple and Samsung. The importance of lithium-ion batteries to our technology and digital lives is best described by the awareness that

> smartphones would not fit in pocket without them. Laptops would not fit on laps. Electric vehicles would be impractical. In many ways, the current Silicon Valley gold rush – from mobile devices to driverless cars – is built on the power of lithium-ion batteries.
>
> (Frankel, Chavez & Ribas, 2016, p. 11)

Yet about 60% of the world cobalt originates in Congo.

Congo's mineral riches continue to play critical role in global technological innovations. It's been argued that the DRC was potentially the richest country in the world as far back as 2010, with its untapped mineral treasure estimated at $24 trillion, which arguably was then equivalent to the GDP of Europe and the United States combined, eclipsing the $18 trillion total value of Saudi Arabia's oil reserve in 2010 (Noury, 2010). But this wealth has brought immense pain and destruction to the Congo. Just as the innovation in automobile manufacturing drew attention to rubber in Congo in the late 19th century resulting in death of millions of people, the mining of Colton has brought death, pain, misery and under-development, and it has fueled and financed civil war (Braeckman, 2004). Cases of child and inappropriate labor practices have been reported, the mining exposes local communities to levels of toxic metals that are linked to sicknesses relating to breathing problems and birth defects (Frankel, Chavez & Ribas, 2016). The abundance of Colton has brought multinational corporations and unscrupulous capitalists to the mines of Congo. With the socio-economic challenges faced by the locals, artisanal mining with crude utensil becomes the source of livelihood for many people, old and young, living in mining areas in order to stave off poverty. Inhumane conditions and bad labor practices have been recorded as some of the experiences of workers in mining companies in the Congo (Stone, 2022). But colonial thinking about digital technology and empire is not only in the sourcing of materials to manufacture digital devices, but also the labor that create the devices. Many of today's technological and digital devices are manufactured by cheap Asian labor in spaces like China, where labor cost is cheaper than manufacturing in the home country of the technology companies. Take the case of Apple, the largest technology company in the world (Ponciano, 2021), that outsources the manufacturing of his products to companies in Asia, such as Pegatron and Foxconn. To meet global demand for technology products workers in these manufacturing outlets work long hours, Foxconn, for example, has increased working hours on its workers to meet Apple's global demands for its products, which led to increased pressures on workers for overtime, resulting in weeks of 60–70 hours of work (Pun, et al., 2016). During high demands, Foxconn and Pegatron have turned also to student interns (Wang, 2020). The working conditions have led to many attempted suicides and suicides among workers. In 2010, 18 young rural migrant workers, between 17 and 25 years of age, attempted suicide at Foxconn facilities in China, resulting in 14 deaths; four survived with crippling injuries (Pun, et al., 2016). The colonial pattern becomes manifest in this global network of technology production: the raw materials and human labor for the manufacturing of digital technologies are provided outside of the Northern home sites of the technology corporations. The Western digital virtuality has real life physical materiality of exploitation in the Global South.

Colonization of communication spaces

Another approach to understanding digital coloniality is studying the trend in the *colonization of communication spaces*. This reveals a pattern where technology corporations colonize communication infrastructure and platforms in many nations, leading to a situation where the communication spaces of nations are dominated by foreign (global) technology and communication corporations. Handful of American-owned digital technology corporations control the communication spaces in many countries of the Global South. Take for instance that Meta owns the dominant platforms for digital communication in Africa and India through Facebook and WhatsApp. WhatsApp has become the most popular messaging application in Africa (Dahir, 2018). Google (Alphabet Inc.), through its search, mail, video platform (YouTube), and its browsing and operating systems (Chrome and Android) controls a huge chunk of the world's digital communication spaces.

They not only control communication spaces, they are providing the conduit for communication. Take the attempts at the provision of Internet access by Meta through Facebook's Free Basics and Alphabet's Google Station in India, Mexico, Indonesia, Philippines, Thailand and Nigeria. Free Basics is an app that gives free access to small selected websites and services, usually without multimedia content. Working with local telecom operators to provide access without Internet connectivity data, the idea is to provide a free taste of the Internet to those without access or who find data expensive. The hope is that people will eventually value buying Internet connectivity data to access the full array of information on the Web, and as a result few people will continue to use Free Basics as many will desire to see the full range of multi-media information available on the web, specifically on Facebook. The Google Station was a service supported by local patterners to provide free WiFi Hotspots in city centers in selected developing countries. This was Google's attempt at expanding Internet access in developing countries with large population of the unconnected to the Internet, an attempt at reaping the potential advertising revenue from the world's unconnected billions.

There is also Meta's (Facebook) investment in *2Africa Pearls* undersea cable that will connect Africa, Middle East, Asia to Europe. Along with partners such as China Mobile International, MTN Global Connect, Orange, Telecom Egypt and Vodaphone this cable is billed, at 45,000km, to be the world's longest undersea cable. This ocean floor cable would connect the coast of Africa providing capacity that is three times the capacity of the current under ocean telecom cables currently serving Africa (Malewar, 2021). There is Google's Equiano subsea cable, which is equally aimed as a conduit for Internet connection in Africa. The cable will connect Africa to Europe, running along the west coast of the African continent with the first phase connecting Cape Town, South Africa to Portugal. There are landing points for the cable in the western Africa coast at Lomé, Togo and Lagos, Nigeria. These cables portend the potential to address the connectivity problem in Africa by connecting millions of people in Africa to the Internet. They will also contribute to further development of Africa's digital economy and contribute to job creation. The market potential of these cables, derived from connecting millions of the unconnected in Africa and the social, political and economic ramifications of Africa's Internet communication conduit provided by foreign global private corporations, shouldn't be lost in the euphoria of connectivity.

Beyond providing conduits for communication, foreign-made communication gadgets from computers to smartphones dominate the African markets. African countries import most of the cellphones used in the continent – exceptions can be noted of the efforts in Rwanda, where the first 'Made in Africa' cell phones were launched. From a factory based in Kigali, Rwanda, the Mara Group launched the first 'Made in Africa' phones to compete with imported phones in the continent. The Mara group, headquartered in Dubai, United Arab Emirates, has also extended phone manufacturing operations to South Africa. Chinese cellphone manufacturer, Transsion (with brands such as Ecno, Infinix, and Itel), is the largest smartphone vendor in Africa with market share of 48% followed by the South Korean Samsung at 20% (Statista, 2022). There are more shipment of feature phones in Africa than smartphones, the Transsion brands also dominate the African feature phone market with a 78% share followed by Nokia (8.6%) and Alcatel (2%) (IDC, 2022).

Foreign domination of the communication device space in Africa is not limited to importation of new technology devices, Africa has become a dumping ground for used electronic products from Western countries. The rapid production of digital gadgets and the alluring marketing effort to create demands imply that technological devices become obsolete quicker, and the old ones need to be discarded. In some cases, used electronic devices end up for re-use, but they mostly end as electronic waste (e-waste) for recycling in developing countries in Africa and Asia. Nigeria is a major receptacle for the developed world's unwanted electronic devices, with cargoes full of used devices arriving frequently. It was noted as far back as 2005 that an estimated 500 shipping containers of used electronic goods entered the city of Lagos, the economic hub of Nigeria, monthly. Of the estimated 8.7 million tons of e-waste created annually in the EU, about 6.6 million are not properly recycled – much of it arrives in Lagos as 'functional' equipment for the second-hand market but eventually ending in the dumps and scrapyards of Lagos (Sullivan, 2014). The dumping of e-waste has led to a booming industry in Lagos. The Lagos 'computer village', where used electronics are being refurbished and sold, is teeming with artisan entrepreneurs working in the refurbishment and sales of used digital devices.

Similar story is found in Ghana – Agbogbloshie, a commercial district, became a dumping ground of e-waste where young boys burnt the world's e-waste to extract and scavenge metal minerals from electronic devices to make a living. The harmful effect of inhaling burning chemicals from the electronic equipment is bound to have a long-time effect on the people directly and indirectly through the chemicals released into the environment (Boateng, 2011). It has been noted that toxins released by e-waste dumping and the burning of electronic equipment to extract metals have seeped into plants, soils and water around the e-waste processing areas. Metals such as cadmium, lead, mercury, and copper are thousands of times more concentrated in the open waters of Lagos' lagoons than levels found in industrial areas without e-waste disposal problems (Sullivan, 2014). Agbogbloshie in Ghana was ranked one of the world's ten worst toxic threats (Heacock et al., 2016). Irrespective of counter argument that the bulk of e-waste imports in developing nations are not waste, but working or repairable equipment, and that domestic waste contributes to electronic discards in developing countries (Lepawsky, 2015), evidence abounds that Africa is one of the world's destinations for obsolete electronic equipment (Schmidt, 2006).

The colonization of communication space spans both the vertical and horizontal integration market structure of the political economy of Africa's communication space. The whole digital/social media environment is largely an oligopolistic American technology empire. As Michael Kwet asserts forcefully, assimilation into the tech products, models and ideologies from foreign powers led by the US is the 21st century form of colonization. He notes that digital colonialism is a structural form of domination, which is exercised through the centralized ownership and control of three core pillars of the digital ecosystem: software, hardware, and network connectivity. This makes Google/Alphabet, Amazon, Facebook (Meta), Apple, Microsoft and other corporate giants the *new imperialist* today (Kwet, 2019). The imperial control over the digital world through control over software, hardware and network connectivity relates to the colonization of communication space, where platform and conduit of communication are controlled by foreign, largely US tech corporations. Equally worrying is the pattern of global surveillance capitalism that describes the extraction, storing, sorting and processing of 'big data' from behavioral patterns of the world's people. These data are eventually used to control and manipulate individuals for commercial benefits of big tech imperial corporations mostly in the US, with potential for political control and state surveillance.

Spatial expansion

Digital coloniality also materializes through *spatial expansion* of the geographical reach of technology corporations. The spatial expansion is both structural and commercial. Just as in the old colonial structure, there is always a local person to head local operations in various outposts. Hence there is a Head of Facebook Africa, a Facebook India head, Google country managers and heads of operations in other countries. The sole job of the country heads is to drive expansion strategies that relate to market and economic growth, while managing relations with the political powers in the specific country. The global reach of tech companies is not only in structural extension, the nature of the market is global with most users and audiences from outside the home base of the tech companies. As observed in 2013, "eight of the world's top 10 Internet companies by audience were based in the United States, though 81% of their online visitors were not" (Wasik, 2015, para 5).

Kwet (2019) suggests the colonial pattern can be understood through a framework that identifies economic domination (through the monopoly power of multinational corporation); imperial control (the direct power over political, economic and cultural domains of life through control of computer mediated experiences); and imperial state surveillance (in which the foreign intelligence agencies partnering with their own tech corporations conduct mass and targeted surveillance in the Global South). This framework becomes relevant considering that a few American-owned corporations control most of the world's digital functions from search engines to digital platforms for commercial transportation. In Africa and other places Uber's commission from every trip and Google's domination of local online advertising ship local revenue to international corporations. The emerging growth of Africa's digital economy has opened up the region for international tech corporations in search of new markets. Historically, Africa was not a very attractive or lucrative communications market, but the digital revolution has benefitted the continent and opened it up for foreign technology corporations. Prior to public access to the mobile telephone, the state of telephony in Africa was a gloomy story. There was a time when there were more telephones lines in Manhattan or in Tokyo than in the whole of sub-Saharan Africa. In 1991 for example, there was one telephone line per 100 people in Africa, compared to 2.3 for all developing countries, and 37.2 for industrial countries. In 1994, Africa accounted for only 2% of world's telephone lines (Castells, 2010).

This was in the era of the dominance of fixed line telephony – although the statistics of fixed line telephony have not really changed but mostly decreased in Africa, mobile telephony has allowed many Africans to talk to one another electronically. The growing penetration of the mobile phone has led to various uses of the phone for fund transfer, health-related information, education and for many other social uses. The growth in mobile phone penetration is also contributing to growth in mobile broadband Internet access, though Internet access remains low in global comparison with only about 43% of Africans connected (World Internet Statistics, 2023). For many, access to the Internet is gained primarily through the smartphone. The growth of the mobile phone penetration, mobile broadband Internet, the observation that many access the web for the first time on smartphones, and the large untapped market of the unconnected have opened up the potential of African market for cellphone corporations and other digital technology corporations to cash in on the potential of this market. Facebook (Meta), for example, launched 'Free Basics' in some African countries in order to corner the African mobile Internet market potential. Free Basics is an app that gives free access to small selected websites and services, usually without videos or photos. It is estimated that smartphone adoption could reach 64% of the African population by 2025, which increases the potential for mobile Internet connectivity (GSMA, 2021). It is then not a surprise that Facebook intends to cash in on this potential by providing 'Free Basics', which literally makes Facebook synonymous with the Internet in much of Africa. The large number of the unconnected to the Internet in Africa opens up potential market opportunity for global technology corporation to exploit this market, which may include providing conduit for connectivity.

But communication and technologies have always been essential to imperial projects. The drive towards global commercial expansion influenced the actions of companies and cartels in world communications in the mid-19th century to early 20th century. Just as commercial rationales shaped the capitalist imperialism of early global communication companies, similar patterns are noticeable in today's digital world. *Capitalism* is the driving force behind the mining of resources, colonization of communication spaces and spatial expansion that define digital coloniality. Capitalist exploitation has always been the overarching motivation for coloniality, the European colonization of other regions of the world was inspired by the commercial exploitation of resources in the colonies. Advertising revenue remains the major source of capital for many tech corporations, this consequently requires that people have to be connected to the Internet in order to harvest their personal 'Big Data' that are sold or used for advertising purposes. But how do corporations generate these big data when billions of the world's population are not connected to the Internet? The strategy is to employ *benevolent capitalism* in order to lure the unconnected in the Global South, where most of the world's unconnected reside.

Benevolent capitalism is a culture of charitable acts in the pursuit of capital. The billions of people without access to the Internet represent potential market to be captured and commodified. Since access to the Internet is hampered by a lack of technological infrastructure and ignorance about what the Internet offers in many developing nations, tech corporations provide 'free access' to the Internet in order to lure the unconnected to the digital domain. Take Facebook's 'free' connectivity with 'Free Basics' or Alphabet's attempt to provide free WiFi hotspots (Google Station), in order to attract the 'unconnected' to the Internet. These are attempts at bringing the unconnected to the marketplace for commodification of their data under the guise of free connectivity. Harnessing the data of the world's unconnected billions presents possibility for monetization of the data for potential advertising revenue. The pattern of exploitation of natural resources, colonization of communication spaces and spatial expansion are driven by capitalism. Typified by the need for global monetization of communication services and the commodification of human social behavior on digital platforms.

A decolonial thinking about technology in Africa

Challenging the colonial and imperialist nature of technology corporations requires a decolonial thinking about the critical understanding of innovations and technologies as seductive tools of coloniality. As Walter Mignolo notes, the idea of Western modernity shaped in the rhetoric about salvation, newness, progress, development, scientific rationality and innovations went hand in hand with the logic of coloniality (Mignolo, 2011). Also Anibal Quijano argues that the universalization of European culture as a form of coloniality was based on the fact that European culture was made seductive. The colonizers imposed a mystified and seductive image of their own pattern of knowledge creation, as such the European culture was made seductive: it gave access to power. After all, beyond repression, the main instrument of all power is its seduction. Cultural Europeanization was a way of participating and later to reach the same material benefits and the same power as the Europeans.

(Quijano, 2007, p. 169)

As such, understanding the seductive nature of innovations and their cultural implication is critical in having a decolonial thinking about technology. Technology and innovations embolden coloniality. But this is not new; technologies, such as guns and other European products were historically traded for slaves in Africa. Technology is seductive; hence, the provision of a free connectivity is a 'Trojan horse' masking the imperialist commercial rationale. American cultural products have always been crafted for seduction. Spectacular glitz and special effect gimmickry have always made Hollywood appealing globally, and the glamour of American TV and popular culture has seduced billions across the world. Seduction is a technology of coloniality.

To decolonize is to innovate. *Innovations as decolonization* becomes critical to decolonial thinking, Africa needs to intensify efforts in scientific, economic, cultural and technological innovations. Local solutions for connectivity should be essential, and not to solely allow foreign technology corporations to dominate and colonize the communication space in Africa. There is a need for African states to provide the necessary support for technological innovations and support private investments and local technology startups. *Innovations as decolonization* implies that Africa needs to be actively involved in a technological turn to address its recurrent social and economic challenges, and participate in scientific and technological innovations that are shaping the world in the emerging fourth industrial revolution, space explorations, transportation and the communication technology revolution. Just as the railway was essential to the industrial revolution and mass transportation to the development of cities, the Internet is the main utility of the 21st century with the 5th generation of Internet connectivity promising a revolutionary culture of connectivity. Africa must not be left behind – it has to invest in Internet connectivity. It cannot continue to be the least connected region of the world; such situation provides the opportunity for global technology corporations to exploit the African market under a guise of corporate benevolence. Just as roads connect suburbs, cities and towns, the backbone infrastructure of today's economy is the Internet. As citizens do not pay to travel on roads, a basic daily amount of free Internet data through public WiFi connection should be a goal of every nation. However, as citizens pay toll for inter-state road connection to raise funds for servicing these roads, citizens pay for expanded WiFi data after exhausting the free basic Internet data.

It is essential to break from the colonization of the African communication environment that sees a few American technology corporations controlling the communication spaces in Africa. Facebook (Meta) and Google (Alphabets Inc) largely control online social networking, mobile texting, chat platforms, online search, online video, and email services. Considering the size of the African market, its potential, and the observation that Africa has a large youthful population, it is commercially vital for the Western (American) tech corporations to secure the large African market. Consider also that many of the American technology platforms are excluded from the huge Chinese market, since China provides indigenous local alternatives, it makes a capitalist rationalization for these corporations to secure the African market. But African states and investors need to support indigenous technology startups that can provide services that many *digital imperialists* provide, and create indigenous platforms of communication and social networking. There are many technology start-ups in Africa that are developing digital solutions, but they are often hampered by lack of state support and meagre local private investment support. Equally, there is cultural coloniality in Africa that shapes disposition to the local alternatives to foreign products. The mentality that foreign (American) innovations are better than indigenous African ones remains a huge hindrance to widening the uptake of local innovations.

While the Chinese model of alternatives to Western social media platforms projects a challenge to the colonizing nature of American social media corporations, several serious caveats and concerns about this model should be engaged. The Chinese model is the antithesis of the core principles of the Internet: openness and interconnection. The model lacks interconnection with Western platforms, thereby highlighting the protectionist and insular nature of the Chinese social media sphere, euphemistically referred to as the 'Great Firewall'. The model creates both an information divide and a geographical divide, as users in China do not have access to American social media platforms. China's pursuit of online and network sovereignty may be construed as an affront to the interconnected ideology of the Internet. There is also concern about government online censorship, by which the authorities can surveil and censor citizens' private communication. Through intense regulation and laws, Chinese authorities have immense power to control social media platforms, resulting in freedom of speech violations to monitor social dissent. Irrespective of all these challenges, Chinese model of indigenous technology innovations as alternative to Western (American) technology domination is commendable.

China's imperialist operations in the telecommunications sector in Africa equally require critical interrogation. Chinese mobile devices are not only dominating the Africa's cellphone market, China is increasingly investing in the African telecommunication sector as part of its strategic presence in key sectors of mining, energy, telecommunication and infrastructure developments in Africa. Chinese presence in Africa serves to divert from Western influence in the continent and places China as a global actor. With a population of about 1.4 billion, Africa also serves as a large market for Chinese products, while providing access to African resources. China has provided funds and line of credit for some African states, it has been involved in infrastructure construction and development across Africa and enacting cultural influence in Africa through language and other cultural artefacts. China's presence in Africa requires a cautious critical assessment of a possible new colonial power, with a forewarning of a re-colonization of Africa.

Currently the American technology corporations' imperialist dominance of communication space presents huge social, cultural, economic and safety concerns. Google (Alphabet Inc.) and Facebook (Meta) house millions of personal data of Africans, and as some states rely on communication infrastructure built by foreign enterprises, increasingly government data are stored in cloud system outside these nations in foreign data centers (Pinto, 2018). The implications of this to state security, civilian control and monitoring, and political maneuverings are ever-present concerns. The colonization of communication spaces also has economic implications for local industries. It bolsters the pattern of exploitation; for example, huge revenue generated from online digital advertising in Africa goes to the American-based technology giants such as Google and Facebook. Africa's current communication sector is shaped by digital coloniality, manifesting in the Western exploitation of its resources, colonization of its communication spaces and a pattern of Western (American) expansion into its digital communication sector. To decolonize the logic of digital coloniality, African states need to encourage innovations, build and allow private indigenous investment in infrastructure. The repercussions of not doing this is the continuation of coloniality explicitly by foreign nations, but mostly through American technology corporations.

References

Aderinola, O. J., Clarke, E. O., Olarinmoye, O. M., Kusemiju, V., & Anatekhai, M. A. (2009). Heavy metals in surface water, sediments, fish, and periwinkles of Lagos lagoon. *American-Eurasian Journal of Agriculture and Environmental Science*, 5(5), 609–617.

Boateng, O. (2011). Ghana burns its health away. *New Africa*, May 2011, 62–65.

Braeckman, C. (2004). The looting of the Congo. *New Internationalist*, 367, 13–16.

Castells, M. (2010). *End of Millennium*, 2nd edn. Malden, MA: Wiley-Blackwell.

Dahir, A. L. (2018, February 14). WhatsApp is the most popular messaging app in Africa. Retrieved May 23, 2019, from Quartz Africa: https://qz.com/africa/1206935/whatsapp-is-the-most-popular-messaging-app-in-africa/

Frankel, T. C., Chavez, M. R., & Ribas, J. (2016). The cobalt pipeline. *Washington Post.* Accessed April 18, 2022 from www.washingtonpost.com/graphics/business/batteries/congo-cobalt-mining-for-lithium-ion-battery/

Geiger, M., and Bamba M.I. (2021). What Hong Kong and Singapore can teach Africa on how to become an economic powerhouse. *World Economic Forum.* Accessed April 13, 2022 from: www.weforum.org/agenda/2021/01/hubs-africa-growth-potential-economics/

Grespin, W. (2010). Blood coltan? *Journal of International Peace Operations*, 6(3), 27–30.

GSMA (2021). *The Mobile Economy Sub-Saharan Africa 2021.* GSM Association.

Heacock, M., Kelly C. B., Asante, K. A., Birnbaum, L. S., Bergman, A. L., Brune, M., Buka, I., Carpenter, D. O., Chen, A., Huo, X., Kamel, M., Landrigan, P. J., Magalini, F., Diaz-Barriga, F., Neira, M., Omar, M., Pascale, A., Ruchirawat, M., Sly, L., Sly, P. D., Van den Berg, M., and Suk, W. (2016). E-waste and harm to vulnerable populations: A growing global problem. *Environmental Health Perspectives*, 124(5), 550–555.

Hochschild, A. (1998). *King Leopold's Ghost: A Story of Greed, Terror, and Heroism in Colonial Africa.* New York, NY: Mariner.

International Chamber of Commerce (ICC) (2007). *Telecoms Liberalization.* Paris, France: ICC

International Data Corporation (IDC) (2022). Africa's Smartphone Market Sees Shipments Decline Amid Global Supply Shortages, but Growth Is Tipped for 2022. Accessed April 27, 2022 from www.idc.com/getdoc.jsp?containerId=prMETA48958222

Internet World Stats (2023). Internet usage statistics 2023. www.internetworldstats.com/stats.htm

Jandrić, P., & Kuzmanić, A. (2015). Digital postcolonialism. *IADIS International Journal on WWW/Internet*, 13(2), 34–51.

Kwet, M. (2019). Digital colonialism: US empire and the new imperialism in the Global South. *Race & Class*, 60(4), 3–26.

Lepawsky, J. (2015). The changing geography of global trade in electronic discards: time to rethink the e-waste problem. *The Geographical Journal*, 181(2), 147–159.

Malewar, A. (2021). Facebook's 2Africa to become world's longest subsea cable. Accessed April 22, 2022 from www.inceptivemind.com/facebook-2africa-become-worlds-longest-subsea-cable/21431/

Mignolo, W. (2011). *The Darker Side of Western Modernity.* Durham, NC: Duke University Press.

Mitman, G., & Erickson, P. (2010). Latex and blood: Science, markets and American empire. *Radical History Review*, 107, 45–73.

Noury, V. (2010). The curse of coltan. *New African*, April 2010, 34–35.

Pinto, R. (2018, July). Digital sovereignty or digital colonialism. *International Journal of Human Rights*, 15(27), 15–27.

Ponciano, J. (2021). The World's Largest Technology Companies In 2021: Apple's Lead Widens as Coinbase, DoorDash Storm Into Ranks. *Forbes*. Accessed April 18, 2022 from www.forbes.com/sites/jonathanponciano/2021/05/13/worlds-largest-tech-companies-2021/?sh=6e492fd769bc

Pun, N., Shen, Y., Guo, Y., Lu, H., Chan, J., & Selden, J. (2016). Apple, Foxconn, and Chinese workers' struggles from a global labor perspective. *Inter-Asia Cultural Studies*, 17(2), 166–185.

Quijano, A. (2007). Coloniality and modernity/rationality. *Cultural Studies*, (2-3), 168–178.

Schmidt, C. W. (2006). Unfair Trade: E-Waste in Africa. *Environmental Health Perspective*, 114(4), A232–A235.

Sharife, K. (2008). DR Congo: The heavy price of the world's high tech. *New Africa*, May 2008, 26–29.

Stanley, T. (2012). Belgium's heart of darkness. *History Today*. Accessed July 31, 2017 from www.historytoday.com/tim-stanley/belgiums-heart-darkness

Statista (2022). Mobile phone shipments in Africa from first quarter 2016 to fourth quarter 2021, by quarter (in million units). Accessed April 27, 2022, from www.statista.com/statistics/791885/africa-mobile-phone-shipment-by-quarter/

Stone, M. (2022). The EV boom is being field by underpaid, underfed, cobalt miners. *The Verge*. Accessed April 18, 2022 from www.theverge.com/2022/2/15/22933022/cobalt-mining-ev-electriv-vehicle-working-conditions-congo

Sullivan, J. (2014). Trash or treasure: Global trade and the accumulation of e-waste in Lagos, Nigeria. *Africa Today*, 61(1), 89–112

United Nations (n.d.). Global Issues: Population. Accessed April 13 from www.un.org/en/global-issues/population

United Nations (2022). Young People's Potential, the Key to Africa's Sustainable Development. Accessed April 13, 2023 from www.un.org/ohrlls/news/young-people%E2%80%99s-potential-key-africa%E2%80%99s-sustainable-development

Verikios, G., & Zhang, X. (2004). The Economic Effects of Removing Barriers to Trade in Telecommunications, 27(3), 435–458.

Wang, Y. (2020). Apple Suspends New Business with Pegatron over Labor Violations. Accessed April 18, 2022 from www.wsj.com/articles/apple-suspends-new-business-with-pegatron-over-labor-violations-11604917504

Wasik, B. (2015, June 4). Welcome to the age of digital imperialism. Retrieved May 6, 2019, from *New York Times Magazine*: www.nytimes.com/2015/06/07/magazine/welcome-to-the-age-of-digital-imperialism.html

World Internet Statistics (2023). Internet Users Statistics for Africa. Accessed July 20, 2023 from www.internetworldstats.com/stats.htm

3 Media for Citizens in Africa

From Nollywood and Naspers to Public Access

Lee Artz

This chapter addresses the media relations between diverse Nigerian video producers and the transnational media company Naspers, which operates Africa Magic and other MultiChoice streaming sites across the continent. To make sense of the structures, social relations, and production practices of Nollywood and Africa Magic, let's begin with a short introduction that defines, unpacks, and summarizes important theories that will be essential for understanding current media practices in Africa. These concepts will also help identify changes that are necessary to create citizen access to media production and distribution. Some of these concepts may be familiar, others may be new: the first three sections presented are only intended to provide a brief overview. Hopefully, the longer case study that follows will prompt your own investigations and discoveries using some of these theories.

Capitalism and Colonialism

Humans survive by interacting with nature. In the process, social relations are constructed with complex economic, political, and cultural manifestations. In each historical situation, dominant social relations reflect and reproduce social positions constructed by existing relations of power, daily activities, and supporting ideologies. Early in human evolution, we produced and created our lives cooperatively by growing food, harvesting, and hunting. Most cultures formed equitable social relations. As surpluses grew, new social relations of production created divisions of wealth and resources. A variety of social forms arose, including African communalism, Iroquois cooperative societies, and other less democratic social forms. In Europe, power was taken by nobles and armies as feudalism expropriated the labor of serfs and peasants, while independent artisans produced needed goods. By the 17th century, merchants, workers, and peasants rebelled, leading to revolutions that appropriated feudal lands and established capitalist private property. Political economy approaches, which investigate the social relations of the production of wealth, explain ownership modes

DOI: 10.4324/9781003352907-4

and relations of production, associated decision-making processes, and the distribution and consumption of goods and services.

Social relations based on the private ownership of the means of producing goods and services are now dominant in most countries. These relations assure capital's capture of labor's surplus value from every product and service provided, enforcing a social class division of labor: corporate owners and shareholders own the means of production (factories, machinery, transport); a professional managerial class owns little but directs the production and distribution; small businesses are individually owned and operated; meanwhile, millions of working people do not own, do not manage, and have nothing other than their own labor power. This social class of labor – about 80% of society – produces the goods and services that become commodities for sale. Of course, labor receives a wage, but that is only part of the value produced. Capital withholds a share of the produced value in its theft of profit.

Despite its triumphant claims, capitalism has inherent contradictions. By the early 20th century, capitalist consolidation from mergers, bankruptcies, and industrial monopolies *within* nations led to a battle *between* nations for new territories with natural resources and markets. National monopolies bolstered by the military might of their respective governments sought colonies for their "national" corporations. *Imperialism* – understood as the stage of capitalism where concentration and consolidation created monopoly capitalism linked with finance and government – led to international conflict. Imperialist and colonial powers conquered less powerful nations and fought among themselves to partition the world. Ultimately, rabid battles for colonial power led to imperialist wars (1914–1918; 1939–1945), devastating Europe while oppressing and exploiting Africa and other continents, allowing the US to become a new global power.

In the post-World War II era, former imperialist powers were confronted with national liberation struggles. Powerful independence movements in Algeria, Kenya, Ghana, the Congo, and around the world, meant Western domination could no longer rely solely on military intervention. The capitalist class soon learned that their social positions of power were best defended through mass consent for their leadership. This social arrangement is called hegemony – mass consent for existing social relations which are protected with coercion. Once the ruling ideas of a society are those of the rulers, then the production and reproduction of dominant social relations (including social inequality) are more stable. Hence, consent for cultural values and norms are essential for economic and political power. Education, religion, and communication that popularize dominant social relations are necessary for every social order.

Competing capitalist nations, seeking to protect the interests of their corporations, accepted the formal independence of their former colonies while restructuring neo-colonial economic control and political influence (Nkrumah, 1965). In the post-colonial world, industrially-advanced capitalist nations offered "development" programs to national elites of developing nations, providing aid, loans, investments, media technology, scholarships, and consumer goods.

In short, European powers and the US found other means for controlling resources and politics in the former colonies. Newly independent nations were often governed by elites trained and assimilated to the cultural norms of their colonial masters. Unequal economic relations were consented to by neo-colonial governments and domestic partners hoping to profit by accommodating their former rulers. These "reconstructed" social relations exhibited many of the same practices, ideologies, and values that predominated during colonial times. Indeed, under neo-colonialism, unequal relations reappeared along with formal independence. Imperialism as an economic-military policy of occupation and exploitation was replaced by neo-colonialism which relied on economic development, resource exploitation, and reimagined cultural practices benefitting Western corporations and nations.

Nations achieving their liberation and formal independence responded energetically to neo-colonialism. Kwame Nkrumah, president of newly independent Ghana, held the All-African People's Congress in 1958 with representatives from every independent African nation, except apartheid South Africa. In 1961, 120 nations united in the Non-Aligned Movement as an independent forum of shared interests. By 1963, 32 nations formed the Organization of African Unity to eradicate colonialism and develop economic and political integration on the continent.

In the 1970s, growing economic inequality seen as the result of the neo-colonial developmental model prompted UNESCO (United Nations Education, Scientific, and Cultural Organization) to address the obvious inequalities in communication across the non-Western world. UNESCO organized the MacBride Commission which drafted recommendations for more equitable media access and representations of the global South. The 1980 final report advocated a New World Information and Communication Order (NWICO) (MacBride, 1982). The US and UK vehemently opposed the report and quit UNESCO, charging that NWICO interfered with the "free flow" of information.

A political economy of media recognizes that media and culture are industrial operations with social relations constrained by ownership structures, production practices using technology and subordinate labor, distribution and consumption of media commodities – all within the larger socioeconomic social order. A political economy perspective also notes that media produce entertainment and symbolic content viewed by mass audiences. The structure and practice of the commercial media industry (including film, TV, advertising, entertainment, and news) create signs, symbols, and images linking meanings, populations, and ideologies (Acland, 2015).

Cultural Imperialism

In tandem with the rise of social movements for liberation and independence – and the neo-colonial adjustments by European powers – critical media scholars and others identified "cultural imperialism" as an effective means of Western influence in the developing world. Critics charged the United States, in particular, with cultural imperialism. Films, television, comics, and advertising were chastised for creating a demand for American goods and services that undermined national cultural practices and values. "Americanization" was understood as the outcome of multinational investment and resource extraction, while the mass export of American films, music, clothing, and fast food replaced local products and traditional ways of life.

Cultural imperialism theories focus on how US culture spreads to developing nations through managerial practices, consumer products, and entertainment. Cultural imperialism creatively imposes the values and practices of a dominant nation onto a subordinate one. Exported US film and television express the norms and models of social and political behaviors amenable to capitalism and consumerism – including individualism, self-interest, and class hierarchy – as also seen in Nollywood videos, for example. Thus, cultural imperialism underwrites and reinforces asymmetrical economic and political power between the West and the rest of the world.

In other words, US and European corporations extend their economic dominance and cultural influence by distributing their entertainment media, music, business practices, and religious and educational activities in developing countries. A leading proponent of the cultural imperialism thesis, Herbert Schiller (1976), explained the idea:

> The concept of cultural imperialism today best describes the sum of the processes by which a society is brought into the modern world system … shaping social institutions to correspond to, or even promote, the values and structures of the dominating center of the system…. This occurs largely through the commercialization of broadcasting.
>
> (pp. 9–10)

Armand Mattelart (1979) further explained how the mass distribution of US comics, cartoons, movies, and fast food promoted US capitalist and cultural values. However, by the 1990s, Herb Schiller (1991) noted that cultural imperialism was no longer sufficient to explain and understand global media structures and practices. He observed that "the domination that exists today, though still bearing a marked American imprint, is better understood as transnational corporate cultural domination" (p. 15). Schiller's insight based on a materialist assessment of shifting media practices in the 1990s suggests that we look the actual economic relations and production practices of national media and their global relations. Thus, we should consider how the global capitalist class has developed a transnational corporate culture that has no specific home nation.

Transnationalism

Some cultural studies and globalization theories argue that the world is flat, that national governments have been replaced by unfettered cultural exchange, or that active audiences are not constrained by media structures or affected by media content. On the other hand, more realistic political economy research finds social relations and social power has been consolidated by transnational media corporations (TNMCs) that have constructed economic relations, political institutions, and cultural norms for our whole way of life.

Neoliberal deregulation led to expanded and consolidated global media, especially in cable, satellite, telecommunications, and digital technology. Transnational relations and forms of production and distribution, including co-productions, joint ventures, and a new international division of cultural labor (Miller et al., 2008), have become less nation-centric. Remarkably, when considering media effects on national cultures many researchers continue to refer to *national* entertainment media rather than a more accurate portrayal as *capitalist* industries, led by transnational corporate media that have little commitment to any particular nation or their publics.

To expand distribution and attract larger and linguistically and culturally diverse audiences, TNMCs have found willing media partners for coproduction and distribution. Transnational co-productions refer to any film or TV program created by producers based in different countries that share financial risks and expectations of profits by reaching broader audiences, investors, and advertisers. Co-productions provide multiple benefits to the partners, including: pooling financial resources; access to government incentives; access to domestic markets and desirable locations; and the opportunity to learn cultural norms and production practices from their partners.

Today, a handful of transnational media corporations (e.g., Disney, Reliance DreamWorks, Dalian Wanda, Warner Bros., Netflix) dominate global entertainment. However, recognizing dominant cultural influences cannot be reduced to national intent nor cultural effect.

Even the most vertically- and horizontally-integrated TNMC commodifies media content and cuts labor costs by downsizing, new technology, and commissioning subcontractors in other nations. Transnational capitalists do not seek to override or dismantle national or cultural boundaries. In fact, they depend on the national and cultural characteristics and actions of their class partners in each country. Transnational capital does not undertake the imposition of some elusive national norm on subordinate cultures, rather it "seeks to accumulate profit on a global scale... [with] no particular interest in destroying or sustaining local cultures apart from the drive for increased profitability" (Sklair, 2001, p. 256).

International political economy scholars have assessed and described the rise of transnationalism organized by an emerging transnational capitalist class (TNCC) (Robinson, 2004; Sklair, 2001). The efforts of this well-organized TNCC have resulted in capitalism conquering and establishing a complete world system. Capitalism has not only overcome all indigenous precapitalist formations, with transnationalism it has also completed the commodification of every meaningful instance of social life, including public institutions, social welfare responsibilities, and national cultural practices. They have all been replaced by privatized, for-profit operations around the world.

Transnational capitalism – partnerships and joint ventures crossing national boundaries – now control most natural resources such as land and water as well as social necessities such as education, health care, and global culture, including media entertainment. In fact, by the end of the 20th century, transnational production exceeded the amount of national import–export trade (Miller et al., 2005). Transnational theories present a materialist, class-based analysis, based on available empirical evidence. Nation-states have not been replaced under transnational relations. Rather, to transform global production and distribution, capitalists favoring global integration direct their national governments to deregulate investment, labor rights, and public protections. While transnational capitalism needs the consent of national governments, it also must recruit the governed who still reside within nations, borders, languages, laws, unions, armies, and cultures.

Importantly for global capital, media do not stand apart from the rest of society, nor do they exist separately from the transnational transformation of global capitalism. Media entertainment is part of a global culture industry seeking profits from sales of tickets, media products, and audiences to advertisers, while presenting engaging stories and images promoting world views, cultural values, and beliefs about gender, race, social class, and market capitalism. In the 21st century, media entertainment is produced and distributed through joint ventures and partnerships among national media across borders and cultures. Regional transnational media – like the Naspers and Nollywood partnerships – indicate shared class interests of national capitalist owners, investors, and subcontractors profiting from a transnational division of cultural labor (Artz, 2016).

Cultural imperialism accurately described media relations among nations in the late 20th century, but neoliberal capitalism has developed new means for the accumulation of wealth, with parallel changes affecting the global production of news and entertainment. The global media industry continues producing and distributing images and information which influence popular beliefs and behaviors, but with diminishing evidence of US media overwhelming local media anywhere in the world (Artz, 2015, 2022).

In fact, ample proof from international political economy research indicates that transnational relations are not imposed nor the result of US dominance; rather, governments responding to their own national capitalist classes invite foreign partners – offering tax incentives and subsidies. As national media and their governments attempt to lure transnational partners, national media also work to replicate the profit-making infrastructure of Hollywood. Global media cities, from Mumbai and Paris to Lagos and Kano now have studios and site facilities financed by private investors hoping to cash in on TNMC productions. Public funds may benefit TNMCs and their domestic partners, but few resources trickle down to media workers or citizens. The result is increased class inequality – as dramatically present in Nigeria. As transnational media consolidation grows, transnationally-interlocked firms centralize creative control, pushing the actual production to contractors and independent studios across nations and cultures (Artz, 2016).

Although this short introduction is no substitute for further study, these short definitions and examples of capitalism, neo-colonialism, transnationalism, and neoliberalism should provide important frames for understanding transnational media relations around the world. The following case study of Naspers partnerships with Nollywood producers provides an important example for how transnational media influence African audiences. Hopefully, these concepts also will indicate what changes need to be made to provide media access for African citizens from Nigeria, Ghana, and South Africa to the entire continent.

Nollywood

Until Nollywood became a hot topic for *Variety, The Hollywood Reporter*, and the *New York Times* in the 1990s, African media was marginal in international communication research. The "market" for media entertainment in Africa was relatively small, so major media did not attend to the continent until very recently. "The rise of Nollywood, with its prolific output, its spectacular popularity and its unprecedented ability to reach remote and non-elite audiences, is the most radical development" in African media history (McCall, 2007, p. 94). Produced by individual entrepreneurs – nascent small capitalists – Nollywood reflected existing Nigerian economic and cultural relations, including ethnic and social class conditions (Haynes & Okome, 2000, p. 51). Yet, Nollywood norms and modes of production, with different social relations based on informal precarious labor, rely on wageworker crews, actors, and distributors. Following the dramatic success of Nollywood and the rise of middle classes in Nigeria, Ghana, Kenya, and South Africa, leading TNMCs (Transnational Media Companies) from Asia, Europe, and the Americas arrived. Indeed, TNMCs are searching for African media partners to attract consumers of movie tickets, pay TV, streaming services, and smartphone entertainment. The field is wide open because across Africa, media entrepreneurs are eager for investors, partners, and distributors – and neoliberal governments adopting structural adjustment programs have deregulated protections of public resources (McColl, 2007). A few TNMCs (Multichoice, Star Times, Netflix, Vivendi) have already established transnational partnerships with Nigerian producers. None of these developments have advanced citizen access to media production.

The issue of cultural imperialism has some residual purchase on media in post-colonial countries like Nigeria, Ghana, Ethiopia, and others because "Africa has a huge hinterland of culture not yet exploited by capitalism" (Haynes, 2018, p. 26). How indigenous cultures and languages are incorporated into neoliberal capitalism remains to be determined, although Nollywood offers some indication. Nollywood films appropriate ethnic traditions to construct a "Nigerian" culture whereby indigenous identities lose their cultural markers (Tsaaior, 2018, p. 149). Exceedingly syncretic and hybrid, Nollywood (and Nigerian music) vigorously adapt, adopt, and wed their dominant themes and forms (Haynes, 2000) with both traditional and contemporary African motifs emphasizing self-interest, wealth acquisition, social hierarchy, and indigenous backwardness. Meanwhile, South African media, which some see as Western cultural imperialism, offer incentives to emerging media producers in sub-Saharan Africa. Yet, boundaries between domestic and foreign cultural influences are not always clearly demarcated (Kraidy, 2005, p. 6). Uchenna Onuzulike (2009) suggests that cultural hybridity synthesizes distinct cultural identities – with distinctiveness elusive. Nigeria itself is a post-colonial amalgamation of more than 300 societies with 500 languages (Ogbe et al., 2020) assembled within boundaries established by British imperialism. Moreover, TV, film, and video are socially and culturally constructed within dominant social relations, political power, and indigenous and class experiences (Tsaaior, 2018).

In Nigeria, in addition to large Yoruba, Hausa, and Igbo groups, hundreds of other ethnicities speak their own languages and practice their own religions and rituals, while sharing similar values toward nature, family, community, and the cosmos. A multiethnic country of almost 200 million, distinct cultures are contested and relative. Even the vaunted African communalism that privileges collective over individual applies chiefly to the local ethnic group. On the other hand, younger urban Africans find cultural differences insignificant because their "life is more or less the same whatever the country" (Ugochukwu, 2013). In both cases, social class is a primary ingredient, as Nollywood's "radically horizontal" structure of production (McColl, 2007, p.96) by multiple entrepreneurs complements the larger global media order. Indeed, most Nigerian video content projects "glamour over substance" (Adesanya, 2000, p. 49). A brief look at Nigerian society unpacks previous observations about social class, transnationalism, and dominant cultural norms.

Neoliberalism and Cultural Production

Nigeria as a nation is a historical construction: first by British colonialism until 1960, then by post-colonial capitalist regimes that ensured social inequality, ethnic and religious animosity, and control over education, media, and employment. By the 1990s, neoliberalism and IMF (International Monetary Fund) structural adjustment programs adopted by the Nigerian government privatized industries, permitted unrestricted foreign investment, and reduced funding for public welfare. Thus, Nigeria is ranked in the top 30 industrial countries with over $450 billion in production each year, but 70% of Nigeria lives in poverty.

The Nigerian nation culture has been constructed by displacing indigenous traditions and religions with institutionalized political and economic forms that feature wage labor, private profit, and transnational investments enabled by corrupt corporate and government officials – disguising actual class relations. Importantly, individual Nollywood creators are an important support for pervasive social inequality, creating entertainment that promotes ideologies of neoliberal self-interest, consumerism, and enforced austerity.

The identification of Nollywood with the national identity of Nigeria is the cultural outcome of a political economy based on transnational economic relations, creating "national" interests to overcome internal regional and class interests through spectacle and self-interest. Indeed, the socioeconomic macrostructures of global capitalism in agriculture, oil, mining, and media production in Nigeria result from social relations of production, social class divisions between labor and capital, and hierarchical forms of private property – all influenced by existing neocolonial, ethnic, and religious oppression enforced by capitalist politicians.

The owners of industrial-scale agricultural land, are former or current military commanders and leading politicians. Workers make about $60 month. Since the 1980s, oil production controlled by Nigerian capitalists with ties to the government has created a dozen new Nigerian oil billionaires, with oil worker's salary averaging $50 month. In addition to transnational investors, twenty-three Nigerian firms mine more than 51% of total production – adding more wealth to the ruling elite, with mine workers earning about $100 month. Nollywood's entrepreneurial practices exhibit similar class and wealth differences. Thus, given the political and economic structures in Nigeria, the wealth of its vast resources are not available to most of its 200 million citizens (Abubakar, 2018).

More than a million people work in media production in Nigeria. Yet, for decades, Nigeria films grossed only $12 million a year. Early Nollywood production consisted almost entirely of short, inexpensive, poorly-produced videos expressing culturally diverse but stereotypical representations of Nigerian indigenous communities based on colonialist tropes displaying "witchcraft, ritual killing, and crass immorality" (Tobechukwu, 2009, p. 76) and other "negative socio-cultural images of the country" (Ogbe, 2020, p. 121). "Emphasis on economic returns" promotes images "of a ritualistic and violent society that thrives on affluence and ebullience, and poor portrayals of women" displaying an "oligarchic society that lives above the rule of law with little or no consequence" (Msugh-Ter Teddy & Msugh-Ter Teddy, 2022, p. 48). At first, lacking access to studio production, thousands of VHS tapes and DVDs replete with voodoo and witchcraft were filmed quickly in the street (Okeowo, 2016) – about 50 per week – and sold informally at kiosks along the streets. Production in Lagos released most films in the Yoruba language. The appearance of Hausa videos in the Islamic north of Nigeria have since spread to Niger and Chad. Ironically, Yoruba and Igbo producers make almost 50% of the Hausa films. Although charges of Yoruba imperialism have yet to be uttered, Adejunmobi (2007) observes that Nigerian videos have become a "dominant force" in West Africa, raising "concerns about the growing influence of Nigerian video films on Ghanian filmmaking" (p. 9–10). Another scholar sees "cultural neo-colonialism of the African continent by Nollywood films" (Ugochukwu, 2013).

Nollywood after 2010

Given the mass response to Nollywood films, the Nigerian government, the World Bank, transnational co-productions, and foreign investment has provided more resources, bigger budgets, and more access to international distribution. Now, those same 1 million media workers produce films that generate $1 billion in yearly revenue (Agency, 2016). Unsurprisingly, Nigerian movie producers "are emulating Western lives" while simultaneously tweaking and complementing the hegemony of the capitalist culture industry (Onuzulike, 2009, p. 184) using African inflections. Many early

Nigerian films used the myths of the colonizers, along with pop music in popular genres displaying romance and singing in Hausa and blood and witchcraft in English and Yoruba. These films feature stories of social instability and suffering, but also offer an entertaining escape from daily life (Zajc, 2009). Yet, despite the richness of cultural diversity available in Nigeria, Nollywood videos articulate a hybrid cultural heritage conducive to consumerism and self-interest.

With new media technologies, the production and sale of video were replaced by television networks, internet access, smartphones, and streaming platforms. Subsequently, since 2010, the political economy of transnational media entertainment has supplanted previous informal structures and practices. As Jonathon Haynes (2018) reports, Nollywood has been corporatized as a new capitalist sector. Nollywood producers have formed partnerships with media in South Africa, France, Britain, and the US. No longer – if ever – are Nigerian videos the "real voice of the people" (Haynes, 2018, p. 4). In fact, rather than representing diverse Nigerian cultures, Nollywood has always been commercial, with an occasional social critique to attract a larger audience.

Haynes (2018) identified several developments of this new political economy of Nigerian entertainment. First, transnational partnerships with Nollywood producers now dominate film and television production. Two, distribution forms have changed from video to television, cable, pay-TV, and internet streaming platforms. Three, due to transnational partnerships that insist on low costs and high returns, series predominate because they are cheaper to produce than longer films. Fourth, multiplexes have reappeared in Nigerian cities, especially in upscale malls that cater to the new professional middle classes that prospered under neoliberal privatization. Additionally, production to scale has increased smartphone use and lowered costs, changing the form of mass exhibition. Moreover, the market-driven Nigerian media industry now "transcends nation-state boundaries" (Arewa, 2015, p. 373). Nigerian on-line platforms such as iROKO and Afrinolly suggest opportunities for "Nigeria to exercise cultural hegemony on the continent" (Msugh-Ter Teddy & Msugh-Ter Teddy, 2022, p. 46).

Naspers and Africa Magic

The largest TNMC presence in Nigeria is Naspers, the South African media company with global media investments. In addition to its 30% stake in China's Tencent, Naspers owns 28% of Russian internet giant Mail.ru, shares in Amazon's Middle East Souq.com, and holdings in videogame maker Zynga. Naspers owns Media24 (the largest publisher in Africa) and Takealot.com (South Africa's largest online retailer). It also operates the African satellite network DStv, the production company M-Net, and

MultiChoice with its satellite bouquet of channels under Africa Magic. Broadcasting to 53 countries. Africa Magic includes stations for Angola, Mozambique, Uganda, Botswana, Zimbabwe, and Ghana, all broadcasting in local languages. Most content for Africa Magic comes from its partnerships with national media, especially Nigerian producers. Africa Magic channels express "corporate cultural politics" (Haynes, 2018, p. 16) even with their "hastily-prepared and poorly-edited subtitles" (Ugochukwu, 2013). Africa Magic Epic is the most popular channel with its traditional, pre-colonial village settings – videos coming from Eastern Nigeria where the lower ends of Nollywood productions are centered. These are not films that reflect contemporary popular culture, but films feeding nostalgia for a fictional, yet comforting prior world. Africa Magic has other channels for urban youth and elite viewers that prefer premium content. Multichoice adjusts each channel to best exploit each audience. Thus, a South African TNMC relies on multiple transnational partners in Nigeria to co-produce profitable content distributed across the continent. In 2022, Multichoice revenue reached $8 billion with 22 million subscribers to Africa Magic and other Multichoice channels.

Naspers has only a few competitors. The most challenging is probably Chinese StarTimes, a broadcast, satellite, and internet company serving 30 African countries with 13 million subscribers. StarTimes has media joint ventures in Tanzania and Zambia. The other major provider in southern Africa has less reach. iROKO, a British-Nigerian internet subscription company, with Swedish and American investors, delivers on-demand Nigerian videos to subscribers in Africa, North America, and Europe. iROKO also offers two channels on Britian's Sky TV. iROKO has distribution deals with YouTube, Amazon, iTunes, and several international airlines. iROKO claims to be one of the "largest funders, co-producers, and commissioners of content in Nollywood" (Okeowo, 2016), with media content partnerships in UK, Zimbabwe, and Latin America. In 2012, Vivendi's Canal+ launched Nollywood TV with French dubbing. None rival the co-production output of Africa Magic.

Commercialization

The commercialism of Nigerian media is most recently illustrated by the hit films *The Wedding Party* (2016, 2017). Not only do the films display celebrity stars, high-production values, and multiple plots and characters, they also feature expensive, glamorous clothing, autos, and settings. The two films grossed over $3 million in an impoverished country. Netflix picked up both films.

One of the co-producers, the vertically-consolidated studio Film One signed a 2019 co-production deal with China's HuaHua to make the first major Nigerian-Chinese movie. Film One also won distribution rights for Disney films in West Africa. Meanwhile, ROK Studio (a division of iRO-KOTV) merged with Canal+ to create more movies in French (Bright, 2019). Of course, transnational partners provide things Nigerian filmmakers have always needed: "bigger budgets from stable sources, superior equipment, good access to international distribution" (Haynes, 2018, p. 13). Yet, in Nigeria, as elsewhere, only a few studios reach the top, creating an oligopoly where before were myriad small producers (see Table 3.1).

As elsewhere, "corporate neoliberalization of Nollywood distribution introduced inequalities" (Haynes, 2018, p. 10) determined by and reinforcing social class. Whether Nigerian produced or pirated from underpaid workers in India, Lebanon, China, Dubai, and across Nigeria, profits made from entertainment commodities were worth more than wages of machine operators, wholesale distributors, retail clerks, and street vendors. Even exhibition is social class structured: luxury flights, film festivals, and theater premiers for the conspicuous rich shown in local Nigerian cinema in exclusive gated neighborhoods and later to pay-TV subscription services. Perhaps in a couple years, affordable DVDs will be available to the general population. For now, Internet streaming and the massive digital divide is social class determined. The neoliberal consumer "boom" and restructured Nollywood production misses the overwhelming majority of Nigeria's population.

Nollywood's transnational development is "gated" by technology and subscriptions available only to capitalists and middle class beneficiaries, just as solidly exclusive as gated communities in Lekki, Ikoyi, Alausa, and elsewhere in Nigeria (Haynes, 2018). In West Africa, colonialism skimmed local economies for profit rather than imposing plantations. Likewise today, post-colonial "national" cultures extract profit from mass entertainment.

Table 3.1 Top five Nigerian films (2016–2020)

Title	Year	Gross	Languages	Distributor
Omo Ghetto:	2020	$2.7 M	English	FilmOne
Wedding Party	2016	$1.7 M	Yoruba, Igbo, English	FilmOne
Wedding Party	2017	$1.65 M	Yoruba, Igbo, English	FilmOne
Chief Daddy	2018	$1.5 M	Yoruba, English	FilmOne
Sugar Rush	2019	$1.1 M	Yoruba, English	FilmOne

Note: All are comedies. All stress wealth and consumption as key to happiness and success in romance, business, and personal relations.

Transnationalism

Today, transnationalism (the collaboration of two or more companies from two or more countries) consolidates social class inequality, as co-productions shift away from traditional cultural identities and austerity crunches film-makers lacking transnational connections. Nollywood's direction has been determined by a new class of capitalist overlords, as TNMC partners profit from "a kind of cultural strip mining: profiting from a cadre of personnel, a star system, a way of working, a style, a set of genres, an assembled audience – that they did nothing to create" (Haynes, 2018, p. 15). Nigeria's Nollywood represents capitalism at the margins, functioning with the same social relations of labor exploitation. As part of TNMC production, work-ers, actors, and writers work for low wages – or they don't work.

Moreover, cultural "authenticity" under these conditions is not possible – unless we accept that select cultural references, colloquialisms, mythologies, and other constructions of indigenous cultures express the lived experiences of average citizens. *Wedding Party*, and other Nollywood films are not dis-rupting the dominant capitalist culture in Nigeria, but providing effective hegemonic overtures to diversity and individualism within neoliberal capital-ism. The cultural autonomy of Nollywood – expressed in films like *Osufia* in London (2003), *Inale* (2010), *At Home Abroad* (2012–2020), *Wedding Party* (2016, 2017), *Lionheart* (2018), and the Netflix series *Far From Home* (2022) – serves as an African ideological spokesmodel for Nigerian social hierarchy accommodating global capital.

Nollywood producers "recycle thematic and aesthetic elements from both dominant and minoritized cultures" exhibiting a mixture of "praise, irony, ambivalence and tentative acceptance ... with large doses of ridicule and negative stereotypes about indigenous culture" (Adenjunmobi, 2007, p. 9). Thus, the best icon for Nollywood videos "would undoubtedly be a Mercedes Benz, which appears ubiquitously as the symbol of the desired good life, the reward of both good and evil, the sign of social status and individual mobility" (Haynes, 2000, p. 2).

Journalist Emily Witt (2017) concludes

globalization did not produce a single cultural capital, but several of them [whereby] humanity now has a visual vernacular: in Hollywood, Bollywood, Nollywood, Korean drama, and the Latin American tele-novela ... the symbols of material wealth are imported bottles of liquor, big watches, sleek cars, and carefully styled hair.... Nollywood marks this phase of self-writing, where the assertion of Nigerian identity is not conducted in opposition to the forces of globalization and multicultur-alism, but within them.

(pp. 112–113)

In short, the spectacle of wealth in most Nollywood films must be understood as obscuring the social relations of production separating producers, writers, crew, actors, distributors, and small merchants.

In structure and content, the political economy of media transnationalism uses class-constructed Nigerian identities to applaud cosmopolitan styles based on self-interest and private profit at the expense of indigenous identities, cultural diversity, and humanity. Building on the introductory definitions, transnational media production distributes stories "selling a neoliberal consumer and professional lifestyle" (Haynes, 2018, p. 16).

Historically South African movies catered to the country's Afrikaans white minority. After apartheid was overturned, films featured poverty and political struggle. Now, as discussed in the introduction, neoliberalism benefits a professional managerial class, transnationally co-produced South African films emphasize wealth – "mansion parties with bouncers, infinity pools soaked in neon lights" with "chicly dressed glamorous housewives and high-powered lawyers" (Goldbaum, 2021). Netflix offers partnerships, as does China's StarTimes, Vivendi's Nollywood TV, and South Africa's ShowMax streaming service, among others. This is not Western cultural imperialism as defined in the introduction. This is the capture of profit from millions of production workers creating entertainment that attracts middle-class audiences and consumers. Collaborating and consolidated national media owners in Nigeria, Ghana, South Africa, and across the continent work with other transnational producers around the world.

The privatization of everyday life, the informal precarious struggle for survival, coupled with video entertainment that promotes self-interest and the ethic of consumption, underwrites tolerance (or acceptance) of inequality and corruption. Multichoice, Vivendi, and Netflix "are not likely to provide support for film projects that do not fit in with their larger concerns" (Adejunmobi, 2007, p. 13) – financially and ideologically. In short, social conditions in Nigeria undercut citizen collaboration, cooperation, and solidarity actions for justice, equality, and a more democratic sharing of abundant resources. Celebrating how "Africans cope with inequality and corruption through informal economics, subsistence agriculture, subversive humor, or subaltern forms of governability" as Johnathon Haynes (2000, p. 16) argues, does little to resolve the gross socio-economic inequality. Indeed, it pushes accommodation to inequality and contributes to the demobilization of any possible social movements for justice. Extreme conditions of social atomization, self-interested survival, while assimilation to and acceptance of inequality have thus far stymied any mass social movement for democracy. Yet, destitution, exploitation, and exclusion from citizen media access should not be applauded as opportunities for creative survival, but recognized as structured negations of humanity.

Towards Citizen Media Access

Social change and social justice are necessary to win public media access. Structurally and politically, the indigenous rural poor, agricultural workers (over 35% of all labor), oil workers, miners, and the urban working class, including informal labor, would likely favor economic and social equality. It happened in South Africa. It happened in Burkina Faso, the Congo, Kenya, and elsewhere on the continent. Indeed, historically social movements like those in Korea, Sri Lanka, Venezuela, Cuba, and elsewhere unified indigenous cultures with the politics of resistance and class solidarity (Koo, 2001; Artz, 2017).

Decades of resistance against South African apartheid led by the African National Congress (ANC) united multiple ethnic groups and urban youth in the Black Consciousness Movement that organized the Soweto Uprising in 1976. Following South Africa's defeat at Cuito Cuanavale by Cuban and Angolan forces in 1988, apartheid was dismantled and Nelson Mandela was elected South African President in 1994. The Independent Communications Authority of South Africa restructured the broadcasting industry, creating three categories of radio: commercial, public, and community. Private media seek profits, advertisements, and consuming audiences (Media Update, 2021). Like other public service broadcasting funded by governments, South Africa's SABC airs programs for the general public. Community radio has a different function – to serve its geographic or community of interest while encouraging community participation in reporting news and events important to residents (Media Update, 2021). Community radio may also serve religion, language, music, or other shared interests. Currently there are more than 200 community radio stations in South Africa, hoping to inform, educate, and entertain their listeners. Seventy percent of community stations serve specific geographic areas, broadcasting in 11 South African official languages, as well as German, Arabic, Urdu, and several other African languages (Kruger, 2020). Soweto's JoziFM has an audience of 570,000, which is larger than 14 private stations and SABC. Overall, more than 8.5 million South Africans listen to community radio each week, primarily in the Gauteng and Capetown provinces (Kruger, 2020).

In contrast, Nigeria is the most populous nation in Africa, but has fewer than 30 "community" radio stations, mostly "run by individuals through bogus communities" (Ntshangase, 2021, p. 37). Such stations largely survive through advertising, undercutting connections to local or indigenous communities. The sorry status of community radio in Nigeria reflects a political economy of atomization in Nigerian society and the lack of collective social movements for democracy.

Latin America illustrates more successful actions for change with important lessons for citizen media and equality. Following the election of Hugo Chavez as Venezuelan President in 1998, the capitalist class and its media organized a coup in 2002 and kidnapped Chavez. Millions of Venezuelans responded by marching on the government center Miraflores in Caracas. The coup leaders – led by the Chamber of Commerce and RCTV – freed Chavez and retreated. Media workers campaigned to modify radio and television regulations. In 2004, the National Assembly adopted the Law on Social Responsibility on Radio and Television: establishing freedom of expression without censorship, respect for human rights, and expanded public access. The Law ensures the right of "active participation and oversight of citizens in all processes of production, distribution, and consumption of media" (Iacobelli & Grioni, 2004). Mass social movements that brought Chavez to power also prompted legislation and constitutional changes to defend and promote democracy and public interest. As the primary means of communication, media are central to power, democracy, and cultural representations. Thus, Venezuelan social movements fought for and won additional laws expanding public access to media (2006, 2010, 2012) – forming some 1000 community radio and TV stations underwritten by a national social fund for community development. Social movements of workers, youth, women, and indigenous peoples also secured free public education, housing, health care, nutrition, and indigenous rights.

Similar processes occurred in Nicaragua in the 1970s through CORADEP (a community radio coalition) following the overthrow of the Somoza dictatorship. In Bolivia, miner's unions won labor rights and media access in the 1950s-1980s. Following indigenous uprisings for water and gas rights in the 1990s, community media were codified in the Bolivian constitution (Artz, 2016). Across Latin America, many governments have since set aside one-third of the national radio spectrum for community stations. Venezuela has instituted the most far-reaching community broadcast system including: dozens of community papers; a pan-Latin American television network, Telesur; hundreds of radio stations; and television stations reaching millions, such as Vives TV, Catia TV, and Petare TV (Artz, 2020). One example of cultural diversity in practice is Afro TV in Balo Vente on the east coast of Venezuela. Afro TV broadcasts the history and contemporary conditions of the Afro-Venezuelan community.

In Caracas, Avila TV – a station organized by youth – is one of the most watched stations in the city (Cassel, 2009). Started in 2006 by the Caracas city government, Avila TV operates under the Ministry of Popular Power for Communication and Information (MinCI) and functions independently. A staff of 30 makes all decisions on programming through its worker assembly. Avila covers the underground culture of Caracas, features hip-hop music from around the world, airs cultural programs, opposes consumerism, and refuses advertising. Additionally, Avila broadcasts local video productions, news and political programs encouraging global solidarity, as well as telenovelas which address gender, indigenous, and Afro-Venezuelan rights. Avila also regularly features criticisms of the Venezuelan government.

Afro TV, TV Avila, other citizen-run TV and dozens of community radio air community-produced documentaries and commentaries – providing examples for Nigerian citizen media production. Across Venezuela, Bolivia, and Nicaragua community media simultaneously express and prompt diverse levels of political consciousness developed and aired by neighborhood social movements. Although in each country, commercial media retain audience dominance, community media in Venezuela, Nicaragua, and Bolivia which operate independent of government have drawn large audiences.

Community media highlight how social being determines social consciousness – something that is sorely lacking in Nigeria, Ghana, and much of sub-Saharan Africa due to the dominance of commercial ideology. Community centered media with direct citizen access to production (not filtered through Nollywood's commercial enterprise) would greatly improve human creativity and allow collective cooperation as a means not just for media and entertainment, but as a pathway to more democratic and culturally-diverse societies in Africa.

References

Abubakar, M. (2018). Globalization and the creative/cultural industries: An assessment of Nigeria's position in global space. *Specialty Journal of Humanities and Cultural Science, 3*(1), 10–17.

Acland, C. R. (2003). *Screen traffic: Movies, multiplexes, and global culture.* Durham, NC: Duke University Press.

Acland, C. R. (2015). Consumer electronics and the building of an entertainment infrastructure. In L. Parks & N. Starosielski (eds), *Signal traffic: Critical studies of media infrastructures* (pp. 246–277). University of Illinois Press.

Adejunmobi, M. A. (2007). Nigerian video film as minor transnational process. *Postcolonial Text, 3*(2), 1–16.

Adesanya, A. (2000). From film to video. In J. Haynes (ed.), *Nigerian video films* (pp. 37–50). Ohio University.

Agency Report. (2016, October 18). Nigeria's broadcast industry to generate $1 billion annually. *Premium Times.* www.premiumtimesng.com/news/more-news/213031-nigerias-broadcast-industry-generate-1-billion-annually-minister.html

Arewa, O. B. (2015). Nollywood and African cinema: Cultural diversity and the global entertainment industry. In I. Calboli & S. Ragavan (eds), *Diversity in intellectual property: identities, interests, and intersections* (pp. 367–383). Cambridge: Cambridge University Press.

Artz, L. (2015). *Global entertainment media: A critical introduction.* Wiley.

Artz, L. (2016). Political power and political economy of media: Nicaragua and Bolivia. *Perspectives on Global Development and Technology, 15*(1–2), 166–193.

Artz, L. (2017). The political economy of attention: Global news agencies and the destruction of democracy. *Medijska istraživanja: znanstveno-stručni časopis za novinarstvo i medije, 23*(2), 59–82.

Artz, L. (2020). A political economy for social movements and revolution: Popular media access, power, and cultural hegemony. *Third World Quarterly, 41*(8), 1388–1405.

Artz, L. (2022). *Spectacle and diversity: Transnational media and global culture.* Routledge.

Bright, J. (2019, July 7). Canal+ acquires Nollywood studio ROK from iROKOTV to grow African film. *Techcrunch.com.* https://techcrunch,com/2019/07/15/canal-acquires-African-film-studio-rok-from-irokotv-to-grow-Nollywood/

Cassel, L. (2009, July 15). Avila TV: Revolutionizing television. (Interview with founder, Victor Rivas). *Venezuelanalysis.com.* https://venezuelanalysis.com/analysis/4519

Goldbaum, C. (2021, May 10). South African Filmmakers Move Beyond Apartheid Stories. *New York Times.* www.nytimes.com/2021/05/10/world/africa/south-african-filmmakers-move-beyond-apartheid-stories.html

Haynes, J. (2018). Keeping up: The corporatization of Nollywood's economy and paradigms for studying African screen media. *Africa Today, 64*(4), 3–29.

Haynes, J. (2000). Introduction. In J. Haynes (ed.), *Nigerian video films* (pp. 1–36). Ohio University.

Haynes, J., & Okome, O. (2000). Evolving popular media. In J. Haynes (ed.), *Nigerian video films* (pp. 51–88). Ohio University.

Iacobelli, D., & Grioni, R. (2004, February 13). Venezuela is one of few countries where right of communities to provide themselves with media is a reality. *Venezuelanalysis.* https://venezuelanalysis.com/analysis/354

Koo, H. (2001). *Korean workers: The culture and politics of class formation.* Cornell University Press.

Kraidy, M. (2005). *Hybridity or the cultural logic of globalization.* Temple University Press.

Kruger, F. (2020, February 12). South Africa has a rich bag of big, small and eclectic community radio stations. *Wits Radio Academy.* www.wits.ac.za/news/latest-news/opinion/2020/2020–02/sas-rich-bag-of-big-small-and-eclectic-community-radio-stations.html

Larkin, B. (2004). Degraded images, distorted sounds: Nigerian video and the infrastructure of piracy. *Public Culture, 16*(2), 289–314.

MacBride Commission (1982). *Many voices, one world: Towards a new, more just, and more efficient world information and communication order.* Paris: UNESCO.

Mattelart, A. (1976). Cultural imperialism in the multinational's age. *Instant Research on Peace and Violence, 6*(4), 160–174.

McCall, J. C. (2007). The pan-Africanism we have: Nollywood's invention of Africa. *Film International, 5*(4), 92–97.

Media Update (2021, August 18). Decoding community radio and its content. *mediaupdate.com.*www.mediaupdate.co.za/media/150981/decoding-community-radio-and-its-content

Miller, T., Govil, N., McMurria, J., Wang, T., & Maxwell, R. (2008). *Global Hollywood 2*, 2nd edn. London: British Film Institute.

Msugh-Ter Teddy, H., & Msugh-Ter Teddy, M. (2022). Nollywood as a soft power tool in the rebranding project of Nigeria. *Nta Tvc Journal of Communication*, 6(1), 41–51.

Nkrumah, K. (1965). *Neo-colonialism: The last stage of imperialism*. Thomas Nelson & Sons. London.

Ntshangase, J. S. (2021). Mapping community radio in sub-Saharan Africa. *Fojo Media Institute*. Kalmar, Sweden. https://journalism.co.za/wp-content/uploads/2021/07/Mapping-Community-Radio-in-Sub-Saharan-Africa-Report_FINAL-24–06–21.pdf

Ogbe, S. J., Ayodele, B. J., Onyeka, E. D., & William, Y. (2020). Film as purveyor of Nigeria's image and socio-cultural development: An analysis of selected Nollywood movies. *Igwebuike: An African Journal of Arts and Humanities*, 6(6), 119–138.

Onuzulike, U. (2009). Nollywood: Nigerian video films as a cultural and technological hybridity. *Intercultural Communication Studies*, 18(1), 176–188.

Robinson, W. I. (2004). *A theory of global capitalism: Production, class, and state in a transnational world*. Johns Hopkins University Press.

Schiller, H. (1976). *Communication and cultural domination*. White Plains, NY: International Arts and Sciences Press.

Schiller, H. (1991). Not yet the post-imperialist era. *Critical Studies in Mass Communication*, 8(1), 13–28.

Sklair, L. (2001). *The transnational capitalist class*. New York: Wiley.

Tsaaior, J. T. (2018). "New" Nollywood video films and the post/nationality of Nigeria's film culture. *Research in African Literatures*, 49(1), 145–159.

Tobechukwu, E. N. (2009). Nollywood, new communication technologies and indigenous culture in a globalized world: The Nigerian dilemma. *International Journal of Social & Management Sciences*, 2(2), 62–84.

Ugochukwu, F. (2013). Nollywood across languages – issues in dubbing and subtitling. *Journal of Intercultural Communication*, 33(5). https://immi.se/oldwebsite/nr33/ugochukwu.html

Witt, E. (2017). *Nollywood: The making of a film empire*. New York: Columbia Global Reports.

Zajc, M. (2009). Nigerian video film cultures. *Anthropological Notebooks*, 15(1), 65–85.

4 Ownership and Market Trends in Telecoms

Tokunbo Ojo

Globally, telecommunications sector is one of the largest and most profitable areas of the world economy (Jin, 2005). Based on the January 2022 data from World Trade Organization (WTO), "the sector accounts for over US$ 1.6 trillion in revenue, of which 65% is from mobile services" at the end of the 2020/2021 fiscal year (WTO, n.d., online). That was about 5.6% of the total revenues of the global trade, which was US$ 28.5 trillion, in 2021 (UNCTAD, 2022, online). In Africa, telecommunications sector is also central to many countries' economic growth and national development. In 2021, the mobile wireless, which currently constitutes about 98% of the African telecommunications sector, "generated around 8% of GDP across Sub-Saharan Africa, a contribution that amounted to almost $140 billions of economic value added" (GSMA, 2022, p. 4). The mobile wireless markets in South Africa, Nigeria and Kenya generate a total revenue of $US 9.67 billion, US$ 8.58 billion, and $US 4.08, respectively, in 2021 (Communications Authority of Kenya, 2022; Nigerian Communications Commission, 2022; Winseck, 2022).

The influential London-based *African Business* Magazine had 17 telecommunications companies on its 2022 list of the continent's top 250 companies from various sectors of economic activities. Combined market capitalization value of these 17 telecommunications companies, which included MTN Group of South Africa, Safaricom of Kenya, Maroc Telecom of Morocco and SONATEL of Cote D' Ivoire, was $US 104.1 billion as at the first quarter of 2022 (African Business Magazine, 2022). This chapter provides an overview of the evolution of the African telecommunications sector. It uses Nigerian mobile wireless market as the case study in its examination of current market structure, key market players and patterns of concentration trend in the last decade (2011–2021).

DOI: 10.4324/9781003352907-5

Market Structure, Competition and Concentration

For media and telecommunications scholars, "questions around monopo-lization, competition, and ownership represent a particularly lively area of interest" because of the central importance of media and telecommunica-tions industries to human experiences and every nation-state's economy, culture and politics (Doyle, 2021, p. 80). The structural configuration of media and telecommunications industries in terms of market operations has wider impacts on public interest, market competition, citizens' choice, ownership and diversity in relations to the broader societal communica-tion *needs* and *wants*. Accordingly, for the media scholars, systematic mapping of concentration and competition levels of media and telecom-munications industries at various levels (national, regional and global mar-kets) provides useful indicators on individual media and telecommunications firms' market and economic power, which directly and indirectly influence the control and available choices to meet the communication *wants* and *needs* of diverse publics, politically, socially and culturally (Doyle, 2021; Albarran, 2010; Winseck & Pike, 2007).

Conceptually, "competition and concentration are two more interre-lated concepts useful in understanding the functions of the media econ-omy" (Albarran, 2010, p. 47). Competition refers to the degree of rivalry among two or more firms, offering goods and services to targeted but diverse groups of customers/audiences/subscribers/advertisers, in one or more geographic markets *or/and* product markets (Hitt, Ireland & Hoskisson, 2017; Picard, 1989). The degree and intensity of the competi-tive rivalry is contingent on the market structure as well as on a variety of other factors that include: product differentiation choices, the number of available buyers, number of firms in the market, market entry conditions and government regulation (Picard, 2011; Doyle, 2013). Concentration refers to the extent of individual firms' market dominance, power and con-trol. Individual firms' market dominance and power are assessed by the size of their market share in a given market. Overall annual revenue or/and overall annual subscription/circulation number are the often used measur-ing indicators in the evaluative assessment of extent of concentration level in a given market, based on Herfindahl-Hirschman Index (HHI) and con-centration ratios (CR) formulae.[1] With the concentration ratios (CR) method, market concentration is determined either by adding up the mar-ket share of the top four firms (CR4) with most market shares or by adding up market share of the top eight firms (CR8) with most market shares. When CR4 is used, the market is considered concentrated if the combined market shares of the top four firms is equal to or greater than 50% of the market share. When CR8 is used, the market is concentrated if the com-bined market share of the eight top firms is 75% or above (Albarran, 2010; Albarran, 2002).

The HHI method squares each firm's market share and then sums the resulting number to arrive at an overall HHI score. The intensity of concentration is identified based on the following thresholds:

- If the overall total score (i.e., HHI score) is less than 1,500, the market is competitive and diverse
- If the HHI score is greater than 1,500, but less than 2,500, the market is moderately concentrated
- If the HHI score is greater than 2,500, the market is highly concentrated.

A monopoly exists when there is only one firm in the market with 100% market share (HHI = 10,000). Though it is rare, if there are 100 firms in the market with 1% market share each, such a market is deemed a highly competitive market.

Monopoly, oligopoly and monopolistic competition are the three common market structures that characterize media communication and telecommunications industries (Albarran, 2010). These market structures "can be thought of as a continuum, where the number of sellers, where the number of sellers increases from one in a monopoly to an unlimited number in perfect competition.... Perfect competition is rarely in the media industries (an exception being websites)" (Albarran, 2010, p. 22–23). In a monopoly market structure, competition is non-existent because there is one firm in the market and that firm has an absolute control over the market operation. Oligopoly market structure generally have few firms, typically between three to ten firms, that are in direct and indirect competition with one another in the geographic or/and product markets. Unlike the oligopoly market structure, monopolist competition exists when there are several firms offering similar goods and/or services, which are "not perfect, substitutes for one another" (Albarran, 2002, p. 34). Since the goods *or/ and* services being offered are similar, each firm uses a combination of methods such as aggressive marketing, advertising and lower prices to differentiate their good and/or services in the minds of targeted citizens for the good consumption or service subscription (Albarran, 2002; Doyle, 2013). Broadly, a careful analysis of the underlying economics, culture and socio-political forces, which shape the scale and dynamics of operation of media and telecommunication companies within countries and globally, broadens perspectives on frequent oscillation of media and telecommunication industries around oligopolistic and monopolistic market structures (Doyle, 2021; Albarran, 2010; Winseck & Pike, 2007). The next section provides an overview of the market evolution of global and African telecommunications. The HHI formula is applied in the case study of the Nigerian mobile wireless market in the third section of this chapter.

Global and African Telecommunication: From Natural Monopoly to Market Liberalization

For much of the 20th century, telecommunications industries operated as the natural monopoly under the authority of the state governments in Africa and many countries of the world. Natural monopoly refers to a single firm's dominance and control of a given market sector of an economy, without any form of competition from any other firm. In the socio-economic sense, natural monopoly, which theoretically bestows market advantage by accident of geography and technological arrangement of production processes, is deemed as an "ideal" structure in an industry whereby competition and market forces can be destructive to the supply of essential products *or/and* services (Plaiss, 2016; Sharkey, 1982). Natural monopoly theoretically bestows market advantage by accident of geography and technological arrangement of production processes (Plaiss, 2016).

Telecommunications was deemed as one of those industries, on the basis that telecommunications services and products were *public utilities.* Hence, natural monopoly would ensure universal telecommunications access and service; "based on the understanding that centralization of operations would be more reliable because monopolies could best tap economies of scale and scope to better achieve growth and equity" (Chakravartty & Sarikakis, 2006, p. 59). The justification of the natural monopoly was also rooted in socio-political logic that the state governments must maintain and control telecommunications infrastructure for national security. For many postcolonial African nation-states, state monopoly of telecommunication operations and services was naturally in tune with the economic and political organizations of their national development agenda, "which emphasized state control, centralized planning, and national sovereignty" (Noam, 1999, p. 3). With the exception of few countries such as the US that had state enabled corporate monopolies, natural monopoly in telecommunications sector was statutorily well-entrenched in the international communication regime until the mid-1980s when the politics of neoliberal regime began to take stronghold in the international system and in turn fostered the acceleration process for the deregulation of public enterprises in European and North American countries.

The authorized divestiture of the AT&T by the US communication regulatory agency and the Conservative government of Prime Minister Margaret Thatcher led deregulation process of the UK telecommunication industry in 1980s marked the beginning of the end of natural monopoly in the global telecommunications sector. "With the election of Margaret Thatcher in Britain in May 1979 and of Ronald Reagan in the United States in November 1980," the 1980s and 1990s "saw the triumph of conservative forces" and neoliberal economic approach in world politics (Noel & Therien, 2008, p. 138). The governments of Thatcher and Reagan strongly championed pro-market policies, globally, through the bilateral and multilateral trade agreements. They leveraged their countries' structural power and influence in the Bretton Wood Institutions (i.e. World Bank and International Monetary Fund) and the World Trade Organization (WTO) for the global diffusion of neoliberal policy norms and ideas. The ascendancy of the WTO as the dominant global forum for international trade negotiation was particularly strategic in this regard.

The WTO's well-profound influence in global and regional telecommunications was self-evident, following its facilitation of the successful negotiation of the 1997 agreement on basic telecommunications services. The agreement was instrumental in accelerating the global waves of deregulation and privatization of telecommunications industries. Seven African countries were among the first 69 signatories of the agreement, which included a strong commitment to market liberalization and opening of telecommunications sector to foreign investment in their respective countries. Côte d'Ivoire, Ghana, Mauritius, Morocco, Senegal, South Africa and Tunisia were the seven African countries that signed the agreement at the time. The geopolitical pressure for the deregulation of the telecommunications through the frameworks of bilateral and multilateral trade agreements was further intensified, with the European Commission's issuance of *Green Paper on the Development of the Common Market for Telecommunications Services and Equipment* in 1987 and the International Telecommunication Union (ITU)'s 1996 *The African Green Paper: Telecommunications Policies for Africa*. The influence of national legislations such as the Telecommunications Act of 1996 in the United States cannot be understated as well (Workneh & Steeves, 2020).

The advancement in communication technologies, particularly with the fiber optics, internet and wireless communication technologies, also accelerated the dismantle of the natural monopoly telecommunication regime, globally. The arguments of high production cost and technological factors, which were among rationales for normalization of the natural monopoly, were no longer logically tenable both in business economic sense and in public policy discourse. The advancement in the fiber optics, satellite networks and new communication technologies offered a new ray of options and possibilities for the support and delivery of telecommunications services. For instance, the technological advancement enabled the system shifts from analogue system to digital and wireless system, while also opening multi-channels and spectrum of communication opportunities with the emergence of cellular mobile network and voice over internet protocol telephony. Couple with the technological advancement and innovation, the inefficiency and poor performance of the state-run monopolies in many jurisdictions further strengthened the argument for the deregulation and neoliberal market-oriented approaches in telecommunications.

In African contexts, the highly touted universal telecommunications service and access were never achieved in many countries under the natural monopoly regime. For example,

> while telephone penetration in the United States in 1994 was almost 65 main lines per 100 population and 47 for all the Organisation for Economic Co-operation and Development (OECD) countries, it was 1.5 in Africa.... In the entire continent of Africa, there were fewer phone lines than in New York State.
>
> (Noam, 1999, p. 3)

International Telecommunication Union (ITU) estimated that Africa as a whole had an average wait time of three to five years to get a fixed telephone line in the mid-1990s, with the backlog of over 3 million customers in the system queue for telephone line and service (ITU, 1998). The low density of the fixed-line telephony and the proliferation of underdeveloped telecommunications infrastructures in many African nations-states were also not detached from the history of colonial rules and resource extraction on the continent. As M' Bayo (1997) wrote:

> the extension of telecommunications to Africa was based primarily on the interest of the Western world, especially European colonialists bent on exploiting the peoples and resources of the African continent. To achieve their aim, they linked African capital cities, strategically located along the coasts of the Atlantic and Indian Oceans with European metropolises through oceanic cables. The effect has been that external telecommunications in almost all of Africa are better developed than domestic telecommunications infrastructures.
>
> (p. 352)

Following the attainment of political independence from the colonial administrations, many postcolonial African nations-states' governments rarely invest in the upgrade or modernization of the inherited telecommunications infrastructures due to other competing national development agenda and socio-political priorities such as education and health care. By the late 1970s and early 1980s, several of the inherited infrastructures were crumbling. The combined ripple effects of the economic downturn, debt crises of 1980s, and political instabilities further ripped apart the archaic telecommunication systems and exposed system-wide deficiencies in many African countries (Djiofack-Zebaze & Keck, 2009). The short-slightness of national development agenda and telecommunications policies of several postcolonial African nations-states' governments cannot be overlooked in this context as well.

Although the pace has not been the same across the continent, the move from authoritarian military rule to a more market-friendly but fragile multi-party democratization process in the late 1990s became pivotal in the structural reforms of African telecommunications industries. The democratic governments were purposefully receptive to the global wave of neoliberal policy regime in telecommunications. As at 2021, telecommunication industries in almost all the African countries have shifted from the state-owned or the state-controlled monopolies to predominately market-driven oligopolies. The 'new' market structure is made up of the consortium of largely multinational and transnational telecommunication companies, and a handful of state-owned companies. In this context, with the exception of Djibouti, Ethiopia and Eritrea, all countries have at least two operators in the mobile telecommunication sector as at 2021. Table 4.1 presents the 2021 market share of mobile telecommunication operators/firms in a cross section of African countries.

Save for a handful of countries such as Ethiopia, transnational firms dominate African telecommunication industries in terms of revenues and market shares at the national and regional level (Orr, 2018).

Table 4.1 Mobile wireless telecommunication operators, 2021

Countries	Subscription Number (2021)	Operators and Percentage of Market Share (Based on the Year 2021 Subscription Number) (%)
Algeria	47,015,757	Algeria Telecom Mobile (42.18), Optimum Telecom Mobile (31.04) & Wataniya Telecom (26.78)
Benin Republic	12,731,782	SpaceTel Benin (local subsidiary of MTN) (70.9) & Moov (29.1)
Botswana*	4,243,124	Mascom Wireless (43.2), Orange Botswana (38.9) & Botswana Telecommunication Corporation (17.9)
Burkina Faso	24,708,389	Orange BF (44.23), ONATEL SA (42.32) & Telecel Faso (13.45)
Cameroon	22,820,000	MTN (46.5), Orange (43.5) & Nexttel Cameroon (10)
Cote d'Ivoire	44,561,505	Orange (43.4), MTN (33.1) & Moov (23.5)
Democratic Republic of Congo	46,885,799	Vodacom (33.86), Airtel (28.55), Orange 27.86) & Africell (9.73)

(Continued)

Table 4.1 (Continued)

Countries	Subscription Number (2021)	Operators and Percentage of Market Share (Based on the Year 2021 Subscription Number) (%)
Ghana	40,450,000	MTN (59.24), Vodafone (20.39), Airtel Tigo (18.27) & Glo (2.09)
Kenya	65,085,720	Safaricom (70.4), Airtel (27.6), Telkom (1.9), Equitel (0.1) & Jamii Telecom (0).
Niger	14,156,225	Airtel (46.56), Zamani (28.38), Moov (22.69) & Niger Telecoms (2.04)
Nigeria	195,463, 898	MTN (38), Airtel (28), Glo (28) & EMTS (also 9mobile –6)
Rwanda	10,902,989	MTN (63.8), Airtel (36.2)
Senegal	19,859,981	Orange (56.44), Free (23.67), Expresso Senegal (19.39), Promobile (1.50) & Hayo (0.02)
Sierra Leone	8,720,300	Africell (51.4), Orange (44), QCell (2.9) & SierraTel (1.6)
Tanzania	54,116,218	Vodacom (29.4), Airtel (27.2), Tigo (24.7), Halotel (13.3), TTCL (3.4), Zantel (2), Smile (0.02)
Tunisia	15,645,000	Ooredoo Tunisia (41.6), Tunisia Telecom (31.5), Orange (25) & Lycamobile Tunisia (1.8)
Zambia	20, 200,000	MTN (42.3), Airtel (39.7) & Zamtel (17.9)
Zimbabwe	14,257,590	Econet (64.9), NetOne (31.4) & Telecel (3.7)

Data Source: Compiled by the author from annual reports and statistical databases of the regulatory agencies of the selected countries, and a variety of business news sources.

While there are liberalized fixed wired telephony markets as well, this segment of African telecommunications industries has become practically non-existent in many countries. The continuous proliferation of mobile wireless telephony, which is rapidly becoming an essential element of everyday life on the continent, has rendered fixed wired telephony redundant in many households. In some territories, fixed wired telephony service is also becoming obsolete due to factors that include unreliable quality of service and frequent service disruption as a result of natural disasters or accidental cutting of copper connection whenever there are construction projects. The continent's teledensity for fixed-wired telephony was 0.6 per 100 inhabitants in 2021(ITU 2022). In contrast, almost 90% of the continent's population were within the mobile-cellular network coverage and teledensity for mobile telephony was 82.7 per 100 inhabitants as at the end of 2021 (ITU 2021; ITU 2022). The next section provides a case study analysis of Nigerian mobile wireless market.

Case Study: Nigerian Mobile Wireless Market

Nigerian mobile wireless telecommunications market has grown tremendously from an obscured nascent market in 1990s to one of the largest mobile wireless telecommunications markets in Africa in 2021. In terms of the number of mobile phone subscribers and generated revenues annually, it ranks among the top three mobile wireless markets on the continent (Ojo, 2017, Southwood, 2022). By the way of example, in 1999, there were less than 35,000 mobile phone subscribers[2] in the country of estimated 140 million people and the services only covered less than 20% of the country's geographical landmass of 923,768km[2] (Ndukwe, 2011). In 2021, the mobile wireless services covered approximately 92% of the country's geographical landmass and there were approximately 195.1 million subscribers (Nigerian Communications Commission, 2022). The country's estimated population in 2021 was 213.4 million (World Bank, n.d., online). The mobile wireless currently drives the Nigerian telecommunication industry, as it accounts for 99.8% of the business activities of the entire industry as at 2021 (Nigerian Communications Commission, 2021). The market generated a total revenue of 2.77 trillion naira (US$8.58 billion) in 2021 (Nigerian Communications Commission, 2022).

The transformation of the Nigerian mobile wireless telecommunications started in 2000/2001 when the Nigerian Communication Commission (NCC), which is Nigeria's telecommunications regulatory agency, conducted digital mobile license auction for the global system for mobile communication (GSM). Of the four GSM service licenses granted at the end of the auction bidding, three went to private corporate entities – Econet Wireless of Zimbabwe (with a consortium of Nigerian investors and partners), MTN of South Africa, and Communication Investment Limited (CIL)[3] that Nigerian oil tycoon Mike Adenuga had 35% ownership stake in (Sutherland, 2018; Southwood, 2022; Ndukwe, 2011). The fourth GSM licence was awarded to the mobile subsidiary (M-TEL) of the state-owned incumbent wired/fixed telephony operator, NITEL. A year after the GSM licenses were granted, the government incumbent operator, NITEL, was put up for sales. Although the sale of NITEL failed to materialize in 2002 due to a combination of legal, socio-political and financial factors, it was eventually sold off as liquidated property assets almost a decade later. In 2007, fifth GSM license was granted to Etisalat, a mobile operator from the United Arab Emirates (UAE).

The award of the GSM licenses to the private corporate entities was part of the NCC's spearheaded full liberalization and deregulation process of Nigerian telecommunications sector. The process, which began in 1992 under the military dictatorship, did not fully take off until Nigeria's transition from military rule to the democratic rule in 1999. The newly elected democratic government, Nigeria's first since 1983, prioritized the deregulation and privatization of telecommunications sector in its national development agenda for the 21st century global economy. The high prioritization of liberalization and deregulation of telecommunication industry was part of the new government's aggressive efforts to improve the country's teledensity and also to boast the country's economic growth through foreign direct investment (FDI). As intended, the telecommunications deregulation and the licensing of GSM operators spurred increase in private capital investment and FDI in Nigerian economy.

> According to the NCC, prior to the licensing of the digital mobile operators, there was about $50m in private investment in the telecoms sector. But between 2001 and 2007, it attracted more than $9.5bn, a substantial part of which is FDI.
>
> (*The Banker*, 2007, online)

In 2021, the sector drew approximately US$ 108 million in FDI (Nigerian Investment Promotion Commission, 2022).

Of the five licensees, only MTN and Glo Mobile have not gone through massive ownership change since licensed to operate in Nigeria. M-Tel (state run mobile operator) is no longer in business operation. Nigerian business segments and brand operation of Econet and Etisalat have been acquired by other corporate entities and investors. Etisalat Nigeria is now 9mobile/EMTS, after the Etisalat International pulled out of Nigeria in 2017 and transferred its 45% holding stakes in its Nigerian venture to a group of loan trustees (Carvalho, 2017). The GSM license, which was initially awarded to the Econet and its consortium of Nigerian investors, is now owned by Airtel Nigeria, a subsidiary of Bharti Airtel of India. From a business economics perspective, firm consolidation, ownership change and acquisitions, as evident with the cases of Econet and Etisalat, are considered purposeful business decisions that foster service efficiencies, sale maximization and strategic competition against other companies in the sector (Croteau & Hoynes, 2001). By implication, such ownership change and organizational restructuring are part of the normative process of growing and maturing corporate firms in a competitive business market. While such perspective might be theoretically valid, there is no guaranteed likelihood of earning above-average returns or increased market power for any firm based on ownership and organizational restructuring. In addition to the general market forces and the firm's organizational business acumen, the outcomes of firm ownership change, acquisition and business consolidation are also predicated on the internal and external forces of economics, socio-cultural practices and politics in the firm's geographical areas of operation.

Structurally, Nigerian mobile wireless market is oligopoly in nature. The market concentration level is relatively high, with the HHI score of 2638 in 2012 and the HHI score of 3105 in 2022. For each year of the past decade assessed, the HHI scores have never been below 2638. Since 2018, the scores have been increasing consistently every year. Table 4.2 presents the sector's HHI scores and each firm's market share from 2011 till 2022. The market share is determined, based on the overall number of active mobile phone subscribers per year across all four firms' networks. Together, three firms (MTN, Glo Mobile & Airtel) have over 80% of the overall market shares in almost every year of the time period assessed. The market share of EMTS/9Mobile has declined every year since Etisalat International pulled out of the operation in Nigeria in 2017. EMTS/9Mobile has lost over 50% of its market share, dropping from 11.70% in 2017 to 5.78% in 2022.

Of the four firms currently present in the Nigerian mobile wireless market, MTN is the most dominant firm. It has the most market share both in terms of the annual generated revenue and the number of subscribers. As shown in Table 4.2, MTN's market share, based on the number of subscribers, hovers over 35% of the overall market size in each year of the period that this chapter assessed. As one of the incumbents in the liberalized mobile wireless market in Nigeria, MTN has consolidated its market presence and built up its market dominance in the country. The extent of MTN's market

Table 4.2 Firms' market share and the sector's HHI scores from 2011 to 2022

Year	MTN (%)	Glo Mobile (%)	Airtel (%)	EMTS(9mobile) (%)	HHI Scores
2011	43.80	20.90	18.90	11.30	2845
2012	42.10	21.40	15.00	13.20	2638
2013	44.60	20.40	19.00	13.40	2948
2014	44.00	21.00	20.00	15.00	3002
2015	43.00	21.00	20.00	16.00	2946
2016	40.10	24.20	22.10	13.50	2864
2017	36.10	26.40	25.70	11.70	2798
2018	39.00	26.00	26.00	9.00	2954
2019	37.30	28.00	27.20	7.40	2970
2020	39.55	26.85	27.25	6.36	3068
2021	37.40	28.10	27.60	6.60	3016
2022	40.06	27.13	27.03	5.78	3105

Source: Author's compilation, based on the Nigerian Communication Commission (NCC)'s various reports and data on the firms' market share and number of subscribers.

dominance is also evident in its annual generated revenue in proportion to the overall mobile wireless market revenue per annum. Whereby it had approximately 49% of the overall mobile market revenue of 1.57 trillion naira (US$ 5.13 billion) in 2017, it had about 54% of the overall mobile market revenue of 2.77 trillion naira (US$8.58 billion) in 2021. Table 4.3 presents MTN's revenue from 2017 to 2021 in proportion to the overall mobile wireless market revenue per year in the time period.

In accordance with the provision in the *Nigerian Communications Act-Competition Practices Regulation, 2007*, MTN holds a dominant position in the market. As the Act stated:

> Subject to any other determination of the Commission under this Part, or to any demonstration by a Licensee in the specific circumstances that the presumption should not apply, the Commission will presume that any Licensee whose gross revenues in a specific communications market exceed forty percent (40%) of the total gross revenues of all Licensees in that market, is in a dominant position in that market.
>
> (part IV, section 20, p. B466)

By the provisions in the above cited 2007 regulatory act as well as in the 2003 *Nigerian Communication Act*, NCC is legally obligated to safeguard fair market competition and also ensure that the conduct of the licensee with the dominant position does not substantially lessen market competition. To fulfill its regulatory obligation, as per the provisions in both acts, NCC does from time-to-time conduct assessment studies on the level of competition in the Nigerian telecommunications. Its 2012/13 assessment study established a pattern of MTN's market dominance in the mobile voice segment. The study also identified MTN and Glo as the joint dominant

Table 4.3 MTN's Annual Generated Revenue from 2017 to 2021

Year	Overall Mobile Wireless (GSM) Revenue Per Year (Currency: naira)	MTN's Annual Revenue (Currency: naira)	MTN's Percentage Share of the Overall Sector Revenue (%)
2017	N 1.57 trillion	N 764.9 billion	48.7
2018	N 1.78 trillion	N 936.7 billion	52.6
2019	N 2.01 trillion	N 1.07 trillion	53.0
2020	N 2.27 trillion	N 1.23 trillion	54.0
2021	N 2.77 trillion	N 1.49 trillion	53.7

Data Source: Author's compilation from NCC's annual reports, and MTN Nigeria's 2021 prospectus and 2021 financial statements.

The presented revenue data in this table is only for the voice and data services of MTN in Nigeria.

operators in the wholesale leased lines and transmission capacity segment of the market. So far, NCC has been cautiously ambivalent in enacting strong regulatory actions to address the issue.

Conclusion

Similar patterns of entrenched high level of market concentration, and market dominance by few firms in the mobile wireless telecommunications have been observed in Kenya, Uganda, South Africa and dozens of other countries as well (Alemu, 2018; Angelopulo & Potgieter, 2016). Broadly, regardless of the progress made with the market liberalization reforms and mobile wireless telephony, there are entrenched patterns of highly concentrated markets in African telecommunications industries. With the growing evolution of African mobile wireless telecommunications and the convergence of telecommunications with the broadcasting and e-banking sectors, high level of market concentration cannot be left unchecked by the national regulatory agencies. Absence of regulatory oversight or interventions in this regard might have dire ramifications for the rights to communicate, customer rights and media democracy. Hence, no product or geographic market should be left to regulate itself – simply based on the law of demand and supply or open-ended fair competition norms that are subject to multiple socio-economic and political interpretations.

Notes

1 There are other formula tools such as Lorenz curve and Noam index, as outlined in Albarran & Dimmick (1996), Birkinbine & Gómez (2020), Iosifidis (2010), and Noam (2016). However, both HHI and concentration ratios, are commonly used measuring tools by several national regulatory agencies around the world, including Ofcom in the UK, and the Federal Communications Commission (FCC) in the United States.
2 It is instructive to note that reference to the number of subscribers in relation to country's population was not to imply that there was one mobile subscription per individual. An individual could have more multiple mobile subscription services. That is, an individual could have more than one mobile telephony service subscription.
3 Communications Investment Limited (CIL) metamorphosed to Glo Mobile, which is owned by Mike Adenuga's company. Southwood (2022) provided a rich contextual explanation of CIL's dramatic evolution to Glo Mobile.

References

African Business Magazine (2022). "Africa's top 250 companies: Firms brace for downturn as global economy lurches." *African Business Magazine*, 493(May), 10–26.

Albarran, A., & Dimmick, J. (1996). "Concentration and economics of multiformity in the communication industries." *Journal of Media Economics*, 9(4), 41–50.

Albarran, A. (2002). *Media Economics – Understanding Markets, Industries and Concepts*, 2nd edn. Ames, IO: Iowa State Press.

Albarran, A. (2010). *The Media Economy*. London: Routledge.

Alemu, R. (2018). *The Liberalization of the Telecommunications Sector in Sub-Saharan Africa and Fostering Competition in Telecommunication Services Markets: An Analysis of the Regulatory Framework in Uganda*. Berlin, Germany: Springer.

Angelopulo, G., & Potgieter, P. (2016). "Media ownership and concentration in South Africa." In E. Noam (ed.), *Who Owns the World's Media: Media Concentration and Ownership around the World* (pp. 986–1008). Oxford: Oxford University Press.

Birkinbine, B., & Gómez, R. (2020). "New methods for mapping media concentration: network analysis of joint ventures among firms." *Media, Culture & Society*, 42(7-8), 1078–1094.

Carvalho, S. (2017, July 10). "UPDATE 1-Etisalat to exit Nigeria after regulators intervene." *Reuters*, online. Available: www.reuters.com/article/etisalat-group-nigeria-idUSL8N1K13H5 (accessed February 3, 2023).

Chakravartty, P., & Sarikakis, K. (2006). *Media Policy and Globalization*. New York: Palgrave.

Croteau, D., & Hoynes, W. (2001). *The Business of Media: Corporate Media and the Public Interest*. Thousand Oaks, CA: Pine Forge.

Communications Authority of Kenya (2022). *Fourth Quarter Sector Statistics Report for the Financial Year 2021/22 (1st April–30th June, 2022)*. Nairobi: Communications Authority of Kenya.

Djiofack-Zebaze, C., & Keck, A (2009). "Telecommunications services in Africa: The impact of WTO commitments and unilateral reform on sector performance and economic growth." *World Development*, 37(5), 919–940.

Doyle, G. (2013). *Understanding Media Economics*, 2nd edn. London: Sage

Doyle, G. (2021). "Economic perspectives on the characteristics and operation of media industries." In P. McDonald (ed.) *Routledge Companion to Media Industries* (pp. 76–95). London: Routledge.

Federal Republic of Nigeria (2007). Nigerian Communications Act – Competition Practices Regulations, 2007. *Official Gazette*, 101(94), pp. B459–B473.

GSMA (2022). *The Mobile Economy Sub-Saharan Africa 2022*. Nairobi, GSMA.

Hitt, M., Ireland, R., & Hoskisson, R. (2017). *Strategic Management Competitiveness & Globalization*, 12th edn. Boston, MA: Cengage Learning.

Iosifidis, P. (2010). "Pluralism and concentration of media ownership: measurement issues." *Javnost – The Public*, 17(3), 5–21.

ITU (2022). Statistics. *World Telecommunication/ICT Indicators database*. Online: www.itu.int/en/ITU-D/Statistics/Pages/stat/default.aspx (accessed December 27, 2022).

ITU (2021). *Digital Trends in Africa 2021*. Geneva, Switzerland: ITU.

ITU (1998). *African telecommunication indicators*. Geneva, Switzerland: ITU.

Jin, D. Y. (2005). "The telecom crisis and beyond: Restructuring of the global tele-communications system." *International Communication Gazette*, 67(3), 289–304.

M'Bayo, R. (1997). "Africa and the global information infrastructure: Prospects, obstacles, preferences and policies for the 21st century." *International Communication Gazette*, 59(4), 345–364.

Ndukwe, E. (2011). "The telecommunication revolution in Nigeria." Convocation Lecture delivered on 2 December at the Igbinedion University, Okada, Nigeria.

Nigerian Communications Commission (2021). *2021 Subscriber/Network Data Annual Report*. Abuja: Nigerian Communications Commission.

Nigerian Communications Commission (2022). *2022 Subscriber/Network Data Annual Report*. Abuja: Nigerian Communications Commission.

Nigerian Investment Promotion Commission (2022, June 9). "Nigeria records N23.982 billion FDI from telecom sector in the first Q1 of 2022." Online: www.nipc.gov.ng/2022/06/09/nigeria-records-n23–982-billion-fdi-from-telecom-sector-in-the-first-q1-of-2022/ (accessed February 2, 2023).

Noam, E. (1999). *Telecommunications in Africa*. Oxford: Oxford University Press.

Noam, E. (2016). *Who Owns the World's Media: Media Concentration and Ownership around the World*. Oxford: Oxford University Press.

Noel, A., & Therien, J. (2008). *Left and Right in Global Politics*. Cambridge: Cambridge University Press.

Ojo, T. (2017). Political Economy of Huawei's Market Strategies in the Nigerian Telecommunication Market. *International Communication Gazette*, 79(3), 317–332.

Orr, D. W. (2018). "A new face of the state: The role of telecom providers in African politics." *Harvard Africa Policy Journal*, 13(Spring), 39–53.

Picard, R. (1989). *Media Economics – Concepts & Issues*. London: Sage.

Picard, R. (2011). *The Economics and Financing of Media Companies*, 2nd edn. New York: Fordham University Press.

Plaiss A. (2016). "From natural monopoly to public utility: Technological determinism and the political economy of infrastructure in progressive-era America." *Technology and Culture*, 57(4), 806–830.

Sharkey, W. (1982). *The Theory of Natural Monopoly*. Cambridge: Cambridge University Press.

Southwood, R. (2022). *Africa 2.0*. Manchester: Manchester University Press.

Sutherland, E. (2018). "Bribery and corruption in telecommunications – the case of Nigeria." *Digital Policy, Regulation and Governance*, 20(3), 244–272.

The Banker (2007). "Special Supplement: Nigeria – Telecoms Renewal – Massive Investment in Telecoms Has Secured Nigeria a Top-10 World Ranking for Mobile Phone Growth." *The Banker*, 1. Online: www.proquest.com/trade-journals/special-supplement-nigeria-telecoms-renewal/docview/225633132/se-2

UNCTAD (Feb 17, 2022). "Global trade hits record high of $28.5 trillion in 2021, but likely to be subdued in 2022." Online: https://unctad.org/news/global-trade-hits-record-high-285-trillion-2021-likely-be-subdued-2022 (accessed December 27, 2022).

Winseck, D., & Pike, R. (2007). *Communication and Empire: Media Power and Globalization, 1860–1930*. Durham, NC: Duke University Press.

Winseck, D. (2022). "Growth and upheaval in the network media economy, 1984–2021." https://doi.org/10.22215/gmicp/2022.01. Global Media and Internet Concentration Project, Carleton University.

Workneh, T. W., & Steeves, H. L. (2020). "State monopoly of telecommunications in Ethiopia: Revisiting natural monopoly in the era of deregulation." In R. Nichols & G. Martinez (eds), *Political Economy of Media Industries: Global Transformations and Challenges* (pp. 127–147). New York: Routledge.

World Bank (n.d.). "Nigeria" https://datacommons.org/place/country/NGA?utm_medium=explore&mprop=amount&popt=EconomicActivity&cpv=activitySource%2CGrossDomesticProduction&hl=en# (accessed January 30, 2023).

WTO (n.d.). "Telecommunication Services" www.wto.org/english/tratop_e/serv_e/telecom_e/telecom_e.htm (accessed December 27, 2022).

5 Decolonizing Journalism Education in South Africa

Kealeboga Aiseng

Institutions of higher learning worldwide serve as diverse communities with linguistic, cultural, sexual, racial, and political diversities. These higher education institutions have brought together a diverse range of people in their spaces. Historically, in South Africa, universities were spaces reserved for the elites and even excluded people on racial grounds. However, things have changed since the first democratic elections in 1994. Universities in South Africa are accommodating predominantly black students; they are also adopting language policies to include indigenous languages in their curricula; there is now racial progress to include more black academics and administrators in universities, and universities have policies promoting gender equality. All these changes did not come easily. They are a product of decades of resistance against the oppressive exclusionary white system. But these changes also call for questions on how and what knowledge we produce.

In 2015–2016 South Africa experienced protests by university students under the movements of #FeeMustFall and #RhodesMustFall. These movements were calling for the decommodification of higher education and critiquing the colonial heritage of higher education in South Africa. Ultimately, scholars such as Bosch (2017) and Naicker (2016) have called South African universities spaces of struggle, spaces of decolonial conflict. Other scholars have expressed similar views about African universities in the past. For instance, Emeagwali and Dei (2014, p. 4) highlighted that

> the decolonization of African academy remains one of the biggest challenges, not only in terms of the curriculum, teaching strategies, and textbooks, but also in terms of the democratization of knowledge, and the regeneration and adaptation of old epistemologies to suit new postcolonial realities.

Martinez-Vargas (2020) also note that if we want to decolonize higher education, we should not only focus on curriculum changes but also reconsider the Eurocentric onto-epistemology of these institutions.

DOI: 10.4324/9781003352907-6

However, the road to the decolonization of higher education is long. Some South African universities and disciplines still struggle with teaching knowledge, not just from the European vantage point. These universities and fields still struggle with situating the histories and knowledge that do not originate from the West in the context of imperialism, colonialism, and power. They still marginalize the wealth of knowledge that comes from Africa. However, discussing measures and ways of liberating the curriculum and broader university culture from selective narratives is still essential.

Decolonization debates are rife in South Africa: decolonizing higher education, the economy, the law, and the justice system. All these debates and attempts are made to achieve equity and justice in the country. To contribute to these debates, the current study focuses on how journalism education can be decolonized in South Africa from a sociolinguistic perspective. To achieve its aim, the chapter will review course descriptions of journalism curriculums at three universities in South Africa that offer journalism education and possible ways to decolonize the curriculums from the sociolinguistics perspectives.

Sociolinguistics is a field of study that has to do with language and society. A branch of linguistics studies the relationship between language, culture, and power. This field of study is interested in explaining why we speak differently in different social contexts, and it is concerned with identifying the social functions of language and the ways it is used to convey social meaning (Holmes, 2014). This is vital because people use language to get their social relationships in a community and construct aspects of their social identity (ibid.).

Asante (1991) proposes using culturally relevant and inclusive language instruction in education. Asante (1991) argues that traditional educational systems often prioritize European languages and cultural norms, marginalizing the languages and culture of non-European communities. Similarly, Ngugi wa Thiong'o (1986) criticizes the historical dominance of European languages in African education systems, which he sees as a continuation of colonial legacies that undermine African languages and cultures. Ngugi wa Thiong'o (1986) asserts that using African languages in education is a matter of linguistic preservation and a means of empowering African communities and fostering a sense of cultural pride and self-confidence.

The focus of this study is on how the inclusion of South African sociolinguistics in journalism programs can help with the decolonization of the journalism curriculum. Some of the sociolinguistic perspectives to be explored include:

1. Learning about the history of the relationship between indigenous languages and colonial languages in South Africa.
2. Studying existing indigenous media case studies

3. Allowing students to write their news stories in indigenous languages
4. Learning indigenous language media
5. Journalism and belonging

Language issues are central to decolonization debates. For a long time in South Africa, learning and teaching in higher education have been conducted only in English and Afrikaans. Universities excluded indigenous languages. This created a problem where African students never got an opportunity to be taught in their indigenous languages. Universities were linguistically marginalizing African students. Universities perpetuated the colonial motives of disregarding the value and status of indigenous languages in Africa.

As part of decolonizing the curriculum, it is vital to consider how the inclusion of indigenous languages in learning and teaching can destroy the colonial system favoring only English and Afrikaans. Some universities, such as the University of KwaZulu-Natal, the University of the Witwatersrand, the University of North West, and the Tshwane University of Technology, have developed language policies to introduce indigenous languages in learning and teaching. This is a breakthrough in the South African education system. These measures allow students to learn in their indigenous languages.

Journalism education in South Africa is divided into universities that teach journalism within communication studies (the University of South Africa, University of Free State, and the University of Johannesburg) and those that offer their program as journalism and media/cultural studies (Rhodes University, the University of KwaZulu-Natal, and the University of Cape Town). Others, such as the University of the Witwatersrand, Stellenbosch University, and the University of Cape Town, only offer stand-alone journalism programs at the postgraduate level (Garman, Malila, van der Merwe, and du Toit, 2015). Garman et al. (2015) contend that this bifurcation between communication studies and media/cultural studies has historical routes with formerly white Afrikaans-language and formerly Bantustan (African/Black) universities aligning their teaching of journalism with intellectual trajectories in communications studies and the formerly white English-language universities aligning their intellectual trajectories with media/cultural studies.

These stratifications of course materials have led to divisions in the curriculum. Journalism educators in the country are pulled between dependency on Western models and materials on the one hand and appeals to African centricity on the other (Berger, 2011). Rodny-Gumede (2018) argues that the problem faced by journalism educators in the global South is that curricula are often copied from journalism degrees in the global North and transferred to media systems in different contexts. This has led to accusations that journalism curricula in the global South are grounded in Western normative ideas of the role and function of journalism (Rodny-Gumede, 2018). This had led to arguments that the African theory of journalism must be developed (Nyamnjoh, 2005) and that journalism training and curriculum in Africa need to become more African and Africanized (Motsaathebe, 2011).

To understand how decolonization in South African journalism education can be addressed and achieved, I analyzed journalism postgraduate course descriptions from three universities in South Africa, the University of the Witwatersrand, the University of KwaZulu-Natal, and the North West University. The module descriptions of these universities require students to develop news writing skills, they teach them media law and regulations, teach them about media and ethics and teach them about digital media. The course descriptions expect students to undertake exams or assessments which they must pass to secure their qualifications. However, no course description of these universities mentions the teaching and learning of indigenous languages, mentions the importance of indigenous languages in journalism and does not mention news gathering or reporting using indigenous oral traditions. Decolonizing higher education framework was applied to review the course descriptions of the three universities and propose how and why sociolinguistics elements should be included in the journalism curriculum as part of the decolonizing journalism education in South Africa.

Below I provide a brief overview of each university's journalism postgraduate course description:

University of the Witwatersrand (BA Honours in Journalism)

This degree consists of five courses that provide a thorough grounding in the practical print and online skills necessary for a journalist, as well as the theory, knowledge and command of journalism issues needed to operate effectively in the profession.

Students will be involved in producing regular media, which ensures they get the hands-on practical experience which will enable them to operate effectively in newsrooms when they graduate. They will be involved in a weekly campus newspaper, an online newspaper, radio programming for campus broadcasts, television news production and social media.

All our teaching is done by experienced professionals and the curriculum includes workshops and seminars with leading journalists and professionals from the media industry.

The University of KwaZulu-Natal (Culture and Media Studies)

Culture and Media Studies is one of the most exciting and relevant disciplines to study at university. We engage with contemporary culture, especially as it manifests in the media of film, television, newspaper, radio and most importantly, the new digital media such as the internet and cell/smart/android phones. We develop the conceptual and creative skills of students to prepare them for professional positions as 'cultural intermediaries' in such careers as advertising, marketing, film-making, journalism, and internet publishing. Although we encourage creative and practical work, students must develop those conceptual skills that give them the ability to understand how culture and the media work, and within which creative work develops.

North-West University (Journalism and Media Studies)

Journalism students are led to discover and master the new world of multiplatform journalism. They are trained to use smartphones and other technology to create content intended for audiences who prefer news in either a printed, broadcast, online or digital format. The NWU also focuses on radio, a field of journalism that reaches people in every corner of South Africa and the world. The focus on practical skills is supplemented by critical reflection grounded in theory about the media's role in a democratic society. The work of a journalist is placed in an ethical and legal context – particularly relevant in an era of fake news. Our journalism lecturers have academic knowledge and extensive professional experience in the field, both in South Africa and abroad.

The above course descriptions do not mention the importance of indigenous languages in South African journalism and journalism education. The current study will propose topics that can be included in these course descriptions to contribute towards the decolonization of journalism education in South Africa from the perspective of sociolinguistics. That is, the chapter will propose possible aspects of sociolinguistics and argue why they should be included in the course descriptions to decolonize journalism education in South Africa.

Literature Review: Decolonizing Higher Education

South Africa, like most African countries, was colonized. This colonization took away many aspects of African ways of living such as language, religion, traditions, and gender and replaced them with Western methods. Rodney (cited in Lebeloane, 2018) argues that although colonization did not introduce education in Africa, it introduced some new sets of education, some of which either replaced or supplemented those which had been in Africa before. Lebeloane (2018) maintains that the establishment of Western forms of formal schools exacerbated the process of colonization by naturalizing and promoting coloniality and or colonialism in the minds of all learners who attended those schools.

This history has haunted many African countries for years. It has led to debates about how the African education system can be decolonized, especially in the higher education sector. Lebeloane (2018) states that one of the aims of decolonizing higher education is to reinstate, re-inscribe and embody the dignity, equity and social justice that was violently devalued or demonized by colonial and imperial systems. Martinez-Vargas (2020) explains that in contexts such as South Africa, it is important to consider what universities teach, under which epistemic systems, and how and by which scholars. These questions are central to decoloniality and decolonization (Hall and Tandon, 2017).

Adebisi (2016) argues that the decolonization of higher education in Africa should be a rigorous, ongoing process of critical engagement that does perpetuate the idea that local or indigenous knowledge is inferior. According to Mampane, Omidire and Aluko (2018), this process is important, especially when considering the various levels at which students are told their home languages cannot be used in higher education. It is for this reason that some African students feel disconnected from the education system as the colonized education system builds cultural inferiority into African students (Mampane et al., 2018).

Fomunyam (2017) states that a departure from such European ideas to a more nuanced and contextual understanding of higher education constitutes the beginning of the decolonization project in Africa. Decolonization of higher education pushes African scholars from seeing Europe and European scholars as the epicenter for higher education and scholarship in general, it leads the former to see the need to reorient scholarship on the continent to make Africa the centre (Ajani, 2019). These reasons make conversations around decolonization quite pertinent for the reshaping of African educational and research agenda to focus on Africa and African educational thought (Ajani, 2019).

According to Boshoff (2010), decolonization would be the reversal, replacement and recentering of Africa as the focus on African higher education, by correcting the ills of colonialism and replacing the continued Eurocentrism in African higher education. Ajani (2019) states that if this is not done, African minds would remain forever colonized. Mafeje (2000) articulated this better when he argues that the peak of colonization is caused by the mental perceptions of the colonized people, who are being manipulated through cultural means. Controlling their minds determines all other economic and political manipulations.

Resolving these issues in African higher education requires Africans to develop African approaches, especially because contextual solutions are required (Mamdani, 2007). To contextualize the African education system is to redirect or redesign the education system to reflect ideal African history, politics, and socio-economic or moral factors (Ajani, 2019). Colonial education systems cannot be destroyed with colonial tools and methods, it requires a culturally responsive approach.

How to Decolonize Journalism Education in South Africa

Leboloane (2018) highlights that the starting point of decolonizing a country is decolonizing the school curriculum. In this section, the chapter presents possible topics that can be included in the course descriptions of these universities to decolonize the journalism curriculum in South Africa from the sociolinguistics perspective. The chapter has identified the following topics as fundamental to the decolonization of journalism education in South Africa:

Learning about the history of the relationship between indigenous languages and colonial languages in South Africa

The language issue has always been a thorny issue in South Africa since the colonial and Apartheid periods. The government and colonial systems used language as a tool of oppression and domination, as a tool of inclusion and exclusion, and as a tool of empowerment and disempowerment. The two oppressive systems led to the onslaught of indigenous languages and only developed English and Afrikaans. The laws of the country led to the marginalization of indigenous African languages and developed only English and Afrikaans as languages of academia, science and technology, commerce, and justice.

Language is at the center of journalism. Journalism is delivered through language. Hence, journalism educators must prioritize the teaching and learning materials that address the above historical issues that led to the dominance of English and the slight usage of Afrikaans over indigenous languages in the South African media. The curriculum should be developed that focuses on topics and information to cover basic material about the history of indigenous and colonial languages in South Africa.

The above course descriptions from the University of the Witwatersrand, the University of KwaZulu-Natal, and the North West University indicate that students will be exposed to a wide variety of study materials that teach them about journalism, news production, new media, and cultural aspects of media and society. However, the inclusion of a topic about the relationship between indigenous languages and colonial languages in the media will enhance the courses and make students appreciate that journalism is an industry that operates using language(s). Hence, learning about the status of indigenous languages in radio, television, newspapers, and cinema about colonial languages takes students beyond the ordinary Eurocentric topics of journalism education. It makes students appreciate what is happening in their context and how journalism operates in their context.

Studying existing indigenous media case studies

In pursuit of creating journalism education that reflects Africanism and a decolonized Africa, studying and learning about indigenous media and different case studies of indigenous media across the world should be paramount. Wilson (2015) defines indigenous media as forms of expression produced, conceptualized, and circulated by indigenous people around the world as vehicles for communication. This is done for purposes of cultural preservation, cultural and artistic expression, political self-determination, and cultural sovereignty.

Through theoretical works and practical exercises, journalism educators in South Africa should include materials on indigenous media. Writing exercises, exams, case study analysis, and media production around indigenous media are some of the methods that can be used to decolonize journalism education. Countries such as Brazil, New Zealand, Wales, Australia, the Philippines, Nigeria, and Ghana are some of the countries that indigenous media case studies that educators can draw from and include in their course outlines. Learning and producing indigenous media content will lead to students graduating with an idea of what it takes to produce unique media content that speaks to the needs of the local people.

The course descriptions of the above three universities do not mention the inclusion of indigenous media case studies as part of their courses. The study of existing indigenous media case studies is one of the fundamental topics that these course descriptions should have as it is one of the topics that show students that they are not only going to learn about the Western methods of journalism, news-making and news gathering. When a topic such as studying existing indigenous media case studies is mentioned in the course descriptions, students become aware that they are going to learn various models of journalism.

Allowing students to write their news stories in indigenous languages

Universities across the country, except for a few, still expect students to write their assessments in English. This is because English is still the medium of instruction in all universities in South Africa. This system is anti-decolonization. As Prah (2017) argues, our real challenge is how to intellectualize African languages, that is, turning African languages into languages that can be used for educating a person in any field of knowledge from kindergarten to university and beyond (Sibayan, 1999).

Journalism educators should allow students to write their news stories, as part of their assessments, in indigenous languages. This is training them to be comfortable and confident in reporting and writing news in their indigenous languages. When students arrive in the workplaces, they can work in English-medium and indigenous-language-medium newsrooms. Course descriptions should clearly state that students have the option to write and report on stories in indigenous languages, especially in the languages that are recognized as official languages of learning and teaching in respective universities. For example, the University of the Witwatersrand's language recognizes English, isiZulu and Sesotho as official languages of teaching and learning in the university. Journalism course outlines should stipulate that students can choose to do their news stories in isiZulu and Sesotho.

Additionally, journalism educators should dedicate time to teaching students about the importance of indigenous languages, especially if journalism is to exist as one of the fields that should contribute to language revitalization strategies. Doing this allows universities to lead the battle against the dominance of colonial languages and restore the dignity and status of indigenous languages. Prah (2017) highlights that Asian societies have completely rejected Western languages and have replaced the role of colonial languages in education and development with native languages and cultures.

Learning indigenous language media

Africa has more than 2,000 languages, but not all of them are used as languages of the media. Most indigenous African languages are still marginalized and undeveloped. This has left a gap in the media market, most media in Africa are still produced in colonial languages. One of the strategies that journalism schools in South Africa can do to change this system is to teach students about indigenous language media. That is, teaching them about the print and electronic media that uses local/indigenous/African languages to publish or broadcast news and information.

As Orao (2009) highlights, indigenous language media use languages of communities determined by geographical location or common interests. Students need to learn about how media can cater specifically for the primordial interests of ethnic groups that are of interest to them. Students should learn about the media produced for and by rural and less formally educated parts of the population. They need to learn about the media that serve the needs of marginalized ethnic groups.

The University of the Witwatersrand, the University of KwaZulu-Natal, and the North West University clearly state that students will learn about radio, new media, television, and newspapers. But they do not articulate clearly that they will also learn about indigenous media, that is, media that are produced in indigenous languages. It has become a norm in journalism schools that students learn about newspapers printed in English, for example, *News24, Mail and Guardian*, and *City Press*, they also learn about radio stations such as *702* and television channels such as *ENCA*. Students should be exposed to indigenous media organizations such as *Isolezwe* (isiZulu and isiXhosa) *Motsosa Kgang* (Setswana), others include *Iwe Eko* (Yoruba) and *Oko-Ane* (Igala). Including such case studies in journalism education is an important step towards decolonizing the journalism curriculum as it shows that universities are starting to appreciate media productions and organizations that use indigenous languages.

Journalism and belonging

Journalism and belonging are one of the most important topics that journalism educators should include in their curriculum if they need to decolonize journalism education in South Africa. Through journalism education, students should learn and appreciate the diverse living experiences and varying cultural, gender, ethnic and racial differences that are found in South Africa. A curriculum that encompasses issues of journalism and belonging can challenge the ways we value diversity in our society and across the journalism industry, it can train and inspire students to produce an equitable and just media landscape.

To that end, journalism schools produce students that appreciate the diversity of the country and that can tell the stories of those that have previously been missing in mainstream media. Journalism schools can commit to proactively fostering diversity, equity and belonging by exposing students to topics such as multilingualism and multiculturalism in the journalism industry. This is because the politics of belonging is central to understanding the decolonization of journalism education in South Africa.

Some voices, bodies, identities, and locations have been excluded and marginalized in the mainstream media. Journalism education schools such as the University of the Witwatersrand, the University of KwaZulu-Natal, and the North West University also do the same by not making it clear in their course descriptions that their courses are inclusive in their approach towards cultures, languages, bodies, locations, and sexuality. These course descriptions should make it obvious that learning journalism in a South African university is about learning respect for diversity/difference and 'others.'

Conclusion

This chapter has tried to draw sociolinguistic perspectives into journalism and show how these perspectives can be included in the journalism curriculum to decolonize journalism education in South Africa. This paper has proposed the inclusion of topics such as learning about the history of the relationship between indigenous languages and colonial languages in South Africa, studying existing indigenous media case studies, allowing students to write their news stories in indigenous languages, learning indigenous language media and journalism and belonging into the journalism curriculum using three universities as case studies. When universities include such topics in their journalism curriculum, they develop and promote the status of indigenous languages in South African higher education.

The paper has demonstrated through its core arguments that language is central to decolonization. Mampane et al. (2018) argue that language is important for knowledge production to ensure epistemic and cultural identity, and to present traditional worldviews. It is for this reason that colonial processes were embedded in the language (Olatunji, 2010). The chapter maintains that journalism students in South Africa should become more African by drawing on African sociolinguistics that characterizes the continent and that can put South African journalism in its place in the curriculum.

This chapter has made recommendations for changes in decolonizing journalism education in South Africa. But universities and journalism educators are best placed to holistically reform their teaching and learning materials to decolonize journalism in the country. However, there is no one size fits all model when it comes to decolonization. Hence, if journalism educators are serious about tackling inequality and social justice and fighting the legacy and impact of colonialism on African higher education, they would do their part.

References

Adebisi, F.I. (2016) Decolonizing education in Africa: Implementing the right to education by re-appropriating culture and indigeneity. *Northern Island Legal Quarterly*, 67(4), 433–451.

Ajani, O.A. (2019). Decolonization of education in African contexts. *African Renaissance*, 16(2), 101–120.

Asante, M.K. (1991). The Afrocentric idea in education. *The Journal of Negro Education*, 60(2), 170–180.

Berger, G. (2011). Networking African journalism educators: Bonding, bridging and linking. *Global Media Journal*, 5(1), 1–23.

Bosch, T. (2017). Twitter activism and youth in South Africa: The case of #Rhodes-MustFall. *Information Communication and Society*, 20(2), 221–232.

Boshoff, N. (2010). South-South research collaboration of countries in the Southern African Development Community (SADC). *Scientometrics*, 84(2), 481–503.

Garman, A. Malila, van der Merwe, V. and du Toit, J. (2015). *Journalism education survey: South Africa*. Accessed on 16th January 2023 online: https://research.tuni.fi/uploads/2020/03/9d972151-je-survey-south-africa-2.pdf

Emeagwali, G. and Dei, G.J.S. (2014). *Indigenous Knowledge and The Disciplines.* Rotterdam: Sense Publishers.

Fomunyam, K.G. (2017). Decolonizing teaching and learning in engineering education in a South African university. *International Journal of Applied Engineering Research*, 12(23), 13349–133358.

Hall, B.L. and Tandon, R. (2017). Decolonization of knowledge, epistemicide, participatory research, and higher education. *Research for All*, 1(1), 6–19.

Holmes, J. (2014). *An Introduction of Sociolinguistics*, 4th edition. London. Routledge.

Lebeloane, L. (2018). Decolonizing the school curriculum for equity and social justice in South Africa. *Koers – Bulletin for Christian Scholarship*, 82(3), 1–10.

Mafeje, A. (2000). Africanity: A combative ontology. *CODESRIA Bulletin*, 1, 66–71.

Mamdani, M. (2007). *Scholars in the Marketplace: The Dilemmas of Neoliberal Reform at Makerere University, 1989–2000.* Dakar: CODESRIA.

Mampane, R.M. Omidire, M.F. and Aluko, F.R. (2018). Decolonizing higher education in Africa: Arriving at a glocal solution. *South African Journal of Higher Education*, 38(4), 1–8.

Martinez-Vargas, C. (2020). Decolonizing higher education research: From a university to a pluri-versity of approaches. *South African Journal of Higher Education*, 34(2), 112–128.

Motsaathebe, G. (2011). Journalism education and practice in South Africa and the discourse of the African renaissance. *Communicatio*, 37(3), 381–397.

Naicker, C. (2016). From Marikana to #feesmustfall: The praxis of popular politics in South Africa. *Urbanization*, 1(1), 53–61.

Wa Thiong'o, N. (1986). *Decolonizing the Mind.* Nairobi: James Currey.

Nyamnjoh, F.B. (2005). *Africa's Media: Democracy and the Politics of Belonging.* London: Zed Books.

Olatunji, S.A. (2010). Thematic changes in postcolonial African literature: from colonialism to neocolonialism. *Sino-US English Teaching*, 7(10), 125–134.

Orao, J. (2009). The Kenyan indigenous languages and the mass media: Challenges and opportunities. *Stellenbosch Papers in Linguistics*, 38(2009), 77–86.

Prah, K.K. (2017). The intellectualization of African languages for higher education. *Alternation*, 24(2), 215–225.

Rodny-Gumede, Y. (2018). A teaching philosophy of journalism education in the global South: A South African case study. *Journalism*, 19(6), 747–761.

Sibayan, B.P. (1999). *The Intellectualization of Filipino.* Manila: Linguistic Society of the Philippines.

Wilson, P. (2015). Indigenous media: Linking the local, translocal, global and virtual. In Susan Mains, Julie Cupples, and Chris Lukinbeal (eds), *Mediated Geographies and Geographies of Media*. London: Springer, pp. 385–398.

Part II

Media Freedom, Democratic Participation and African Media Culture

6 Internet Shutdowns in Africa

Triggers and Rationalization

Tendai Chari

The Internet has spawned numerous opportunities for citizens of the African continent, enabling access to information that counters state propaganda, thereby asserting their digital citizenship. Citizen journalists, bloggers, vloggers, cyber activists and clicktivists utilize the Internet to express their opinions, support certain causes as well as expose misgovernance and other malfeasance in the corridors of power. Some governments in Africa have resorted to Internet shutdowns of different guises to counter online free expression, citing different reasons for their actions. However, there is very little scholarship, if any, examining triggers of Internet and justifications for Internet shutdowns in Africa. Consequently, there is a knowledge lacuna with regard to what sets off Internet shutdowns and justifications given. Using the concept of digital rights as a conceptual lens, and based on literature review, this chapter examines triggers and justification of Internet shutdowns in Africa and their justifications by the governments which impose them.

Internet shutdowns are becoming more widespread in Africa (Stremlau & Dobson, 2022). For instance, between 2014 and 2019, 22 African countries implemented shutdowns. Of these, 77% were categorized as "authoritarian" while the rest fell into the so-called "hybrid" or "semi-authoritarian" states (CIPESA, 2019). This underscores the close connection between Internet shutdowns and the suppression of citizen rights. In 2021, there were several African countries that implemented different types of shutdowns, with 12 countries cutting Internet access 19 times, an increase of three countries compared to the previous year (Access Now, 2021b). In the run-up to the August 2021 elections, the Zambian government allegedly slowed down the Internet, while Eswatini imposed an Internet blackout in June 2021, citing "security reasons" after the country was rocked by violent protests against King Mswati III (Reuters Foundation, 2021). In June 2021 Nigeria banned the use of Twitter two days after Twitter removed president Muhammadu Buhari's post where he "threatened to punish regional secessionists" (Reuters Foundation, 2021). Earlier the same year, Uganda had ordered an Internet shutdown on the eve of the country's

DOI: 10.4324/9781003352907-8

presidential election, allegedly to "avoid outside in the election." Ethiopia also imposed an Internet shutdown after the country's elections were postponed for the second time in May 2021. It was the thirteenth shutdown since April 2018 (Reuters Foundation, 2021). These examples demonstrate the extent to which Internet shutdowns are increasingly becoming part and parcel of the menu of manipulation in Africa.

Given the close connection between Internet shutdowns and democratic participation, Internet shutdowns deserve more scholarly scrutiny in media and communication studies.

Internet shutdowns deserve scholarly scrutiny because of the following reasons:

- The internet is critical for ensuring democratic participation and enables citizens to access services provided by the state and other entities.
- It is a source of information alternative to that provided by state and gives the disenfranchised groups in society a voice.
- The Internet makes it possible for citizens to monitor performance of the state, thereby enhancing accountability.
- It is an enabler of other non-epistemic rights such as the right to education, right to health care, and the right to participate in economic activities.
- It enables citizens to share information among themselves and to mobilize for political activities.

The rest of the chapter will proceed as follows: After this introduction, the first part explains key terms and concepts. The following section discusses triggers and justifications for Internet shutdowns in Africa. The final section provides concluding remarks and critically reflects on implications of Internet shutdowns for democratic participation in Africa.

Definition of an Internet Shutdown

Internet shutdowns take various forms in different contexts, ranging from subtle forms as Internet slow-downs or throttling of Internet bandwidth, switching off access to social media applications or "network shutdowns" (Rydzak, Karanja, & Opiyo, 2020) taking down of individual blogs to total blackouts (Marchant & Stremlau, 2020). The following are some of the definitions of Internet shutdowns:

- "An international disruption of the Internet or electronic communications, rendering them effectively unusable, for a specific population or within a location, often to exert control over the flow of information" (Access Now, 2016).

- "A deliberate significant disruption of the entire channels of the electronic communication within a given geographical area and/or affecting a pre-determined group of citizens" (Rydzak, Karanja, & Opiyo, 2020, p. 4265).
- "Internet shutdowns are an absolute restriction placed on the use of Internet services due to an order by a government body. It may be limited to a specific period, time or number of days. It can even extend indefinitely. An Internet shutdown may be limited to mobile Internet that you may use on smartphones or the wired broadband that usually connects to a desktop or both at the same time" (Internet Freedom India, n.d.).

While the first two definitions emphasise the intentionality, spatiality and temporality of Internet shutdowns, the third definition accentuates the impartiality of Internet shutdowns as well as the fact that the perpetrator is usually a government institution or body. All the three definitions, however, bring to the fore the notion that Internet shutdowns negatively impact on citizens' right to access information.

The Human Rights Council gives a broader and illuminating definition of Internet shutdowns which identifies government as the main perpetrator of Internet shutdowns, and intentionality, scope and unintended impacts, thus:

> measures taken by a government, or on behalf of a government to intentionally disrupt access to, and the use of information and communication systems online. They include actions that limit the ability of a large number of people to use online communication tools, either by restricting the accessibility and usability of services that are necessary for interactive communications, such as social media, and messaging services. Such shutdowns inevitably affect many users with legitimate pursuits, leading to enormous collateral damage beyond their intended purposes.
>
> (The Human Rights Council, 2016: pp2–3)

In the context of this chapter, Internet shutdowns are thus defined as the intentional total or partial disruption of the Internet, social media networks and mobile telecommunications services by the government for legal, moral, social, political, technical whatever reason, resulting in the suppression of citizens' rights. It is crucial to view Internet shutdowns as instruments whose effect goes beyond "the suppression of information" (Wagner, 2018) because they interfere with a spectrum of citizens' rights beyond the realm of digital rights.

Defining Digital Rights

One way of illuminating into how citizens' access to information online is undermined by Internet shutdowns is the digital rights theoretical lens developed by Mathiesen (2014). The concept of digital rights is rather vague and malleable to the extent that it has been debated from diverse perspectives (Karppinen & Puukko, 2020). Despite the lack of consensus, scholars generally agree that the term digital rights entails rights in the digital era (Media Defence, 2022; Kaye & Reventlow, 2017). It means that fundamental human rights such as access to information should be promoted and protected. While digital rights are subject to varied interpretations, dominant literature conflates digital rights with Internet rights (Karppinen & Puukko, 2020; Kaye & Reventlow, 2017). This locates digital rights within the realm of broader struggles for communication rights. In this chapter digital rights are a viewed as a subset of the communication rights discourse which dates back to the New World Information and Communication Order (NWICO) debate in the late 1960s (CRIS, 2005; Thomas, 2005).

Debate rages as to whether the Internet should be a human right or not and if so, how can it be implemented and by whom (Milderbrath, 2021; Pollicino, 2019; Barry, 2019; O'Reilly, 2015; Mathiesen, 2014; Cerf, 2012). Internet rights protagonists assert that any disruptions or manipulation of the Internet content is a violation of human rights. Mathiesen (2014, p. 3) equates access to online information with a "moral standing to claim something due to one as a particular individual or particular group." Thus, any disruptions to the smooth functioning of the Internet becomes a violation of citizens' rights. Mathiesen acknowledges the distinction between primary human rights and derived human rights but places emphasis on the notion that all human rights have an ethical dimension because they oblige states to "act so as to respect and fulfil" those rights (ibid., p. 8). Having rights to seek and access information online implies that one has the "moral standing to claim something due to one as a particular individual or a particular group" (ibid., p. 3). The "human dignity" aspect of human rights requires that people "live minimally good lives," giving people "ample opportunities to exercise agency," ensuring that they "they are able to exercise important human capabilities" (ibid., p. 4).

States are obliged to put in place institutional arrangements for citizens to have access to the technology needed for Internet access (ibid., p. 4). Ensuring that citizens have access to infrastructure for accessing the Internet inserts the state into the contentious terrain of politics of digital infrastructures, thereby setting up the state against private enterprises which own and control such infrastructure. Although private enterprises have an important role to play in protecting digital rights they are driven by commercial motives (Human Rights Council, 2011, p. 13). The dominance of the liberal market system precludes states from interfering with the production of public goods, leaving citizens to the vagaries of the market. This contradicts the argument that states must guarantee citizens' access to the Internet because without Internet other human rights such as the right to work, basic education, and the right to life may not be realizable (Barry, 2019).

However, some scholars reject the notion that the Internet should be a human right, because a human right is something that humans need for them to "lead healthy meaningful lives," of which the Internet is not (Cerf, 2012). Cerf argues that the Internet is a derivative right which enables other rights to be realized. Thus, "it is a mistake to place any particular technology in this exalted category (of human rights) since over time we will end up valuing the wrong thing" (Cerf, 2012). O'Reilly's (2015) stance is less nuanced, contending that the Internet is neither a necessity nor a human right. He argues that it is unreasonable to regard the Internet as a human right because people can live without it.

However, advocates of Internet rights argue that the Internet has a natural affinity with epistemic rights, which are rights pertaining to "epistemic goods such as information, knowledge, understanding and truth (Watson, 2018, p. 89). Epistemic rights "afford their bearer a complex set of entitlements that provide a justification for their performance and prohibition of certain actions regarding epistemic goods" (ibid.).

Triggers of Internet Shutdowns

Globally, political instability such as demonstrations, protests, stalled elections, insurrections, and similar forms of collective action have been identified as the major triggers of Internet shutdowns (Howard et al., 2011; Chari, 2022). Thus, shutdowns tend to be planned and purposefully executed before or at the onset of protests as "weapons of control and impunity" (Access Now, 2022). Thus, Internet shutdowns are viewed as "markers of deteriorating human rights situations" since they tend to occur in particular contexts such as periods of conflict, heightened political tensions like electoral crises or large-scale protests (The Human Rights Council, 2022, p. 6). Stauffer (2022) notes that governments are increasingly resorting to shutdowns during crisis times on the pretext of public safety or "curbing the spread of misinformation." According to Bergin et al., (2022) Internet shutdowns signal that "something bad is about to happen" leading to the perception that Internet shutdowns are closely aligned with human rights abuses because they are a "cloak of darkness." Rydzak, Karanja, and Opiyo (2020, p. 4271) reflect on how Internet shutdowns camouflage human rights thus:

> When authorities claim an existential threat to the government, rank – and- file security units or militias are deployed as protectors and enforcers of the status-quo. This goal often takes precedence over facilitating

citizen rights as in the massacre of peaceful protectors by militias from the Rapid Support Forces in Sudan in June 2009. In this way, shutdowns often act as invisibility clocks for abuses by street level forces.
(Rydzak, Karanja, & Opiyo, 2020, p. 4271).

Thus, claims to existential threats to the state or government are used to legitimise Internet shutdowns and unleashing of acts of brutalities against citizens. This means that Internet shutdowns should be viewed as synonymous with deprivation of citizen rights, both online and offline.

Demonstrations/Protests

The Human Rights Council (2022, p. 6) notes that almost half of the Internet shutdowns recorded between 2016 and 2021 occurred in the context of protests and political crises, with 225 of them recorded during public demonstrations. Such shutdowns are generally aimed at "quelling demonstrations relating to a range of social, political, or economic grievances" (ibid.). Such protests are often followed by additional repressive measures meant to undermine possible political mobilisation by citizens, resulting in quick, severe restrictions on protests or demonstrations, regardless of whether they are peaceful or violent. Within the African context, there are several incidences of Internet shutdowns that have been triggered by demonstrations and or protests. One such notable example was the Egypt Revolution where Egyptian citizens, predominantly young people converged in the Tahrir Square and other places in and around the country on 25 January 2011 to express their aspirations for political change through peaceful demonstrations and social media mobilisation. The demonstrations continued for several days until President Hosni Mubarak stepped down on 11 February 2011 leaving the military in charge (Global Freedom of Expression, 2018). However, before that, on 28 February, 2011, the country experienced one of the most unprecedented shutdown of all communications, including cuts in mobile and fixed telephony communication services, social media and the Internet. Three of the country's telecommunication operators, Vodafone, Mobnil and Etisalat complied with the state's order to shut down the Internet in order to curb the extent of the demonstrations. The demonstrations themselves were met with unprecedented violence by the police, resulting in the death of hundreds while thousands were injured. While suspension of mobile services lasted for a day, the Internet shutdown continued until 2 February 2011 (Global Freedom of Expression, 2018).

Similar incidents where Internet shutdowns were instituted to quell demonstrations/protests were reported in Eswatini in 2021. On June 29, the Eswatini government cut the Internet to crack down on large scale protests which had started in May 2021 after the unexpected death of a university student (Access Now, 2021a; Southern Africa Litigation Centre, 2021). The three network companies, namely, Eswatini Post and Telecommunications, eSwatini MTN Mobile and Eswatini Mobile were ordered to disconnect the Internet. This was followed by the imposition of a curfew and closure of schools. In an ironic twist of events, a statement signed by the acting Prime Minister, Themba, N. Masuku provided an email as "an alternative channel" through which they were expected to ventilate their grievances. Like in all cases where the state uses Internet shutdowns to curtail collective action by citizens, the statement sought to delegitimize the protests by framing them through moral panics and illegality tropes, describing them as "alarming," "upsetting," "violent," "unruly" and destructive of the social fabric. Thus:

> We witnessed violence in several parts of the country perpetuated by an unruly crowd where people have been attached, property destroyed, businesses looted and public roads blocked…. Unfortunately, the protests we are seeing of late have been hijacked by criminal elements. Such cannot be accepted under circumstances. No one can hide behind a glass wall of grievances to administer harm to others and cause unrest and anarchy…. The law will be held against all those who perpetuate anarchy and threaten the lives and livelihoods of emaSwatini. Our security forces are on the ground to maintain law and order. We request the Nation to cooperate with security forces as they are deployed to protect the lives of all emaSwati and residents of this beautiful Kingdom, including private and public property.
>
> (Government of the Kingdom of Eswatini, 2021, p. 6)

The above quotation illustrates how Internet shutdowns triggered by citizen collective action such as demonstrations and protests need to be legitimated through the strategic and tactful deployment of communication devices which justify wanton use of violent methods against citizens. This shows that the natural proclivity between Internet shutdowns and gross human rights violations (Chari, 2022). In the case of Eswatini in June 2021, there were several images depicting police brutality and heavy-handedness in the handling of protests which surfaced showing various acts of police brutalising citizens during protests and the shutdown was meant to mask such brutalities. Thus, Internet shutdowns triggered by demonstrations/ protests are characterised by high levels of opaqueness and lack of accountability on the part of the state because they are meant to gloss over human rights violations whereby "the dark alleys of the state become havens for unbridled human rights violations" (Chari, 2022, p. 89).

Like in Eswatini, Internet shutdowns in Zimbabwe have curiously "coincided" with planned demonstrations and citizens protests for political reforms, which timing has exposed government's ulterior motives. In the recent past plans for demonstrations and or protests which are widely publicised on social media platforms have been thwarted by government through disruptions of the Internet or social media platforms. The two main Internet shutdowns, the one in 2016 and the other in 2019 happened in the context of high political tension in the country occasioned by citizen led protests and or industrial action (Majama, 2019: Mare, 2020). The July 2016 disruption was a "partial shutdown" which targeted the instant messenger application, WhatsApp, after Zimbabwean citizens heeded a call to stay at home in order to put pressure on the government to address prevailing economic challenges, human rights abuses and other citizen grievances (Mare, 2020). The protest was championed by a digital activist movement, #This Flag campaign led by cleric, Pastor Evans Mawarire. In a move to disrupt social media platforms used by protester organiser to mobilise citizens to participate in the stay away government ordered the major telecommunication companies to disable WhatsApp after which the application stopped working for four hours. The 2019 total shutdown which entailed disruption of all Internet and social media services came against the backdrop of widespread and violent protests across the country after a 150% increase in the price of fuel was announced by the state-president, Emmerson Mnangagwa. Again, government, through the Minister of State Security, Owen Ncube ordered all Internet Service Providers (ISPs) to switch off the Internet and social media services (Mare, 2020). In the days that followed, Internet and social media services were intermittently blocked. Observers accused government of attempting to use the Internet shutdown to hide violent crackdowns on citizens by the security services sector, during which hundreds of people were arrested on public order charges while 400 others were charged by magistrates throughout the country (*Aljazeera*, 2019a). While government was evasive about the motives of the Internet blockade, government officials view citizen access to the Internet as a potential threat to national security (Chimhangwa, 2019) with then deputy minister of Information, Publicity and Broadcasting Services, Energy Mutodi stating that the Internet shutdown was not illegal, adding that government would not hesitate to shut the Internet in future by invoking the Interception of Communications Act (2007 "because it was part our law" (Freedom House, 2019). Mutodi reportedly referred to citizens as "primitive people (...) who don't understand the meaning of peaceful demonstrations." Then Minister of Information and Communication Technologies (ICT), Kazembe Kazembe issued a warning against the abuse of the Internet and social media in the state-owned daily newspaper, The Herald, stating that:

> There is a lot of photoshopping and negative falsehoods which are being peddled on social media. What really has gotten into us as people? Let's

be very careful with what we see on social media. Not everything that we see on social media is true.

(Chimhangwa, 2019).

The preceding quotation suggests that government perceives citizens access to the Internet and protests as mutually interlinked, which justifies the heavy-handed way Internet shutdowns are handled. Perhaps, the most unequivocal statement which signals the Zimbabwean government's standpoint with regard to Internet shutdowns and demonstrations came from the current Minister of Information, Publicity and Broadcasting Services, Monica Mutsvangwa, who, when answering a question at the Internet Governance Forum (IGF) in November 2022 hinted at the necessity of Internet shutdowns "to prevent the use of digital platforms and social media to spread propaganda and fake news, which may result in more bloodshed, loss of life and even genocide" (Simanje, 2022).

Electoral Conflicts

Apart from demonstrations and or protests Internet Shutdowns in Africa are also triggered by electoral contexts. The Human Rights Council (2022) notes that between 2016 and 2021 Internet shutdowns affected 52 elections, while in 2019, 14 African countries disrupted the Internet during elections, thereby hindering electoral campaigns and public dialogue. Internet shutdowns implemented during elections are particularly problematic because they create obstacles that damage electoral processes and the free flow of information, thereby jeopardising the public trust in electoral processes and the escalation of hostilities (The Human Rights Council, 2022). The Human Rights Council (2022) notes that disruptions of the Internet during elections are particularly problematic for opposition political parties that depend on the Internet for mobilisation due to little resources. Similarly, journalists and media organisations are also seriously affected because it becomes difficult for them to play their watchdog role. This may affect the transparency and fairness of elections – the very essence of democracy. Below we highlight a few cases on Internet shutdowns which were triggered by elections in Africa:

- In 2021 Uganda shutdown the Internet, social media and messaging platforms on the eve of the January 2014 general elections. Uganda's communications regulator, the Uganda Communications Commission, ordered mobile network companies to disable selected social media platforms, namely, Twitter, Facebook, WhatsApp, Instagram, Snapchat, Skype, Viber, Google Play Store, as well as some telegram services like short messaging services (Business Human Rights Resources

Centre, 2021). The election campaign was characterised by excessive use of force against the opposition by the police and security agencies, resulting in disruption of opposition rallies, intimidation, arrest of opposition figures and death of several opposition supporters (Reuters, 2021). Although President Museveni later apologised for the social media blackout, he justified it on the grounds that Facebook had removed some accounts which were supporting his party, the ruling National Resistance Movement (NRM) and claimed that Facebook was biased in favour of the opposition (Reuters, 2021).

- During the Zambian presidential elections which took place on August 21, 2021, the government deliberately switched off the Internet and social media platforms (Africa Report, 2021; Fight Inequality, 2021). Access Now, an organisation that monitors Internet disruptions globally reported that social media platforms such as Twitter, Instagram, and Facebook were blocked, thereby undermining citizens' ability to access news and information about the election, while also adversely affecting their lives, work, education, and communication. Journalists could not upload stories about the election on their websites and could not access information on elections from the tallying centre. Open Observatory of Network Interference (OONI) data indicated that the shutdown was coordinated between the different Internet Service Providers in the country as the same censorship techniques were used to implement the shutdown (Access Now, 2021b). Like the Ugandan shutdown discussed above, the Zambian shutdown came against the backdrop of gross human rights violations during the run-up to the election, characterised by political violence (Fight Inequality, 2021). These could not be broadcast to the outside world after the implementation of the Internet shutdown.

- The Democratic Republic of Congo (DRC) also implemented a total Internet and SMS shutdown ahead of the December 30, 2019 presidential elections. The blackout continued for the next twenty days and was only lifted after the country's constitutional court confirmed Felix Tshisekedi as the winner (*Aljazeera*, 2019b). One of the major telecommunications companies in the country, Vodacom reportedly confirmed that it had cut web access following a government directive (Dahir, 2019). Government justified the blackout on the grounds of preventing circulation of "fake results online and to avert "chaos" and a "popular uprising"". Like the other cases discussed above, the shutdown occurred in the context of a highly contested election marred by insecurity, delays and violence as well fake news and misinformation which gave government the ammunition to implement an Internet blackout.

As seen from the three cases discussed above, Internet shutdowns triggered by electoral contexts take place in the context of high intense political contestation, insecurity and gross violation of human rights. Shutting the Internet during such moments severely undermines citizens' ability to participate in democratic processes.

While demonstrations/protests and elections appear to be the main triggers of Internet shutdowns in Africa, armed conflicts such as military or violent takeovers of government, public examinations, and fortuitous events such as cyclones and earthquakes have also caused Internet shutdowns. However, due to space constraints, and also because these have not been frequent in Africa, this chapter has mainly addressed triggers of Internet shutdowns linked to political factors.

Justification for Internet Shutdowns

Justifications for Internet shutdowns vary but typically range from the following:

- protecting national security – where it is alleged that some internal or external force(s) pose a threat to the legitimacy of the state.
- curbing misinformation and disinformation – the intention (in the case of the latter this is deliberate) circulation of ideas and information by individuals, the media or organisations which is not supported by facts.
- combating fake news – being news that "does mischief with truth" because it lacks truth and truthfulness (Jaster & Lanius, 2018).
- curbing hate speech – offensive speech or discourse targeting a particular group of people or individual based on their race, ethnicity, gender, creed or region.
- securing public safety – speech that may undermine or compromise public safety.
- economic arguments – divulging information that may undermine the economic interests of the nation.
- technical reasons – technical faults e.g., electrical disruptions, network disruptions due to natural disasters.
- preventing cheating during public examinations – for example, if there is suspicion that there may be cheating during public examinations.

Twelve categories of Internet shutdown justifications collapsed into two main themes have been identified, namely, preserving the public good and protecting political authority (Howard et al., 2011, p. 226). Table 6.1 shows the two main themes on Internet shutdowns and their sub-categories.

Table 6.1 illustrates the most common justifications for Internet shutdown from a global perspective. Since Internet shutdowns are shaped by political contexts, not all these justifications could apply to the African context. National security has been cited as the most common justification for

Table 6.1 Justification of Internet shutdowns

Theme 1: Protecting Political Authority	What sub-categories entail	Theme 2: Preserving the Public Good	What sub-categories entail
Protecting political authority and state institutions	Intervention meant to curb the spread of information detrimental to public authorities, e.g., the President.	Preserving cultural and religious morals	Intervention attributed to preventing the spread of blasphemous or offensive information that challenges the religious and moral authority of the state
Election crisis	Where the incumbent responds to events around elections e.g. election violence/protests	Protecting individuals	
Eliminating propaganda	Where intervention happens because of the spread of misinformation/ disinformation	Protecting children	Intervention meant to stop threats to children, for example, child pornography.
Mitigating dissidence	Intervention attributed to reducing dissident civic action	Cultural preservation	Interventions attributed to the need to stop outside influence or threats to national interests.
National security	Intervention attributed to threats to national security/state security	Protecting individual privacy	Intervention attributed to threats on individual privacy
		Dissuading criminal activity	Intervention aimed at stopping illegal activities such as gambling

Source: Howard et al., 2011, p. 15

Internet shutdowns under the first theme, while "preserving cultural and religious morals" was the most cited justification for disrupting the Internet under the second theme (Howard et al., 2011). In Africa, as in most parts of the world, national security argument is the most cited reason for Internet shutdowns resonates (ibid.). The Ethiopian government has successfully deployed the "National Security" narrative in a manner that resonates with the Global War on Terror to gain credibility in international circles as a state committed to peace and stability, while masking its oppressive tactics, thus "leaving Ethiopians and the West with the stark choice of either accepting political repression or risking an onslaught of violent extremism" (ibid.).

Conclusion

This chapter employed the concept of digital rights to illuminate on triggers of Internet shutdowns in Africa and the justifications provided by these governments for implementing Internet shutdowns. The chapter locates access to the Internet within the broader realm of communication rights whereby any disruptions or manipulation of the Internet is viewed as a violation of human rights. Consequently, states are obliged to put in place institutional arrangements to ensure that citizens have access to the Internet. The triggers of Internet shutdowns and the justifications given discussed in this chapter demonstrate that Internet shutdowns create conditions for human rights violations.

The opaque way in which Internet shutdowns are implemented suggests that Internet shutdowns foster lack of transparency and accountability by authoritarian governments. This shows that Internet shutdowns are associated with unstable political climates linked to citizen collective action and mobilization activities such as demonstrations, protests, contested elections and similar circumstances. Common justifications provided by African governments include, protection of national/state security, elimination of propaganda, preventing misinformation and protecting authority/state institutions and safeguarding the integrity of elections.

While international organizations and local civil society groups tend to view Internet shutdowns as an extreme form of information control and censorship characteristic of "digital authoritarianism" (Access Now, 2021b, p. 4) or "abuse by political actors seeking to silence critics or manipulate elections" there is need for further research to ascertain whether there could be legitimate justifications for Internet shutdowns (Stremlau & Dobson, 2022, p. 17) or whether they could be used as a last resort, particularly in the context of rising misinformation, disinformation and fake news. As the situation stands there is more compelling evidence to show that Internet shutdowns cause more harm than good. As demonstrated in this chapter there is near consensus that Internet shutdowns are explicitly motivated by selfish interests by political actors fearful of losing power. It is irrefutable that Internet shutdowns are antithetical to democratic participation as much as they impinge on the free-flow of information. How to distinguish between legitimate and illegitimate reasons for implementing them is a challenge. The indiscriminate nature of Internet shutdowns shows that they are a blunt instrument which with both intended and unintended targets. There is need for further research to ascertain if there could be alternative methods of dealing with threats to national security, fake news, misinformation and disinformation during delicate political moments such as elections without interfering with citizens' digital rights.

Given the limited studies on Internet shutdowns in the African context, there is need for further explorations to ascertain the hidden harm caused by Internet shutdowns to citizens and national economies. More accurate data on Internet shutdowns will help governments to weigh the costs and benefits of Internet shutdowns. Existing data on the costs of Internet shutdowns focuses more on tangible costs while neglecting intangible costs such as suppression of citizens digital rights. This gap in research needs to be addressed. While most national constitutions guarantee freedom to access and receive information, they do not specifically address the issue of digital rights, which is a fairly new phenomenon. National states should take the necessary steps to address this anomaly by promulgating laws that secure the digital communication rights of their citizens in an unambiguous way in order to deepen democratic cultures and promote citizen participation in governance processes.

References

Access Now (2021, 14 September). "Shutdown in Zambia on Election Day: How it affected People's Lives and well-being." Retrieved from www.accessnow.org/shutdown-in-zambia-on-election-day-how-it-affected-peoples-lives-and-wellbeing/. Accessed 21 March 2023.

Access Now (2016). "No More Internet Shutdowns! Let's #Keep It On." Retrieved from www.accessnow.org/no-internet-shutdowns-lets-keepiton/. Accessed 27 October 2020.

Access Now (2021a, 21 October). "#KeepION: Eswatini authorities shutdown Internet to quell protests, ask people to email grievances." Retrieved from www.accessnow.org/keepiton-eswatini-protests/. Accessed 19 March 2023.

Access Now (2021b, 24 May). The Return of Digital Authoritarianism. Internet Shutdowns in 2021. Retrieved from www.accessnow.org/cms/assets/uploads/2022/05/2021-KIO-Report-May-24–2022.pdf. Accessed 14 February 2022.

Access Now (2022, 23 February). Weapons of Control and Impunity: Internet Shutdowns in 2022. Retrieved from www.hrw.org/world-report/2020/country-chapters/global-5. Accessed 18 March 2023.

Africa Report (2021, 8 August). "Kenya, Uganda, Zambia … Internet Shutdowns (or not) during polls." Retrieved from www.theafricareport.com/230536/niger-uganda-zambia-internet-shutdown-during-elections/. Accessed 21 March 2023.

Aljazeera (2019a, 20 January). "DR Congo Internet Restored after 20-day suspension over elections." Retrieved from www.aljazeera.com/news/2019/1/20/dr-congo-internet-restored-after-20-day-suspension-over-elections. Accessed 21 March 2023.

Aljazeera (2019b, 18 January). "Zimbabwe Imposes Internet Shutdown amid crackdown on Protests." Retrieved from www.aljazeera.com/news/2019/1/18/zimbabwe-imposes-internet-shutdown-amid-crackdown-on-protests. Accessed 19 March 2023.

Barry, J. (2019). *Information Communication Technology and Poverty Alleviation: Promoting Good Governance in the Developing World.* London: Routledge.

Bergin, Julia, Lim, Louisa, Nyein, Nyein, and Nachemson, Andrew (2022). "Flicking the Kill Switch: Governments Embrace Internet Shutdowns as a Form of Control." Retrieved from www.theguardian.com/technology/2022/aug/29/flicking-the-kill-switch-governments-embrace-internet-shutdowns-as-a-form-of-control. Accessed 18 March 2023.

Business Human Rights Resource Centre (2021). "Uganda Shuts Down Internet Ahead of General Election." Retrieved from www.business-humanrights.org/en/latest-news/uganda-shuts-down-internet-ahead-of-general-election/. Accessed 21 March 2023.

Cerf, G. V. (2012, 4 January). "Internet Access is not a Human Right." *New York Times.* Retrieved from Opinion | Internet Access Is Not a Human Right – The New York Times (nytimes.com). Accessed 30 January 2021.

Chari, T. (2022). Between State Interests and Citizen Digital Rights: Making Sense of Internet Shutdowns in Zimbabwe. In Farooq A. Kperogi (ed.), *Digital Dissidence and Social Media Censorship in Africa* (pp. 76). London: Routledge.

Chimhangwa, Kudzai (2019). "What Zimbabwe's Internet Disruptions say about the State of Digital Rights in the Country?" *Global Voices.* Retrieved https://globalvoices.org/2019/07/19/what-do-zimbabwes-internet-disruptions-say-about-the-state-of-digital-rights-in-the-country/. Accessed 22 October 2020.

CIPESA (2019). "Despots and Disruptions: Five Dimensions of Internet Shutdowns in Africa." Retrieved from https://cipesa.org/2019/03/despots-and-disruptions-five-dimensions-of-internet-shutdowns-in-africa/. Accessed 18 May 2022.

CRIS (2005). *Assessing Communication Rights: A Handbook.* London: CRIS Campaign. https://archive.ccrvoices.org/cdn.agilitycms.com/centre-for-communication-rights/Images/Articles/pdf/cris-manual-en.pdf. Accessed 12 April 2022.

Dahir, A. L. (2019). "An Internet Shutdown is the Latest Frustration Hitting Voters in Dr Congo." Retrieved from https://qz.com/africa/1513023/drc-shuts-down-internet-sms-ahead-of-election-results. Accessed 21 March 2023.

Fight Inequality (2021). "Internet Shutdown and Human Rights Violations in Zambia." Retrieved from www.fightinequality.org/news/internet-shutdown-and-human-rights-violations-zambia. Accessed 21 March 2023.

Freedom House (2019). "Freedom on the Net 2019: Zimbabwe." Retrieved from https://freedomhouse.org/country/zimbabwe/freedom-net/2019. Accessed 19 March 2023.

Global Freedom of Expression (2018). "The Case of Communications Suspension and Internet Shutdown During the 2011 Egyptian Revolution." Retrieved from https://globalfreedomofexpression.columbia.edu/cases/communications-suspension-and-internet-shutdown-case-during-the-2011-egyptian-revolution/. Accessed 19 March 2023.

Government of the Kingdom of Eswatini (2021). "Acting Prime Minister's Statement." Retrieved from www.accessnow.org/cms/assets/uploads/2021/06/APM-Statement-29-June-2021-final-1-1.pdf. Accessed 19 March 2023.

Howard, N. Philip, Agarwal, D. Sheetal and Hussain, M. (2011). When Do States Disconnect Their Digital Networks? Regime Responses to the Political Use of Social Media. *The Communication Review*, 14(3), 216–232.

Human Rights Council (2011). Report of the Special Rapporteur on the Promotion and Protection of the Right Freedom of Opinion and Expression, Frank La Rue. A/HRC/17/27. Retrieved from https://digitallibrary.un.org/record/706200. Accessed 23 December 2022

Human Rights Council (2016). Oral Revisions of 30 June. The Promotion, Protection and Enjoyment of Human Rights on the Internet. United Nations, A/HRC/32/L.20. https://www.article19.org/data/files/Internet_Statement_Adopted.pdf. Accessed 23 July 2022.

Human Rights Council (2022). "Internet Shutdowns: Trends, Causes, Legal Implications and impacts on a Range of Human Rights Report." Retrieved from https://reliefweb.int/report/world/internet-shutdowns-trends-causes-legal-implications-and-impacts-range-human-rights-report-office-united-nations-high-commissioner-human-rights-ahrc5055-enarruzh. Accessed 18 March 2023.

Internet Freedom India (n.d.). "What are Internet Shutdowns?" Retrieved from https://internetfreedom.in/shutdowns-faq/. Accessed 14 February 2023.

Jaster, R. and Lanius, D. (2018) What is Fake News? *Versus*, 2(127), 207–227.

Karppinen, K. and Puukko, O. (2020) Four Discourses of Digital Rights: Promises and Problems of Rights-Based Politics. *Journal of Information Policy*, 10, 304–328.

Kaye, D. and Reventlow, N. (2017). "Digital Rights are Human Rights." Retrieved from https://slate.com/technology/2017/12/digital-rights-are-human-rights.html. Accessed 6 July 2023.

Majama, K. (2019). The Bigger Picture: Assessing Zimbabwe's Internet Blockade. Retrieved from https://www.apc.org/fr/node/35336. Accessed 20 May 2023.

Marchant, E. and Stremlau, N. (2020). A Spectrum of Shutdowns: Reframing Internet Shutdowns from Africa. *International Journal of Communication*, 14, 4327–4342.

Marchant, E. and Stremlau, N. (2019). *Africa's Internet Shutdowns: A Report on the Johannesburg Workshop*. Programme in Comparative Media, Law & Policy. Oxford: Oxford University Press. Retrieved from http://pcmlp.socleg.ox.ac.uk/wp-content/uploads/2019/10/Internet-Shutdown-Workshop-Report-171019.pdf. Accessed September 2020.

Mare, A. (2020). State-Ordered Internet shutdowns and the Digital Authoritarianism in Zimbabwe. *International Journal of Communication*, 14, 4244–4263.

Mathiesen, K. (2014) Human Rights for the Digital Age. *Journal of Mass Media Ethics*, 29(1), 2–18.

Media Defence (2022). "Introduction to Digital Rights." Retrieved from www.mediadefence.org/resource-hub/introduction-to-digital-rights/. Accessed 23 March 2023.

Milderbrath, H. (2021). "Internet Access as a Fundamental Right: Exploring Aspects of Connectivity." Brussels: European Parliamentary Research. Retrieved from   www.europarl.europa.eu/RegData/etudes/STUD/2021/696170/EPRS_ STU(2021)696170_EN.pdf. Accessed 7 July 2023.

O'Reilly, Michael (2015) "What is the Appropriate Role for Regulators in an Expanding Broadband Economy?" Remarks of Commissioner Michael O'Reilly Before the Internet Innovation Alliance, June 25, 2015. Retrieved from http://transition.fcc.gov/Daily-Relrases/Daily_Business/2015/adb0625/DOC-334113A1.pdf

Pollicino, O. (2019). The Right to Internet Access: Quid Iuris. In A. Von-Arnaild, K. Von Der Decker and M. Susi (eds), *The Cambridge Handbook of New Human Rights* (pp. 1–14). Cambridge, UK: Cambridge University Press.

Reuters Foundation (2021, April). "Slowdowns and Shutdowns: Africans Challenge Internet Restrictions." Retrieved from www.globalcitizen.org/en/content/africans-challenge-internet-restrictions/?gclid=EAIaIQobChMIgYzktuCS_QIVhJlmAh0STwGcEAAYAiAAEgKYufD_BwE. Accessed 13 February 2023.

Reuters (2021). "Uganda bans Social Media ahead of Presidential Election." Retrieved from www.reuters.com/article/us-uganda-election/uganda-bans-social-media-ahead-of-presidential-election-idUSKBN29H0KH. Accessed 21 March 2023.

Rydzak, J., Karanja, M. and Opiyo, N. (2020). Dissent Does not Die in Darkness: Network Shutdowns and Collective Action on African Countries. *International Journal of Communication*, 14, 4264–4287.

Simanje, N. (2022, 12 December). "Zimbabwe Government tries to Justify Shutting Down the Internet." IFEX. Retrieved from https://ifex.org/zimbabwe-government-tries-to-justify-shutting-down-the-internet/. Accessed 19 March 2023.

Southern Africa Litigation Centre (2021) "Statement: Internet Shutdown in Eswatini Challenged in the High Court." Retrieved from www.southernafricalitigationcentre.org/2021/07/05/statement-internet-shutdown-in-eswatini-challenged-in-the-high-court/. Accessed 19 March 2023.

Stauffer, B. (2020) "Shutting Down the Internet to Shutdown Critics." Retrieved from www.hrw.org/world-report/2020/country-chapters/global-5. Accessed 18 March 2022.

Stremlau, N. and Dobson, N. (2022) Information Controls and Internet Shutdown in African Elections: The Politics of Electoral Integrity and Abuses of Power. *Journal of African Elections*, 21(2), 1–22.

Thomas, P. (2005). CRIS and Global Media Governance: Communication Rights and Social Change: Paper Presented at the 21st Century Conference. Center for Social Change Research, Queensland University of Technology, Queensland, 28 October 2005. Retrieved from https://espace.library.uq.edu.au/view/UQ:102463. Accessed 31 December 2022.

Thomas, P. (2006). The Communication Rights in the Information Society (CRIS) Campaign: Applying Social Movement Theories to an Analysis of Global Media Reform. *The International Communication Gazette*, 68(4), 291–312.

Wagner, B. (2018). Understanding Internet Shutdowns: A Case Study of Pakistan. *International Journal of Communication*, 12, 3917–3938.

Watson, L. (2018). Systematic Epistemic Rights Violations in the Media: A Brexit Case Study. *Social Epistemology*, 32(2), 88–102.

7   Media Censorship in East Africa during Elections

George Nyabuga and Shitemi Khamadi

The media should be at the heart of political and democratic processes. However, recent political developments in Kenya, Tanzania, and Uganda show increasing intolerance to freedoms of expression and the media particularly during elections. While such freedoms are constitutionally guaranteed, a culture of political intolerance is created by the desire of those in power to enervate the opposition and independent media. Through laws and policies, use of police force, and fiat media shutdown, the media has been considerably emasculated.

In Kenya, freedom of expression and the media are guaranteed by Articles 33 and 34 respectively of the Constitution of Kenya, 2010. In Tanzania, Section 18 (1) of the constitution guarantees freedom of expression. In Uganda, freedom of speech and expression "which shall include freedom of the press and other media" is guaranteed by Article 29 of the Uganda Constitution 1995 which also protects and promotes fundamental and other human rights and freedoms including conscience, movement, religion, assembly and association. Despite such constitutional guarantees, however, there are serious concerns about levels of intimidation, harassment and clampdown on media and journalism in the three East African countries.

In addition, regardless of regular multiparty elections, the three countries can be best described as "pseudo" or "fake" democracies (Mutua, 2022) because they exhibit both democratic and autocratic characteristics. Granted, there is no gainsaying that elections, however flawed, have had a significant effect on the democratization process (cf. Lindberg, 2006). "The process of holding an uninterrupted series of *de jure* participatory, competitive, and legitimate elections," argues Lindberg (2006, p. 3) "not only enhances the democratic quality of the electoral regime but also ... civil liberties in ... society." Such optimism is, however, tempered with pessimism given the fact that recent elections in Kenya, Tanzania and Uganda have not been genuinely competitive, and legitimate and thus not free and fair. In Kenya, for example, Nyabuga (2012) points out that there are serious problems with the quality of its democracy and good, accountable and

DOI: 10.4324/9781003352907-9

responsible governance and political leadership. The same has been experienced in Tanzania (particularly under the late President John Pombe Magufuli (29 October 1959 – 17 March 2021) (Bamwenda, 2018) and Uganda under Yoweri Museveni (Ojambo, 2022; Reid, 2017).

While the freedoms and rights mentioned above are key to the practice and consolidation of democracy, this chapter is concerned with media freedom and the regular clampdown of independent media especially around election time. More specifically, this chapter examines the issue of censorship, whether preemptive or punitive (meaning that censorship happens before and after media events or reporting respectively). Regardless, there is evidence that preemptive or punitive censorship "work in tandem: one punishment serves as a warning to others" (Watson and Hill, 2012, p. 35). This often creates fear among journalists and media who consequently steer clear of certain issues that may be seen as offensive to those in power. Censorship is seen as "the curtailment, usually by or on behalf of those in authority, of the major freedoms – of belief, expression, movement, assembly and access to information" (ibid.). Often, censorship is "applied by the self: a thing is not expressed because of the risk of external censorship – from the law, from organizations, and institutions … thus we have censorship by omission or evasion" (ibid.).

The histories of Kenya, Tanzania and Uganda are similar in many ways. They became one party states a few years after independence as the immediate post-independent leaders sought to centralize or consolidate power through legal and extra-legal means. These strategies included the suppression of opposition, detention, imprisonment or even assassination of opposition political figures, changes in constitutions to make the countries one-party states or coups. The countries, however, enjoyed relative political "stability" until the overthrow of Uganda's Milton Obote by Idi Amin on 25 January 1971. The either *de facto* or *de jure* single-party political arrangement lasted until the 1990s in Kenya and Tanzania. Kenya and Tanzania liberalized their politics in the early 1990s and paved way for multi-party democracy even as the world was moving away from the cold war with the collapse of the Union of Soviet Socialist Republics (USSR). That collapse marked the start of the winds of change that swept across Africa. Nonetheless, changes in Uganda came through either military coups or civil war. For example, the National Resistance Movement of Yoweri Museveni ascended to power in 1986 after five years of an armed uprising against Obote's government that begun on 6 February 1981. President Museveni has been in power since 1986 often by manipulating political and democratic process, "sham" elections and use of violence (see, for example, Kanyamurwa, Kakuba, Kaddu and Babalanda, 2022).

Whatever the political arrangement, however, the three countries exercise similar control and influence of the media landscape. The three have state owned and government-controlled media. The Kenya Broadcasting Corporation, Tanzania Broadcasting Corporation and Uganda Broadcasting Corporation are all state controlled, and those in power often get a lion share of news coverage especially around election time. The "independent" media is also often influenced by the political class who use state advertising to control or manipulate coverage.

A look at the political and electoral landscape provides a glimpse into the difficulties media face. For example, Kenya's 2017 and 2022, Uganda's 2016 and 2021 and Tanzania's 2015 and 2020 elections show the rough political landscape the media and journalists had to navigate. The environment was replete with threats, intimidation and violence as those in government sought to control or influence political and democratic narratives and public opinion.

To better illustrate the issues above, a discussion of presidential elections in Kenya, Tanzania and Uganda is apt. Presidential elections mainly because they are the most contested, emotive and divisive in the countries as power often rests with those elected president. And power is considered the "most fundamental [issue] in ... politics" (Goverde, Cerny, Haugaard and Lentner, 2000, p. 1) because it deals with, among other things, control, of state resources, and sometimes media. Democracy is seen as the "distribution of power through democratic institutions" (Goverde, Cerny, Haugaard and Lentner, 2000, p. 11) although as evidence from Kenya, Uganda and Tanzania show, control of those "democratic institutions," like parliament, also rests with those in power, with the media sometimes providing some checks and balances through information and criticism of those in power.

The three East African countries are at different stages in terms of post-colonial or post-independent political and democratic development even though all gained independence in the 1960s. Tanzania was the first to get its independence on 9 December 1961 followed by Uganda on 9 October 1962 and Kenya on 12 December 1963. However, events in the three countries, and particularly the systems of government defined their political trajectory. Tanzania, for example, under the first President Julius Nyerere followed what he called *Ujamaa* (a system of African socialism) while Kenya and Uganda embraced different forms of capitalism.

The media has become an important actor in ensuring legitimacy by focusing on how government exercises power. This is done through provision of information, and a platform through which people share ideas, and discuss issues that concern them. Seen as public sphere (cf. Habermas, 1989[1962]), the media provides the space to share and discuss information, ideas that ultimately contributes to the formation of public opinion (Dahlgren, 2005). Thus, reining in media becomes important to state actors keen on manipulating public opinion and political will. Accordingly, state- and self-censorship, suppression of information, use of force, arrest and intimidation are often used by governments to trample on media and journalists' freedom to report on politics and elections. This is mostly because political uses of the media

> matter because they have some effect upon the way the political process works, and the interests that motivate the media also shape the outcomes of that process. The media have power: they determine the fate of politicians and political causes, they influence governments and their electorates.
>
> (Street, 2001, p. 231)

Mediatization of politics

However manipulated the political and democratic processes are, political leadership in Kenya, Tanzania and Uganda is now determined through elections. Consequently, the informed participation of as many people as possible is the cornerstone of legitimacy, openness, fairness, and effectiveness of the electoral and, indeed, the democratic process. In a democracy, popular participation is key to legitimation of power, decisions and thus the formation and existence of governments. Popular or mass participation gives governments the authority or right to exist. A government without the support of the people cannot be said to be democratic. As the great political thinker John Stuart Mill (1910, pp. 215–217) noted

> the only government which can fully satisfy all the exigencies of the social state is one in which the whole people participate; that any participation, even in the smallest public function, is useful; that the participation should everywhere be as great as the general degree of improvement of the community will allow; and that nothing less can be ultimately desirable than the admission of all to a share in the sovereign power of the state.

Mazzoleni (2008) has defined mediatization of society as "the extension of the influence of the media … into all spheres of society and social life." Hjarvard (2008, p. 113) calls mediatization "the process whereby society to an increasing degree is submitted to, or becomes dependent on, the media and their logic" while Asp and Esaiasson (1996, pp. 80–81) see it as a "development towards increasing media influence." In the foregoing definitions, the argument that the media is increasingly playing an influential role in society and political and democratic processes is clear yet problematic especially because of concerns about "the excessive power of the media expanding beyond the boundaries of their traditional functions in democracies [and because] no constitution foresees that the media be accountable for their actions" (Mazzoleni and Schulz, 1999, p. 248). Even though it is not by any means the only socializing agent, the media has and continues to play a critical role in politics and electoral politics in Kenya, Uganda and Tanzania and thus its control is seen as critical to influencing public opinion and to some extent political and democratic processes and electoral outcomes.

Often, the role of the media is considered vital to the consolidation and expansion of democracy because it "perform[s] not only cognitive functions of information dissemination but also interpretative functions of analysis, assessment and comment" (McNair, 2011, p. 67). Arguments abound about the role of the media in the public sphere (Habermas, 1984) particularly the provision and interrogation of information and ideas. Habermas (1984, p. 49) contends that the public sphere is the

> realm of our social life in which something approaching public opinion can be formed. Access is guaranteed to all citizens. A portion of the public sphere comes into being in every conversation in which private individuals assemble to form a public body.

In addition, McQuail (2010) has written eloquently about the role of the media in political and democratic processes. To him,

> [T]here is no doubting the … significance of mass media in contemporary society, in the spheres of politics, culture, everyday social life and economics. In respect of politics, the mass media provide an arena of debate and a set of channels for making policies, candidates, relevant facts and ideas more widely known as well as providing politicians, interest groups and agents of government with a means of publicity and influence. In the realm of culture, the mass media are for most people the main channel of cultural representation and expression, and the primary source of images of social reality and materials for forming and maintaining social identity. Everyday social life is strongly patterned by the routines of media use and infused by its contents through the way leisure time is spent, lifestyles are influenced, conversation is given its topics and models of behaviour are offered for all contingencies.
>
> (McQuail, 2010, pp. 1–2)

The arguments above demonstrate the increasing importance of media to inform and influence politics and society. Besides, in a world that is increasingly reliant on the media, arguments abound that "mass audiences encounter mediated politics via the media" because most people do not "encounter politics in a direct (firsthand) manner, involving active participation" (Louw, 2005, p. 31). In this context, audiences encounter politics as a "set of secondhand (manipulated and distorted) media images." This conclusion supports arguments of increased mediatization of politics, the idea that "political institutions increasingly are dependent on and shaped by mass media" (Mazzoleni and Schulz, 1999, p. 247). This is mostly as a result of the "increased importance of the mass media as a source of political information and the decline of the party press" and because "politicians have become more dependent on the mass media in general" (Kepplinger, 2002, p. 973). However, as Mazzoleni and Schulz, (1999) posit, the fact that the media is sometimes irresponsible and unaccountable means regimes in the three countries have always found excuses to accuse it of seeking to manipulate the will of the people. Thus the

> absence of accountability can imply serious risks for democracy because it violates the classic rule of balances of power in the democratic game, making the media (the "fourth branch of government") an influential and uncontrollable force that is protected from the sanction of popular will.
> (Mazzoleni and Schulz, 1999, p. 248)

"Unaccountable" and "'irresponsible" powerful media

Kenya, Tanzania and Uganda enjoy a relatively robust media environment. The countries have numerous radio and television stations, and a growing internet penetration. Tanzania had 183 radio stations, 43 TV stations, 229 newspapers and magazines as of March 2020. It also had a vibrant online media. Internet penetration stood at 37.60% (Bazira, 2021). Reports indicate that Uganda has over 309 licensed radio stations, numerous public and private TV stations, and is experiencing a rapid growth in internet accessibility and usage (Internews, 2021). In Kenya, the Communication Authority which licenses TV and radio stations indicate that there were 327 TV, and 257 radio stations as of March 2023. The organization also indicates that data/Internet subscriptions stood at 47.96 million out of which 67.1% were on mobile broadband. This means that almost 90% have access to the Internet.

Despite the growth, and growing reliance, of the media, notions of irresponsible and unaccountable and "powerful" but irresponsible media abound. The concerns have been used on numerous occasions to clamp down on media and journalism. Following widespread claims that, for example, the media contributed to the genocide in Rwanda in the 1990s, and post-election violence in Kenya in 2007/2008 following the disputed presidential election, the media has always been under scrutiny. In Rwanda, the genocide claimed more than 800,000 civilians mostly Tutsis, but also moderate Hutus. The post-election violence that followed the contested elections in 2007 killed more than 1,333 people displaced over 650,000 people and forced around 2,000 Kenyans to seek refuge in the neighboring countries especially Uganda and Tanzania according to the Commission of Inquiry into the Post-Election Violence (CIPEV), an international commission of inquiry established by the Government of Kenya in February 2008 to investigate the clashes. Parts of the CIPEV report blamed the media for inciting hate and violence prior to the post-election violence, a decision that had led to banning of live broadcasting by the government on 31 December 2007 ostensibly to arrest violence and harm. The decision was justified by the then Permanent Secretary of the Ministry of Information and Communications Dr. Bitange Ndemo who said in the CIPEV report that the action was in "good faith" and done with the "overriding national interest in mind" (CIPEV, 2008, p. 297). Since the post-election violence and subsequent accusations of complicity in the mayhem self-censorship has become common in Kenya. In such tense situations, the media often chooses to "keep the peace" by blacking out violence, not publishing hate speech, and not giving politicians space to antagonize ethnic relations in Kenya's highly polarized and ethnicized political environment. Thus, crude censorship, the manipulation of messages and sometimes propaganda continue to be part of the media environment in Kenya, Tanzania and Uganda.

The censorship that has been used to restrict media's coverage of elections has had both legal and extra-legal means in the three countries. This is particularly prevalent in Tanzania and Uganda. In Tanzania, for example, Cheeseman, Matfess and Amani (2021) argue that the ruling Chama Cha Mapinduzi (CCM) party has often used coercion to limit media coverage of election. The 2020 elections were particularly bad for the media although clampdown started much earlier.

Legal and extralegal restrictions

Immediately after taking over office in 2015, the regime of former President John Pombe Magufuli begun enacting new legislations, amending old ones or using provisions that were not being actively used against media freedoms (Cheeseman, Matfess and Amani, 2021). The government targeted media in general, political parties and civil society during the Magufuli's time in power. He served as Tanzania's fifth President from 2015 until his sudden death in 2021.

Human Rights Watch (2019) documented different legal impediments or instruments used to trample on media freedoms. The 2015 Cybercrimes Act restricts free expression online. The Statistics Act, 2015, criminalizes the publication of statistics without government approval and bans publication and dissemination of independent research. Elections often require data on the number of voters, trends, candidates, voting patterns, etc. and thus banning such publication is deleterious to democracy and a free and fair election. The Statistics Act was only amended in June 2019. Furthermore, the 2018 regulations to the Electronic and Postal Communications Act subject bloggers to excessive licensing fees. The Media Services Act, 2016, gives government agencies broad power to censor and limit the independence of the media by creating stringent rules for accrediting journalists. This severely restricts press freedom, and makes it difficult for journalists and the media to operate freely. During the 2020 elections, John Pombe Magufuli used state ownership of media outlets and state regulatory powers over the media to guarantee himself and his party, CCM favorable coverage (Paget, 2021). Media houses that gave space to opposition figures were often harassed and threatened. Government advertising was stopped to punish "independent" media.

Accordingly, from 2015, there were serious concerns about media freedom and freedom of expression in Tanzania as Magufuli became increasingly authoritarian. In 2019 Amnesty International and Human Rights Watch reports accused the president of presiding over rising levels of abuses against journalists, human rights defenders, political opponents and others since his first election in 2015. This followed his blanket ban in July 2016 of political activities until 2020. During this period, state and self-censorship intensified as radio and newspapers were shutdown, and live transmission of parliamentary debates stopped. TV and stations were severely punished for any reporting considered anti-government.

Magufuli's regime jailed or detained many critics, banned publications for criticizing his style of leadership. For example, publications such as *Mawio Weekly* and *Mwana Halisi* were banned. The Tanzania Editors Forum reported that by 2017 at least five newspapers and two radio stations had been suspended for three to 36 months in connection with the publication of false information, incitement of rebellion or threatening national security. *Mwana Halisi* was closed down for "repeated unethical reporting, publishing a fabricated and inciting article and endangering national security" as per The Media Services Act, 2016 which gives the government the right to suspend or close media organizations that publish information that is seditious or that which is likely to cause fear and alarm. The arrest and prosecution of investigative reporter Erick Kabendera illustrates the point of misuse of law to settle scores. He was apparently interrogated for alleged sedition and publication of false information in an Economist Intelligence Unit, a publication of the popular international magazine the Economist. The article documented Magufuli's abuses of power.

In another case, former Regional Commissioner of Dar es Salaam Paul Makonda stormed Clouds FM accompanied by armed police officers. He ordered the station's staff to broadcast a video incriminating Josephat Gwajima, a Protestant church leader, in drug trafficking. Subsequently, the Minister of Information and Communication Nape Nnauye was fired after visiting the station and condemning the attack. Instead of reprimanding the Regional Commissioner, President Magufuli praised Makonda and promised him support as he continued clamping down on government critics and opponents (Reporters Without Borders, 2017). The situation worsened especially for opposition politicians who were regularly targeted by the government. For example, in 2017, unidentified assailants shot an opposition member of parliament, Tundu Lissu. In 2018, unidentified assailants killed Daniel John and Godfrey Luena, two officials of the main opposition party, Chadema.

The Cybercrimes Act was also used to harass opposition politicians, journalists and activists. In addition, police and others assaulted, abducted and arbitrarily arrested journalists for doing reports critical of government or Magufuli's' rule. Magufuli's regime was thenceforth considered as an enemy of the media, rule of law and democracy (Bamwenda, 2018). According to Bamwenda

> accusations against Magufuli also ... [his] authoritarianism, which includes inadequate following of the rule of law, established governance procedures, and abiding to the principles of the separation of powers of the three governance pillars.... He believed that the criticism of his person and the style of conducting policy hindered the implementation of [his policies] ... the opposition [and] his critics had to face the penalty of imprisonment [for any criticisms].
>
> (2018, p. 137–138)

This conclusion is shared by Cheeseman, Matfess and Amani (2021, p. 86) who posit that "under Magufuli, the prospects for democratization and good governance looked bleak. Civil society could not mobilize, elections were neither free nor fair, the media were hamstrung, advocates of democracy and accountability" were persecuted, detained or exiled. In short, Tanzania became a democratic rogue state because of Magufuli's intolerance for criticism, and his decimation of numerous freedoms including those of free speech, media, and association (see, for example, Bamwenda, 2018; Cheeseman, Matfess and Amani, 2021). In fact, Cheeseman, Matfess and Amani (2021, p. 85) posit that

> the recent intensification of authoritarian practices in Tanzania underlines the risks of engaging with new democracies while wearing rose-tinted glasses.... Magufuli has been presented as a uniquely authoritarian force, but he was enabled by this system and the realities of one-party rule. Tanzania's reputation as a "success story" of gradual democratization rests on a selective view of the country's politics and an overlooking of the threat inherent in one-party dominance.

In Uganda, the Covid-19 pandemic provided a perfect environment for the regime to restrict information spaces like the internet and social media. Describing the situation as bleak, Nanfuka (2021) termed it as a textbook strategy often used by authoritarian regimes to retain or centralize power. Disruption of the internet, rampant disinformation campaigns, and harassment of the media and civil society were also commonplace.

The disruption of the internet by President Museveni's government and its shutdown was not, however, new in the 2021 elections. It happened in the 2016 elections, in what was seen as attempts by the regime to reduce the spread of information election anomalies, including vote rigging and manipulation. However, in the 2021 elections, Facebook suspended a number of accounts including those of leading National Resistance Movement (NRM) luminaries for spreading coordinated disinformation, a move that led the government to ban the social media platform. Facebook remains inaccessible in Uganda except with the use of Virtual Private Networks (VPNs) (Enywaru and Ndung'u, 2021).

Kenya's situation is not much different. Cheeseman, Matfess and Amani (2021) contend that in the 2017 elections, the incumbent regime in Kenya led by President Uhuru Kenyatta, used state resources to influence media coverage of his campaigns. He, for example, used government advertising to arm-twist media houses. In the aftermath of the repeat presidential 2017 election boycotted by opposition leader, the media came under heavy censure for covering the "illegal" self-swearing in of opposition leader Raila Odinga as the "people's president." To demonstrates its power, the government shut down all TV media houses that broadcast the ceremony. These included major TV stations like NTV, KTN and Citizen TV. Fred Matiang'i, the then Cabinet Secretary for the Ministry of Interior and Coordination of National Government under whose docket security fell, accused "elements" in the media of facilitating the "illegal act" and putting lives of thousands of Kenyans at risk. Subsequently, the government refused to obey a High Court order to lift the ban. Prior to the shutdown, the government had summoned top editors to State House, the official residence of the president, waring them against broadcasting the swearing-in. The repercussions of the intransigence were dire, and the drastic decision to shut down the television stations remains a blot in Kenya's postcolonial political and media history. Granted, the 2017 general election saw an increase in disinformation and cyber propaganda (Maweu 2020). The presidential election was the target of most attacks. In the election, the ruling party Jubilee was seeking to retain power against a resurgent main opposition, National Super Alliance (NASA) – a coalition of opposition parties. But is often the case, the most critical casualty in the era of extensive disinformation and misinformation is truth, which denies citizens "truthful" information upon which their decisions are based. This continued into the 2022 general election. Maweu (2020) points out that disinformation and propaganda succeed mostly because they reinforce societal myths and stereotypes. These are often deeply embedded within a people, making it difficult to recognize the messages as mere propaganda.

Elections in Kenya, Tanzania and Uganda

Kenya, Tanzania and Uganda have always held regular elections every five years. This started in the 1990s after the reintroduction of multipartyism. However, the integrity of the elections is often questionable. This is largely because of widespread irregularities, election-related fraud and intimidation, opacity and lack of a level playing field. For example, the Tanzania Elections Watch, a group of regional experts monitoring the last election in Tanzania concluded in October 2020 that the vote "marked the most significant backsliding in Tanzania's democratic credentials" due to the "climate of fear" created by, among other factors, a clampdown on the media, and the heavy deployment of military and police which curtailed people's rights and freedoms.

Besides, neopatrimonialism is often commonplace in East Africa. The ruling parties and their presidential candidates often use state resources to contest and buy loyalty and following of the general population. That is if they cannot rig the elections.

In Uganda, the regime of Idi Amin that came to power after the overthrow of the independence leader Milton Obote in 1971, seriously limited people's political rights and freedoms. So when Museveni came to power on 26 January 1986 and promised to end the culture of "overstaying" in power (although the first "competitive" elections were held 20 years later on 9 May 1996), people were optimistic things would change for the better (cf. Ojambo, 2022; Reid, 2017). Promising to be different from other African leaders and step aside after serving a five-year term and pass on the baton to a "democratically elected successor," Museveni said in his speech after being sworn that "the problem of Africa in general and Uganda in particular is not the people, but leaders who want to overstay in power" (see also a collection of his speeches published in Museveni, 2000). Ironically, he is still in power 37 years later. This is reinforced by his increasing consolidation of power, intolerance to opposition politics, criticism and use of state machinery to silence independent voices and clamp down on the opposition and critics. What is more, on December 20, 2017, the Ugandan Parliament passed an amendment to the Constitution scrapping presidential age limit to ensure he continues to stand in subsequent elections. Before then, candidates vying for the presidency were expected to be under 75 years of age. The removal of term limits was arguably done before the 2021 elections during which he would have been 76 years old and thus ineligible to contest. He was declared winner in the 2021 election with 59% of the vote compared to 35 per cent of his then closest competitor, the 38-year-old former pop star Bobi Wine (real name Robert Kyagulanyi). This is despite widespread violence and reports indicating that, for example, "at least twenty-eight people died in violent clashes between Ugandan security forces and supporters of a detained opposition presidential candidate" (*France 24*, 2020). Amnesty International also reported that "security forces used intimidatory tactics to suppress political opposition members and supporters in the context of the January elections, including arbitrary arrests, abductions, prolonged incommunicado detention, enforced disappearances and prosecutions. The rights to freedom of expression, peaceful assembly and association were severely restricted; the authorities targeted organizations working on human rights and shut down the internet for five days" (Amnesty International, 2022, p. 377). Amnesty International's findings were supported by a report by the Human Rights Watch which indicated on 21 January 2021 that:

> The weeks leading up to Uganda's recently concluded elections were characterized by widespread violence and human rights abuses.... The abuses included killings by security forces, arrests and beatings of opposition supporters and journalists, disruption of opposition rallies, and a shutdown of the internet.... Since election campaigns began in November 2020, security forces have clamped down on opposition members and journalists, violently arresting scores of people, including the presidential candidates Patrick Amuriat of the Forum for Democratic Change and Robert Kyagulanyi, of the National Unity Platform.

Based on the arguments above, and other studies, Ojambo (2022, p. 9) has concluded that Museveni is an impediment to the growth of democracy in Uganda largely because of his reliance on "overt and latent military force, coupled with a growing personality cult which considers Museveni indispensable." This view is shared by Cheeseman, Lynch and Willis (2021, p. 85) who point out that Museveni has used a "combination of threats and outright violence, and control of state media, state officials and patronage to secure victory" in elections.

Conclusion

As the arguments above show, the media is critical to political and democratic processes in Kenya, Tanzania and Uganda mainly because they provide important information vital for people's participation in electoral activities and democracy. Concomitantly, the expansion of the media space (despite political and economic challenges), constitutional guarantees of freedom of expression and people's increasing interest and participation in electoral politics indicate growing levels of democracy. This is despite serious concerns about the quality of democracy and democratic activity, and political inclusion and participation. Consequently, it is clear that what Kenya, Tanzania and Uganda have is a pseudo or fake democracy because of the intolerance shown towards freedom of expression and freedom of the media. There are, of course, differences in terms of levels of democracy based on the extent of intolerance. It is also evident that Kenya, Tanzania and Uganda have had mixed fortunes in terms of the expansion of both the political and media space. Whilst Kenya and Tanzania have been relatively peaceful, and use elections to change political leaders, Uganda has been "autocratic" over the years. Granted, Kenya and Tanzania have had their share of political upheavals, particularly under the one-party dictatorships or autocratic regimes crafted by the independence parties namely the Kenya African National Union (KANU) in Kenya and Chama cha Mapinduzi (CCM) in Tanzania respectively as a way of consolidating power.

More worrying in the context of this chapter is the growing intolerance towards press freedom, particularly by those in power, and the consequent rise in preemptive or punitive censorship. In short, political intolerance and clampdowns on media freedom have affected the capacity of the media to provide information and space vital to people's participation in electoral activities and decisions. This may, in the long term, affect not only the capacity of the media to provide information critical of government but also information that would enhance citizen's knowledge about and understanding of issues, and their contribution to ideas and debates, and ultimately political opinion and will. In short, participatory democracy has suffered as a result of increasing intolerance towards individual freedom of speech and expression as well as that of the media. State-censorship sometimes leads to self-censorship, an insidious problem affecting the quality of media content, and the credibility and reliability of media and journalism particularly around election time. Compounded by media capture, censorship has compromised the place of media in society, and affected its ability to hold power to account and promote democracy in East Africa.

References

Amnesty International (2022). *International Report 2021/2022: The State of the World's Human Rights*. London: Amnesty International.

Asp, Kent and Esaiasson, Peter (1996). The Modernization of Swedish Campaigns: Individualization, Professionalization, and Medialization. In Swanson, David and Mancini, Paolo (eds), *Politics, Media, and Modern Democracy: An International Study of Innovations in Electoral Campaigning and Their Consequences*. Westport: Praeger, pp. 73–90.

Bamwenda, Emilia (2018). The Symptoms of the Shift Towards an Authoritarian State in Tanzania's President John Pombe Magufuli's Rule. *Politeja*, 56, 123–150.

Carbone, Giovanni and Pellegata, Alessandro (2020). *Political Leadership in Africa: Leaders and Development South of the Sahara*. Cambridge: Cambridge University Press.

Cheeseman, Nic, Lynch, Gabrielle and Willis, Justin (2020). *The Moral Economy of Elections in Africa: Democracy, Voting and Virtue*. Cambridge: Cambridge University Press.

Cheeseman, Nic. Lynch, Gabrielle and Willis, Justin (2021). *The Moral Economy of Elections in Africa. Democracy, Voting and Virtue*. Cambridge: Cambridge University Press.

Cheeseman, Nic, Matfess, Hilary and Amani, Alitalali (2021). Tanzania: The Roots of Repression. *Journal of Democracy*, 32(2), 77–89.

Commission of Inquiry into the Post-Election Violence (CIPEV) (2008). CIPEV [Waki] Report.

Communication Authority (of Kenya) (2023). *Third Quarter Sector Statistics Report for the Financial Year 2022/2023 (1ˢᵗ January – 31ˢᵗ March 2023)*. Nairobi: Communication Authority (of Kenya). Report available online at www. ca.go.ke/sites/default/files/2023–06/Sector%20Statistics%20Report%20 Q3%202022–2023.pdf

Cottle, Simon (2006). *Mediatized Conflict*. Maidenhead: Open University Press.

Dahlgren, Peter (2005). The Internet, Public Spheres, and Political Communication: Dispersion and Deliberation. *Political Communication*, 22(2), 147–162.

Enywaru, Pius and Ndung'u, Leah Kahunde (2021). Debunking Election Disinformation during Uganda's Internet Shutdown. *Code for Africa [online]*, 26 March. Available at https://medium.com/code-for-africa/debunking-election-disinformation-during-ugandas-internet-shutdown-d82f8345b634

France 24 (2020). 28 die in violent start to Uganda's election season. *France 24* [online], 20 November. Available at www.france24.com/en/live-news/20201120–28-die-in-violent-start-to-uganda-s-election-season

Goverde, Henri, Cerny, Philip G., Haugaard, Mark and Lentner, Howard H. (eds.) (2000). *Power in Contemporary Politics: Theories, Practices, Globalizations*. London: Sage.

Habermas, Jürgen (1984). *The Theory of Communicative Action*, 2 vols. Cambridge: Polity Press.

Habermas, Jürgen (1989 [1962]). *The Structural Transformation of the Public Sphere: An Inquiry into a category of Bourgeois Society*. Cambridge: Polity Press.

Hjarvard, Stig (2008). The Mediatization of Society: A Theory of the Media as Agents of Social and Cultural Change. *Nordicom Review*, 29(2), 105–134.

Human Rights Watch (2019). *"As Long as I am Quiet, I am Safe": Threats to Independent Media and Civil Society in Tanzania*. Human Rights Watch [online], 28 October. Available at www.hrw.org/report/2019/10/28/long-i-am-quiet-i-am-safe/threats-independent-media-and-civil-society-tanzania

Human Rights Watch (2021). *Uganda: Elections Marred by Violence*. Human Rights Watch [online], 21 January. Available at www.hrw.org/news/2021/01/21/uganda-elections-marred-violence

Internews (2021). *The State of Radio in Uganda: A 2020 Review and the New Reality of COVID-19*. Washington, DC: Internews. Report available online at https://internews.org/wp-content/uploads/2021/05/State_of_Radio_Uganda_2021–05_Internews.pdf

Kanyamurwa, John Mary, Kakuba, Juma Sultan, Kaddu, Ronald and Babalanda, Stanley (2022). Elections and Domestic Peace in Africa: Assessing Peace Opportunities in Uganda's 2021 Presidential Elections. In Muzee, Hannah, Sunjo, Tata Emmanuel and Enaifoghe, Andrew Osehi (eds), *Democracy and Africanness: Contemporary Issues in Africa's Democratization and Governance*. Cham, Switzerland: Springer, pp. 161–176.

Kepplinger, Hans Mathias (2002). Mediatization of Politics: Theory and Data. *Journal of Communication*, 52(4), pp. 972–986.

Lindberg, Staffan (2006). *Democracy and Elections in Africa*. Baltimore, Maryland: The John Hopkins University Press.

Louw, Eric (2005). *The Media and Political Process*. London: Sage.

Maweu, Jacinta Mwende (2020). "Fake Elections"? Cyber Propaganda, Disinformation and the 2017 General Elections in Kenya. *African Journalism Studies*, 40(4), 62–76.

Mazzoleni, Gianpietro (2008). Mediatization of Society. In Donsbach, Wolfgang (ed.), *The International Encyclopedia of Communication*, vol. VII. Maiden, MA: Blackwell, pp. 3052–3055.

Mazzoleni, Gianpietro and Schulz, Winfried (1999). "Mediatization" of Politics: A Challenge for Democracy? *Political Communication*, 16(3), 247–261.

McNair, Brian (2011). *An Introduction to Political Communication*, 5th ed. Abingdon: Routledge.

McQuail, Denis (2010). *McQuail's Mass Communication Theory*, 6th ed. London: Sage.

Media Innovation Centre (2021) *Media Viability in Kenya*. Nairobi: Graduate School of Media and Communications, Aga Khan University and DW Akademie.

Mill, John Stuart (1910). *Utilitarianism*. London: Dent and Sons.

Museveni, Yoweri (2000). *What is Africa's Problem*. Minneapolis: Minneapolis University Press.

Mutua, Makau (2022). Kenya's Fake Democracy Part 1. *Nation* [online], October 30. Available at https://nation.africa/kenya/blogs-opinion/opinion/kenya-s-fake-democracy-part-1-4002028.

Nanfuka, Juliet (2021). Uganda's 2021 Election: A Textbook Case of Disruption to Democracy and Digital Networks in Authoritarian Countries. Cipesa [online], January 13. Available at https://cipesa.org/2021/01/ugandas-2021-election-a-textbook-case-of-disruption-to-democracy-and-digital-networks-in-authoritarian-countries/

Nyabuga, George (2012). *Mediatising Politics and Democracy: Making Sense of the Role of the Media in Kenya*. Nairobi: Media Focus on Africa Foundation.

Ojambo, Robert (2022). The 1995 Constitution as a Tool for Dictatorship in Uganda: An African Dilemma in Constitutionalism. In Muzee, Hannah, Sunjo, Tata Emmanuel and Enaifoghe, Andrew Osehi (eds), *Democracy and Africanness: Contemporary Issues in Africa's Democratization and Governance*. Cham, Switzerland: Springer, pp. 3–20.

Okoye, John-Bell, Owino, Ruth Aoko, Anyasi, Laura and Mule, Daniel (2019). The Alternative Platform: Kenya's Television Stations Navigation During the Switch Off of Raila Odinga's "Swearing-In". *Journalism Practice*, 13(9), 1091–1105.

Paget, Dan (2021). Tanzania: The Authoritarian Landslide. *Journal of Democracy*, 32(2), 61–76.

Reid, Richard (2017). *A History of Modern Uganda*. Cambridge: Cambridge University Press.

Reporters Without Borders (RSF) (2017). President Magufuli Praised Makonda and Promised him Support as He Continued Clamping Down on Government Critics and Opponents. RSF [Online], March 23. Available at https://rsf.org/en/brazen-interference-media-tanzania-s-government

Street, John (2001). *Mass Media, Politics and Democracy*. London: Palgrave.

Watson, James and Hill, Anne (2012). *Dictionary of Media and Communication Studies*, 8th ed. London: Bloomsbury Academic.

8 African Public Sphere Discourse

Culture and Community Radio

Siyasanga Tyali

Research results continues to be generated from the community radio sector of South Africa (Berger, 1996; Teer-Tomaselli, 2001; Bosch, 2003). A majority of the generated research has focused on multiple themes, including the health communication role of the industry, its history and development within the country. Using a case study approach, the focus of this chapter is on theorising and grappling with the role of the community radio sector by understanding its contribution in the liberation of African culture that is emerging from settler colonial and apartheid South Africa. In the attempt to understand the role of community radio within these scenarios, the chapter thus also manages to probe the community radio role in relation to the history and memory of a "particularised" African community[1] that is served by the broadcasting platform. The chapter managed to focus on these objectives as a result of zooming in on the everyday role of such a station in relation to the discourse about and contribution of the community broadcaster in the everyday developments within an African community setting. As per the dictates of the broadcasting act of South Africa (1999), community radio broadcasters need to be closely aligned to the interest of the broadcasting community. Thus, this chapter further probes as to whether a community radio station in Africa and serving an African community can display the characteristics of an African public sphere?

The chapter was drawn from a bigger study (Tyali, 2017) that aimed to understand the trajectories that have been made in the Africanisation and decolonisation of the broadcasting sector of South Africa. Some historical media research has suggested that media institutions, including the radio broadcasting sector, were designed to advance European colonial objectives and ambitions in Africa (Mano, 2011; Rønning & Kupe, 2000; Rosenthal, 1974; Switzer and Switzer, 1979; Mhlambi, 2015). The role of the media in colonial advancement has also been pursued by Fanon (1965, p. 69) who argues that in Algeria for instance, "Radio-Alger, the French broadcasting station which has been established in Algeria for decades,

DOI: 10.4324/9781003352907-10

a[s] re-edition or an echo of the French National Broadcasting System operating from Paris, is essentially the instrument of colonial society and its values." In this sense, the modern media industry is directly connected to the many colonial and cultural institutions that were used to buttress the colonial culture and thus in a way, shaped the contemporary public sphere in Africa (Ziegler and Asante, 1992). Thus, in thinking about decoloniality and decolonisation within the context of the media, reference needs to be made on the history of these institutions and their current roles in the liberation of African cultures (in the aftermath of a settler colonial state) in South Africa. The question of a media institution as an African public sphere is thus aligned to this quest of understanding the liberation role of media institutions in post-colonial states such as South Africa.

The section below outlines the case study that informed the research that is underpinning this chapter. The objective is to understand and situate the arguments outlined in this chapter within a certain context of South Africa.

Brief notes on the case study: Making sense of Vukani Community Radio (VCR)

In the year, 1996, the democratic government of South Africa initiated a process of awarding broadcasting rights (initially on a temporary basis) to the then newly established community radio stations of the country. In this country, the sector had been officially recognised during the pre-democracy negotiations. Among the licence granted community broadcasters in 1996 was a university student aligned broadcasting institution named Vukani Community Radio (VCR).[2] This community radio station was and still is situated in a small IsiXhosa speaking semi-rural town known as Cala,[3] in the Eastern Cape province of South Africa. It was established by a group of students who were then known as the Cala University Students Association (CALUSA).[4] The community radio station started broadcasting on 9 April 1996 and it has since grown and established itself as a stable community broadcaster with "healthy" day-to-day broadcasting activities (Tyali, 2017).

From its initial development and association with a group of university students, the history of VCR is similar to that of a number of community radio stations in South Africa. In their initial development phases, some of South Africa's eminent community radio stations were incubated at and sometimes hosted by university campuses. An example of such include: Forte Community Radio, Unitra Community Radio, Bush Radio and VCR. In some cases, and at the height of the anti-apartheid movement (Bosch, 2003), some of the projects which eventually became community radio stations were established by students who acquired broadcasting skills from university campuses and then later used their skills to build broadcasting facilities in their respective communities (Cape Flats, Cala etc). In its initial years of establishment, VCR started operating through a temporary licence, but in the year 2000, the broadcaster was granted a renewable medium-term licence that allowed it to broadcast for a four-year period. It is this same broadcasting licence condition that still allows VCR to broadcast until today. Broadcasting on the 90.6–98.4 frequency, VCR together with Bush Radio (Bosch, 2003) are some of South Africa's oldest community radio broadcasters whose focus has traditionally been the communities underserved by the broader mainstream media of the country.

The section below outlines the concept of community radio. This is important as the golden thread that underpins the discussion of this chapter is the idea of community radio as constituting a form of an African public sphere.

Understanding the nature of the medium: on community radio philosophy

Research literature suggest that in its ideal nature, the community radio sector signifies the "democratisation" of communications and more especially the airwaves (Mtimde et al., 1998). It is a media sector who's philosophical mandated is to be transparent and participatory in its conduct for the benefit of the communities it serves. However, and in spite of the general perceptions that are often imposed on the sector, scholarly debates indicate that there is no single, definitive and all-encompassing global definition that exists for the community radio sector (Librero, 2004). The World Bank Institute (2007) advances this point by indicating that, there are as many models of community radio as there are community radio stations across the world.

Research discourses on community media, however, also indicate that the broad guiding philosophy of the community radio sector should emphasize and be underpinned by the involvement of people in the use of such radio platforms so as to facilitate and speed up the process of dealing with challenges related to infrastructure development. The medium is about people empowerment. Writing for AMARC-Africa, Mtimde et al. (1998) defines the sector by stating that in its purest sense, a community radio station is a media platform that allows communities to participate as planners, producers and performers of the broadcast content. It is the means of expression by the community, rather than for the community (Mtimde et al., 1998; cf. Mgibisa, 2005 and Olurinnisola, 2002). The emphasis is therefore on the community being directly involved in all aspects of the community radio station. The Media Institute of Southern Africa (MISA) (2000) notes that a community radio station is a broadcasting medium that is built by community members; is used by these members and ideally in service of the interests of that specific community. They state that the defining indicators of such broadcasting platforms include the ownership aspect, the self-governance, and participation by the community as well as the representation of these communities. The emphasis is primarily on local content and such content is produced by the community for their own benefits and consumption (MISA, 2000).

The philosophical characteristics mentioned above (AMARC-Africa, 1998 and MISA, 2000) compliment the criteria of the sector as outlined by the Broadcasting Act of South Africa. According to the Broadcasting Act of 1999, No. 4, community radio stations in South Africa should (1) be fully controlled by a non-profit entity and used for non-profit purposes, (2) serve a particular community or people associated with promoting the interest of *such a* community, and (3) allow people to participate in the selection and provision of programmes to be broadcast. The Act indicates that these stations should be funded by donations, grants, sponsorship, advertising or membership fees, or a combination of all of the above. Lastly, the Act concludes that the programming services of a community radio station must reflect the needs of the constituency it represents including cultural, religious, language and demographic needs of the community. According to Jo Tacchi (2003), there are two types of community radio station. These include a community radio station serving: i) a geographical community; and ii) those serving a community of interest.

The community of interest stations may be defined as having a specific, ascertainable common interest. This common interest is what makes such a group of persons or sector of the public an identifiable community. These common interests may vary from being institutional, religious or cultural communities depending on the licensing conditions (Tacchi, 2003; cf. Teer-Tomaselli, 2001). Therefore, a relationship between audiences and a community radio station is likely to be influenced by the classification and the mission of that specific station. One of the distinguishing features of community media, including community radio, is that it allows citizens to be active in one of many (micro) spheres relevant to their daily life and to exercise their right to communicate (Carpentier, Lie and Servaes, 2008). It is also stated that community media offers different societal groups and communities the opportunity for extensive participation in public debate and for self-representation in the public sphere, thus entering the realm of enabling and facilitating macro-participation (Carpentier, Lie and Servaes, 2008). For the purpose of this chapter, the parameters of understanding the sector in South Africa and in the rest of the African region will be guided by the definitions and indicators that have been outlined by MISA, 2000; AMARC-Africa, 1998; and the Broadcasting Act of South Africa, 1999. Largely this is a result of the synergy and how the sector as defined in their documents compliments one another.

Community radio and community culture

The question and challenges facing African media today is how to be technologically progressive while maintaining allegiance and being rooted in the African cultures of the broadcasting constituencies (Chinweizu, 1999). History of the media industry in this continent (Fanon, 1968) suggests that it is important to create media systems that speak to African cultures and address issues that are African oriented in nature. That is because Africa as a lived reality has historically either been erased or distorted by media institutions that were established in this continent by colonisers (Sesanti, 2010).

Cultural relevance of media content attest to audience familiarity or interest to messages embedded in the content. The decision to consume such media content can also be dependent on the available alternative content that each media consumer has at their disposal. In other words, do media consumers have access to relevant international, nation or regional media? My aim in this chapter is to explore the different ways in which community radio can be a site for representing the African cultures and interests of the communities in which they are rooted in. This is particularly more important in making sense of a community radio station as an African public sphere that is representative of African ways of being in the world. In the context of the case study that is underpinning this chapter, these need to be understood as cultures to which the community radio stations and the "community"/audience have a sense of relevance or proximity by the virtue of representing the community of reception. Hall (2011) argues that there are two ways to understand the concepts of culture and identity. He notes that on one hand, cultural identity can be understood by one's shared culture, meaning that it is an individual cultural identity and outlook. However, this individual self is said to be positioned among many other selves, including "more superficial or artificially imposed 'selves', which people with a shared history and ancestry hold in common" (223).

Cultural identities may include Africanity, ethnicity or languages or any other cultural lineages that people see as important to them. Hall (2011) further argues that, in such instances, cultural identities point to historical experiences and cultural indicators that portray people's common culture. In other words, this could be understood on a communities shared sense of African cultural identities that is common in that particular community. Hall (2011) identifies a second and important point on the issue of cultural identity. He states that cultural identities have origins or history – meaning that they emanate from somewhere. Thus, we are made to understand that culture has historical basis, but such identities are bound to undergo constant transformations and evolvement of sorts.

Far from being grounded in a mere "recovery" of the past, which is waiting to be found, and which when found, will secure our sense of ourselves into eternity, (cultural) identities are the names we give to the different ways we are positioned by, and position ourselves within, the narratives of the past.

(Hall, 2011, p. 225)

Cultural identities can also be seen as fluid and, though partly anchored in history, such identities can undergo transformations with the passage of time. The media as a cultural product plays an important role in the creation, affirmation and re-construction of identities and culture. Straubhaar (1991) has therefore proposed a strategy on how those who are on the periphery of media power can build their own cultural industries that speak to their identities. He indicates that "these include decreasing audio and video technology costs that allow for increased local production, and, more broadly, the development of the technique required to use such hardware to create cultural products" (Straubhaar, 1991, p. 43). Because of its proximity to the communities it represents, the community radio sector is a cheap, accessible medium that is actively involved in the reflection of a community's cultures. After all, as part of the media fraternity, the community radio sector is a member of the cultural industry. This factor is also vital when we assess community broadcasters operating today and how the communities surrounding such broadcasters relate to them as their African and community public sphere platforms.

Making sense of the public sphere: A conceptual departure point

Media platforms such as newspapers, magazines, radio and television are understood as platforms of the public sphere (Habermas, 1989; McQuail 2000). This means that they are ideally open to all members of the society as receivers, interpreters and senders of information that is in the public interest. However, this role of such media platforms (the public sphere platforms) does not always allow citizen participation. Sometimes this can be attributed to more urgent matters that need to be represented or discussed within the public sphere platforms. For instance, Wasserman and Garman (2012) noted that in South Africa, the high levels of inequality have prevented the majority of citizens from participating in the public sphere and making decisions at local level that impact their daily lives. In other words, the social ills affecting a community can shift the participatory interest of communities in the public sphere and make the community focus on life's more urgent problems. According to Habermas (1997, p.105 cited in McKee, 2005) the public sphere is a domain of our social life where such a thing as public opinion can be formed and possibly, where citizens can deal with matters of general interest without being subject to coercion to express and publicise their views. Habermas further states that it is in this public sphere space where citizens can exchange ideas and discuss issues, in order to reach agreements about matters of "general interest" to the community (cf. McQuail, 2000).

Generally, three types of public spheres have been known to exist: micro, meso and macro public spheres (Keane, 2004). Micro public spheres can include spaces such as small discussion circles, the church, the clinic and most casual political chats with friends or acquaintances. These public spheres tend to be small involving an institution, a community or an association that may be advocating for certain interests. Citizens in these sites question the pseudo-imperatives of reality and counter them with alternative experiences of time, space, and interpersonal relations. Micro public spheres are today a vital feature of all social movements. They are also vital for building community relations and community identities. These are spaces in which citizens enter into a dispute about who does what and who ought to get what, when, and how (ibid.). The meso encompass millions of people watching, listening, or reading across vast distances. These meso public spheres are mediated by large circulation newspapers as well as through electronic media (ibid.). Lastly, the macro public sphere operates at a global level as well as in regions of the globe. Macro-publics of hundreds of millions of citizens are the consequence of the international concentration of mass media firms previously owned and operated at the nation-state level.

For the purpose of this chapter, the interest is on a community radio as a micro African public sphere platforms existing for the purpose of broadcasting to the Chris Hani municipality of the Eastern Cape province in South Africa. Historically, the theoretical concept of the public sphere and it's mainstream understanding has largely been popularised by "western" (Hall, 2011) scholarship on public gathering and the discourses accompanying such gatherings. In fact, it was Habermas (1989) who traced the European role of the public sphere and argued on the role of a rationale public sphere as exemplified by the early coffee shops in Germany for instance. The problem with such discussion forums as theorised by Habermas, was that they were seen to be elitist in their nature and were thought to encapsulate the views of selected members of their societies. However, as a cosmos of discussion on social matters, the concept of the public sphere has also been widely debated by scholars (Hungbo, 2012; McGuigan, 2005; Habermas, 1989) and this has pointed to various notions of a "cultural public sphere." Thus it is safe to conclude that within African based communities, we have noticed an "appropriation" disruption, the complication and the rethinking of the Euro idea of a public sphere. This has largely been exemplified by the rationales of African local debates concerned with African thought processes, cultural interests and concerns (cf. Rønning, 1993). In this chapter the concept of the public sphere is understood within the context of how the local Chris Hani community is making use of VCR as a community radio public sphere. This is illustrated by the communities ability to satiate their broadcasting and discursive needs within the airwaves of VCR as a community discursive platform. Thus, the chapter presents the community radio station as a discursive forum for matters that are of interest to the local African community of the Chris Hani District.

Brief discussion on the research approach

When considering the African worldviews and local rationalities, there is a need to rethink how we engage with the structure of colonial or neo-colonial research system and how they impact research agendas in Africa. In recent years, discourse on the need to decolonise "research methods" has gained momentum and interest (cf. Smith, 1999; Tomaselli & Dyll-Myklebust, 2015; Tuck & Yang, 2012; Sithole, 2014). Smith (1999, p. 1) in her seminal work on "decolonising methodologies" argued that as a practice, research as a scientific tool has traditionally been associated with the worst excesses of colonialism and continues to be remembered with execration by those who have been subjected to the darker side of modernity. This means that, "just knowing that someone measured our 'faculties' by filling the skulls of our ancestors with millet seeds and compared the amount of millet seed to the capacity for mental thought offends our sense of who and what we are" (Smith 1999, p. 1). Therefore, the study underpinning chapter was conducted using a critical "qualitative case study" approach. The aim was to disrupt the colonial method (Smith, 1999) by experimenting with the idea of decolonising research. For the purpose of the study underpinning this chapter, insight into VCR as an African public sphere from the following stakeholders (Table 8.1):

Furthermore, the opinions of the internal stakeholders of the community radio station were balanced by the following external stakeholders that are the community members within the broadcasting location. A conversation with the following external stakeholders assisted in balancing the views of the internal stakeholders (Table 8.2):

For research purposes, the study underpinning this chapter identified the relevant internal stakeholder respondents who were deemed vital in the conceptualisation, building and maintenance of the station's identity and broadcast patterns. These were individuals who were either in the management position of the community radio station or were involved in the creation and selection of content that was ultimately received by the audiences through community broadcasts. For the purpose of the study underpinning

Table 8.1 Details of the internal stakeholder research participants

Name	Age	Race	Designation	Gender
Malixole Teketa	27	African	On-Air Presenter & Producer	Male
Mnyamezeli Mpumela	42	African	On-Air Presenter & Producer	Male
Thandeka Mbobozi	39	African	News editor/Acting Programmes Manager/On-Air Presenter & Producer	Female
Viwe Mfundisi	28	African	Music Compiler	Male
Xola Nozewu	40	African	Station Manager/ On-Air Presenter & Producer	Male
Sinethemba Nota	34	African	Technical Manager	Male
Linda Magazi	25	African	On-Air Presenter & Producer	Female

To protect the identity of the respondents, it was decided that all names appearing on the table should be pseudonyms. This was to ensure anonymity and protect the identity of the respondents.

Table 8.2 Details of the external stakeholder research participants

Name	Age	Race	Gender	Designation
Fezeka Silwana	48	African	Female	Chris Hani Community Member
Mvuyo Mhlekwa	52	African	Male	Chris Hani Community Member
Weziwe Dodo	44	African	Female	Chris Hani Community Member
Nolusindiso Ncapai	32	African	Female	Chris Hani Community Member
Phumla Xokashe	31	African	Female	Chris Hani Community Member
Nompucuko July	30	African	Female	Chris Hani Community Member

the chapter, the sampled population had to be members of the community who have the basic working knowledge of the community radio station. This rationality is connected to the basic need of allowing a community radio to be run by the community. For the purpose of data collection, a semi-structured conversation was used. These are conversation strategies that are designed to overcome the problems that are associated with the structured interviews – including the question of allowing the participants to participate meaningfully in the conversation.

Semi-structured conversations involve open ended questions but are based on the topic that the researcher wants to cover (Hancock, 1998). A decolonial twist to these interviews was introduced by conducting the interviews in a conversational approach and in an African language – IsiXhosa. This approach eliminated any formality that might be associated with structured or semi-structured interviews. Wellington and Szcerbinski (2007) indicate that semi-structured conversations allow researchers to query, observe and investigate matters that have been identified. They therefore allow researchers to probe individuals.

In the section below, I provide a discussion on the question of community radio as an African public sphere. The intention behind this thematic discussion was to illustrate the role that is played by VCR as an African public sphere platform. Broadening the discourse around the concept of the public sphere has also meant that we need decolonise the idea of the public sphere as popularised by Jurgen Habermas' (1989) theorisation.

Community radio as a micro African public sphere: The VCR effect

As discussed above, media platforms (magazines, newspapers, radio and television) are often regarded as public sphere platforms that constitute areas of public concern (Habermas, 1989; McQuail, 2000). Ideally, they are meant to provoke and facilitate discussion in order to make sense of humanitarian concerns and aspirations. However, in recent times, the concept of the media as an inclusive public sphere platform in South Africa has been critiqued as a result of inequalities that have forced people to be preoccupied with poverty and other social ills affecting the citizenry (cf. Wasserman and Garman, 2012). In reflecting on general aspects of the community, the data for the study underpinning this chapter suggests that VCR can be seen as a "subaltern" (cf. Spivak, 1988) African public sphere that is instrumental in creating debate and discussion around community concerns. Conversation with respondents demonstrate that such community concerns can vary from making sense of changing African traditions to engaging public officials on service delivery concerns. Whereas the concept of the public sphere has been criticised because of its apparent elitist nature (cf. Habermas, 1989), the role of VCR as a notional public sphere for the discussion of community concerns seems to be geared towards easy access for the community members in their arena of public discussion. Through interview responses, it was indicated that the community radio station is readily available to listen to community members when these communities have matters to discuss. Research data indicates that the radio station also facilitates these discussions by cutting the costs of dialogue inclusion to the broadcasting platform as a public sphere. For instance, this happens by incurring costs of teleconferences so that the voices of the "subaltern" identified African community can participate in social discourse. Thus, in this sense, this community radio station becomes a "counter public sphere" within the broader notion of micro public spheres (Keane, 2004). Largely this is because it represents "smaller" voices within the notion of dominant western-centric narratives and discussion occurring in some public sphere debates. Furthermore, through its role as a widely accepted community arena of discussion, the community radio station is instrumental in "centre-ring" African subjects in discussions that are inevitably about these very subjects. This role is congruent with Asante's (2003) and Mazama's (2003) Afrocentric theory where Africans need to be central in any discussion that concerns their worldly interests, views, values and their urgency to partici-pate in discussions that concern them. The role of the community concerns that are discussed on the stations programming was explained by one of the content producers responsible for a discussion programme:

> It is a show with a broad focus on this broadcasting platform. It looks at people's needs and interests. It helps people who are facing challenges in solving those challenges. And so, the show facilitates the role of bringing those in authority and those that are not. And issues that affect them in playing the role of coming into contact and solve their challenges.
>
> (Malixole Teketa, VCR Producer & On-Air Broadcaster,
> Imbadu, 30 March 2016)

In the context of African societies, Rønning (1993) has argued that the public sphere needs to be seen as a gathering arena on social and cultural interests that are linked to issues of gender, social as well as cultural inter-est groups. This type of public sphere is especially applicable to the deco-lonial discourse as decolonial struggles in Africa took place within the broader ideas of a counter public sphere (ibid.). In reflecting on community concerns, the data of the study underpinning the chapter suggests that the community radio station also demonstrates the role of community centred media by discussing topics that often do not feature in national/mainstream media agencies. Furthermore, as a means of facilitating discussion between the community and governing authorities, the producer of a talk program at VCR indicated:

> It works like this, it is a show where every beginning of the month there is a platform where the listeners are given an opportunity to call and state what they wish for the radio station and this show called Mbadu should help them with. Once they do that, we start the process of helping them with regards to their needs. And then we put them in conversation with government people, the NGO's, with any person, with Chiefs, headmen and anyone who is responsible for answering their questions.
> (Malixole Teketa, VCR Producer & On-Air Broadcaster,
> Imbadu, 30 March 2016)

Thus, as an African public sphere that is "centre-ring" community discourse, the role of VCR is not only preoccupied with the idea of cultural discussions but in facts transcends these to include additional community concerns that are part of the everyday. As explained by another study respondent, the station is in fact readily available to the community that it serves:

> I would say Vukani is very important because, it is able to be accessible to people, even when we have a problem at Chris Hani they do come.
> (Nompucuko July, VCR Lisener, Komani Resident;
> March 31, 2016)

Thus, the elitist nature of the public sphere (Habermas, 1989) is overcome by VCR through a number of strategies, including shying away from arbitrarily controlling on-air discussions by asking listeners to suggest the topics of the week and discussion angles. In this instance, the community radio station is also subscribing to the concept of a participatory media platform that gives access to surrounding communities to be involved in the broadcast content of such media platforms through participation and direct representation (MISA, 2000; Tyali and Tomaselli, 2015). The availability of VCR as a means of communicating and discussing community interests has also been hailed by most respondents of the study underpinning the chapter "this radio station is very important to me and the people of this area because we tend to access information on things that would otherwise not be easily accessible" (Vuyo Mhlekwa, VCR Listener – Cala resident; March 31, 2016). As illustrated above, it was also repeatedly asserted that unlike mainstream media, the community radio station was readily available to listen and assist with community concerns. The idea of a readily available media platform to engage and report on community concerns is therefore another indication of how the concept of the public sphere continues to be re-thought, localised and decolonised by alternative media platforms that have an interest in small-medium community set-ups. Asked about the value of VCR as an African and local public sphere, a volunteer of this community responded:

> I would say they [communities] walk away with information, they learn obviously because you notice that a lot of people from villages like to hear as to what is happening around.
>
> (Linda Magazi, VCR Producer and On-Air Personality; March 30, 2016)

Though the concept of the public sphere has been criticised for its emphasis on rationale debate (Habermas, 1989), the idea of an African public sphere as exemplified by VCR is indeed a continuous stride towards an inclusive public sphere that is not concerned with the Euro-North American normative standards of debates. The concept of participation through VCR and the range of strategies that have been put in place to ensure community access to the media platform illustrate that the community radio station has a rationale role in ensuring that Africans use media platforms according to their wishes and agency.

Conclusion

In this chapter, the focus was on the question of community radio as an African public sphere platform. With an overall objective of understanding the Africanisation community media broadcasting platforms, the chapter set out to understand the role that is being pursued by VCR in contributing to the formation or development of African interest discussion arenas. Thus, by understanding the discussion role that continues to be played by the community members in bringing their community concerns into the fore. Through VCR, we are able to observe a pattern where small African community interests are to be discussed in the realms of a media institution.

Notes

1 On the question of who is an African, this chapter acknowledges and distinguishes between continental citizenship and African descent. African in the context of this chapter is squarely focused on continental descent (cf. Prah, 2004).

2 This is a community radio station that started as a student radio project. The project has grown and matured throughout the years. It is now firmly among the list of community radio stations that can be described as established and sustainable. This list includes radio stations such as Bush FM, Jozi FM and Radio Zibonele. For further historical details on VCR, visit their website at: www.vukanifm.org/

3 Some body of research work has been produced about the relevance of the Cala community and its contribution to the fight against apartheid South Africa. Further reading the town's contribution in the fight against apartheid can be accessed on the following link: http://calusa.co.za/era-secret-slaughter-murder-batandwa-ndondo/#page-content

4 Some of the illustrious alumni's of this organisation include: Prof Lungisile Ntsebeza, Adv Dumisa Ntsebeza, Godfrey Silinga and Siphiwe Liwani.

References

AMARC. (1998). What is community radio? A resource guide. AMARC Africa & Panos Southern. Africa. Retrieved from https://www.media-diversity.org/additional-files/documents/A%20Guides/what%20is%20community%20radio%20A%20resource%20guide%20[EN].pdf

Asante, M.K. (2003). *Afrocentricity: The Theory of Social Change*. Chicago: African American Images Press.

Berger, G. (1996). What is the Community Media?. Paper presented at the *Community Voices Conference*, October 6–11, Malawi. Retrieved from www.journ.ru.ac.za/research [accessed 13 February 2014].

Bosch, T. (2003). Radio, community and identity in South Africa: a rhizomatic study of Bush radio in Cape Town. Ohio University, USA, Unpublished PhD Thesis

Broadcasting Act, No 4 Of 1999 of South Africa. Retrieved from www.gov.za/sites/www.gov.za/files/a4–99.pdf [accessed 15 March 2015].

Carpentier, N. et al. (2008). Making Community Media Work: Community Identities and their Articulation in an Antwerp Neighbourhood Development Project. In Servaes, J. (ed.), *Communication for Development and Social Change*. India: Sage Publications

Chinweizu (1999). Towards the African Renaissance media. In Makgoba, M.W. (ed.), *African Renaissance*. Cape Town: Tafelberg Publishers.

Fanon, F. (1965). *A Dying Colonialism*. New York: Grove Press.

Habermas, J. (1989). *The Structural Transformation of the Public Sphere*. Great Britain: Polity Press.

Hancock, B. (1998). Trent Focus for Research and Development in Primary Health Care An Introduction to Qualitative Research. University of Nottingham. http://faculty.cbu.ca/pmacintyre/course_pages/MBA603/MBA603_files/IntroQualita

Hall, S. (2011). *Questions of Cultural Identity: Identity, Genealogy, History*. London: Sage.

Hungbo, J. (2012). The public sphere and representations of the self: radio talk shows in post apartheid South Africa. Witwatersrand University, Johannesburg, Unpublished PhD thesis

Keane, J. (1995). The Structural transformation of the public sphere. Retrieved from www.johnkeane.net/wpcontent/uploads/1995/01/jk_public_sphere_full.pdf [accessed 17 June 2015].

Keane, J. (2004). The structural transformation of the public sphere. Retrieved from http://www.johnkeane.net/wp-content/uploads/1995/01/jk_public_sphere_full.pdf

Librero, F. (2004). *Community Broadcasting: Concept and Practice in Philippines.* Singapore: Eastern University Press.

Mano, W. (2011). Why radio is Africa's medium of choice in the global age. In Gunner, L., Ligaga, D. & Moyo, D. (eds), *Radio Africa: Publics, cultures, communities.* Johannesburg: Wits University Press.

Mazama, A (2003). *The Afrocentric Paradigm.* Trenton: Africa World Press.

McGuigan, J. (2005). The Cultural Public Sphere. *European Journal of Cultural Studies,* 8(4).

McKee, A. (2005). *The Public Sphere: An Introduction.* United Kingdom: Cambridge University Press.

McQuail, D. (2000). *McQuail's Mass Communication Theory.* London: Sage Publications.

Media Institute of Southern Africa (MISA). (2000). *Community level baseline research into community media attitudes and needs in Zambia and Namibia.* Windhoek: MISA.

Mhlambi, T. (2015). Early broadcasting history in South Africa: Culture, modernity and technology. University of Cape Town, Cape Town. Unpublished PhD Thesis.

Mgibisa, M. (2005). It's the community in community radio. *Rhodes Journalism Review* (RJR), 25(47).

Mtimde, L., Bonin, M., Maphiri, N., & Nyamaku, K. (1998). What is community radio? A resource guide. AMARC-Africa and Panos Southern Africa. Retrieved from https://www.media-diversity.org/additional-files/documents/A%20Guides/what%20is%20community%20radio%20A%20resource%20guide%20[EN].pdf

Olurinnisola, A. (2002). Community radio: participatory communication in Post-Apartheid South Africa. *Journal of Radio Studies,* 9(1).

Prah, K. (2004). Africanism and Africanisation: Do they mean the same thing? In Seepe, S. (ed), *Towards an African Identity of Higher Education.* Pretoria: Vista University and Skotaville Media.

Rosenthal, E. (1974). *You have been listening…The early history of radio in South Africa.* Cape Town: Purnell Publishers.

Rønning, H. (1993). Institutions and representations. In Zhuwarara, R. et al. (eds), *Media, Democratization and Identity.* Harare: University of Zimbabwe, Department of English.

Rønning, H. & Kupe, T. (2000). The dual legacy of democracy and authoritarianism: The media and the state in Zimbabwe. In Curran, J. & Park, M. (eds), *De-westernizing Media Studies.* London: Routledge.

Smith, L.T. (1999). *Decolonising Methodologies.* Dunedin: University of Otago Press.

Sesanti, S. (2010). The concept of "respect" in African culture in the context of journalism practice: An Afrocentric intervention. *Communicatio,* 36(3).

Sithole, T. (2014). Achille Mbembe: Subject, subjection, and subjectivity. University of South Africa, Pretoria, Unpublished Thesis.

Sithole, T. (2016). Researching the African Subject: Decolonial meditations. Unpublished paper.

Spivak, G.C. (1988). *Can the Subaltern Speak?* In Nelson, C. and Grossberg, L. (eds), *Marxism and the Interpretation of Culture*. New York: Macmillan Education.

Straubhaar, J.D. (1991). Beyond media imperialism: asymmetrical interdependence and cultural proximity. *Critical Studies in Mass Communication*, 8(1).

Switzer, L. & Switzer, D. (1979). *The Black Press in South Africa and Lesotho*. Boston, United States: G.K. Halland.

Tacchi, J. (2003). Promise of citizens' media: Lessons from community radio in Australia and South Africa. *Economic and Political Weekly*, 38(22).

Teer-Tomaselli, R. (2001). Who is the community in community radio? A case study of community radio stations in Durban, KwaZulu-Natal. In Tomaselli, K. & Dunn, H. (eds), *Critical Studies on African Media and Culture: Media, Democracy and Renewal in Southern Africa*. Colorado: Colorado Press.

The World Bank Institute. (2007). Good practices in development and operation of community radio: Issues important to its effectiveness. Retrieved from http://siteresources.worldbank.org/INTCEERD/Resources/WBI5-CountryStudy.pdf

Tomaselli, K. & Dyll-Myklebust, L.E. (2015). Public self-expression: decolonizing researcher researched relationships. *Community*, 4(3).

Tuck, E. & Yang, K.W. (2012). Decolonization is not a metaphor. *Decolonization: Indigeneity, Education & Society*, 1(1).

Tyali, S.M. (2017). Africanising community radio broadcasting: the role of Vukani Community Radio (VCR). University of the Witwatersrand, South Africa, Unpublished PhD thesis.

Tyali, S.M. and Tomaselli, K.G. (2015). Investigating beneficiary community participation in HIV/AIDS communication through community radio stations: A case study of X-K FM. *Communicare*, 34(2).

Wasserman, H. & Garman, A. (2012). Being South African and belonging: the status and practice of mediated citizenship in a new democracy. *The 7th Global Conference on Pluralism, Inclusion and Citizenship*, Prague, Czech Republic, 12–14 March 2012. Retrieved from www.inter-disciplinary.net/wp-content/uploads/2012/02/garmanpaper.pdf

Wellington, J. & Szcerbinski, M. (2007). *Research Methods for the Social Science*. London: Continuum International Publishing Group.

Ziegler, D. & Asante, M.K. (1992). *Thunder and Silence: The Mass Media in Africa*. New Jersey: Africa World Press.

9 Historical Overview of the Nigerian Film Industry

Khadijat Adedeji-Olona, Ganiyat Tijani-Adenle and Lai Oso

Societies across the ages have developed unique means of transmitting their cultural heritage, mores, norms, and values from one generation to the other. In most African communities, several story-telling techniques are effectively used to relay societal values and norms to younger generations, thus integrating them into the dominant societal culture (Amodu et al., 2019). With the expansion of societies and globalisation, came the need for more efficient means of reaching larger numbers of people. This need was soon met by the development of mass media technologies, which became the apparatuses of information dissemination and cultural preservation, through which people gain knowledge and insight about their world (Oso, 2011). One of such significant inventions, the motion picture, forms the foundation of modern-day film industry (Vaughn, 1990).

With the invention of the motion picture, films became a notable platform through which the identity, character, images, and cultures of societies are impressed on the minds of their people (Sunday, 2009). Working with a similar feature as photography but combining moving images and sounds, films create lasting impressions and influence thoughts and perspectives (Adedeji, 2014). The discovery of the video film technology marked a major turning point in the history of communication, because, while it shares similar features with previous technologies, its ability to combine moving images, sounds and creative effects provide the potential to tell compelling stories and achieve desired outcomes. With its unique features, film conquered the limitations of language and cultural barriers to become a powerful platform for filmmakers to share their ideas and advocacies on topical issues with a global audience in an enduring format (Opubor et al., 1979; Sunday, 2009). While it cannot be said that films have completely taken over the role of traditional institutions, it is safe to acknowledge that the development of films, "has further aided the process by which generationally held beliefs are handed from one generation to another" (Amodu et al., 2019, p. 264).

DOI: 10.4324/9781003352907-11

Birthed by the pioneering activities of the *Yorùbá* Travelling Theatre, sustained by the commercial activities of the *Igbo* (or *Ibo*) entrepreneurs and transformed by improved technology and digitisation, the Nigerian film industry, also known as *Nollywood*, has evolved, over the years to become Africa's most productive film industry in terms of the number of productions and value (Giwa, 2014; Haynes & Okome, 2000). The popularity of *Nollywood*, even beyond the shores of Nigeria, to a continental level, is such that "nowhere else in Africa has a domestic market for audio-visual entertainment been captured so successfully" (Haynes & Okome, 2000, p. 51).

Thus, this chapter, in two sections, reviews the evolution of Nigerian film across the different phases of the country's historical development. The first section provides brief explanations of the key concepts in the chapter, while the second section highlights the advancement of Nigerian film industry from the *Travelling Theatre era* to the *New Nollywood era*.

Understanding the Basics

This first section explains (very briefly) a few of the concepts that will aid an understanding of the contexts that moderate the evolution of the Nigerian film industry.

Hausa: The Hausa are the dominant tribe in Northern Nigeria. They speak the Hausa Language, which is also spoken in some countries in West and Central Africa. Nigeria's Northern region also has a viable film industry, and it is referred to as *Kannywood*, after Kano State, the commercial hub of Northern Nigeria.

Home Video: Home Videos are recorded films sold or rented for viewers to play/watch in their homes using VHS players. The VHS (Video Home Systems) are devices that are used to play home videos. Currently out of popular usage, VHS tapes are played on VHS players and watched on Television sets connected to the VHS players.

Igbo (Ibo): The Igbo (or Ibo) is the dominant tribe in Eastern Nigeria. They speak the Igbo Language and are prolific film producers and marketers. They produce films in English Language, Igbo Language and Pidgin-English.

Nigeria: Nigeria is popularly referred to as the Giant of Africa. It is the most populated country on the continent, with over 200 ethnicities and languages. With several mineral resources and crude oil, the West African country is a developing economy with diverse industries. Colonized by Great Britain, the regions in present-day Nigeria were amalgamated and formed into a country in 1914. Nigeria secured her independence in 1960.

Nollywood: Nollywood is used interchangeably with the Nigerian film industry in this chapter, to refer to that section of the Nigerian film industry domiciled in the southern part of the county (West and East) and headquartered in Lagos (Haynes, 2012). Nollywood films, therefore, refer to

Nigerian films that have English and/or Pidgin as their major language of conversation. Igbo/Ibo and Yorùbá language films are also classified under Nollywood, especially when translated into English Language. The Hausa (Northern) section of the Nigerian film industry (referred to as *Kannywood*) is not discussed in this chapter.

Yorùbá: The Yorùbá are the dominant tribe in Western Nigeria. They speak the Yorùbá language, which is also spoken by minorities in a few other West African countries. They are very enterprising and Yorùbás are the predominant members of Nigeria's Travelling Theatre group. The headquarters of Nollywood is in Lagos State in South-Western Nigeria, the nation's commercial capital. Lagos State is a majority Yorùbá language state.

Now that some of the key words in the rest of the chapter have been briefly explained, we will now present the main discourse, the highlights of the history of Nigerian film industry.

A Nation and its Film Industry

This second section details the various stages of Nigeria's film development from the Yorùbá *Travelling Theatre era* to the *New Nollywood era*.

Without a doubt, the story of contemporary Nigerian society cannot be told without its film industry, otherwise known as *Nollywood*. At every stage of the country's development, the film industry has, since colonial times, been used to project the country's people and cultures, while offering insights and commentaries on prevailing socio-political, economic, and cultural contexts (Haynes & Okome, 2000). Haynes (2016) alludes to the symmetrical relationship between *Nollywood* and Nigerian society, when he asserts that Nollywood films are "a record and interpretation of contemporary Nigeria, a social and emotional history" (Haynes, 2016, p. xxiv). Similarly, Nollywood has been affected by Nigeria's political terrain and the economic policies of successive governments. Because of this, Farinde (2008) considers Nollywood a significant indicator of Nigeria's developmental level.

Although Nigeria had its first recorded contact with film in 1903, there is a unanimous view among scholars that indigenous filmmaking in Nigeria is rooted in the activities of the Yorùbá Travelling Theatre troops which held sway between 1946 and 1981 (Adesanya, 2010; Azeez, 2019; Farinde, 2008; George, 2018; Haynes & Okome, 2010). Jeyifo (1984, cited in George, 2018) specifically dates the emergence of the travelling theatre to 1946, spanning through a 35-year period.

According to him,

In 1946, in a Lagos bustling with post-World War II economic and social "revitalization" – the kind of "revitalization" possible in a colonial society – a thirty-year-old ex-teacher, church organist and composer,

Hubert Ogunde, resigned his job as a policeman and became a full-time producer and performer of a quasi-dramatic musical entertainment then known as Native Air Opera. Ogunde proceeded to launch a professional troupe composed of male and female performers and musicians, and thus emerged in 1946 the first professional modern theatre company in Nigeria, the company that was to initiate the contemporary Yorùbá travelling theatre movement.

(Jeyifo, 1984, as cited in George, 2018, pp. 15–16)

Indeed, the Nigerian film industry has come a long way and its films have become significant vehicles through which societal concepts such as family life, language, marriage, spirituality, societal cohesion and other Nigerian identities are transmitted across generations (Abah, 2009).

Scholars, including Azeez (2019) and Ernest-Samuel & Uduma (2019) have identified different phases in the evolution of the Nigerian film industry. For instance, Azeez (2019) traced the evolution of Nigeria's film industry under two broad eras, namely: the colonial era; and the post-colonial era. Ernest-Samuel & Uduma (2019), on the other hand, identified five phases in the development of the film industry in Nigeria. They are: the colonial era; the independence or post-colonial era; the indigenisation era; the television era; and the *Nollywood* era. For discussion purposes in this chapter, these phases are harmonised and modified into six as detailed in the following sub-sections: The Colonial Era; The Independence Era; The Indigenous Film Era; The Television Era; The Home Video Era; and The New Nollywood Era.

The Colonial Era

Historical records have it that by the turn of the 19th century, the British colonialists, who were in Nigeria for political, cultural, and economic imperialism, had introduced film, as a medium of entertainment to their subjects in the colony (Enwefah, 2009; Onabajo & Odoe, 2009; Sunday, 2009). Some scholars, however, believe that it was the successful screening of the first set of silent films in 1903, at the Glover Memorial Hall in Lagos between August 12 and 22 by Spanish Balboa Film Company, that reinforced the desire to deploy film as a tool for furthering the objectives of colonialism (Azeez, 2019; Ernest-Samuel & Uduma, 2019). The colonial government, therefore, wasted no time in establishing the Colonial Film Unit (CFU) as its propaganda arm. The Colonial Film Unit was primarily tasked with the production of newsreels and documentaries using mobile cinema technologies (Azeez, 2019). Events of the First World War lent further credence to the profound powers of films; hence, the British Colonial Government released its absolute hold on the film industry by allowing for the independent distribution and exhibition of films. So, Nigeria's first distribution and exhibition company – West African Pictures, was birthed in 1930 by two Lebanese nationals. With this pioneering act came the establishment of more distribution and exhibition companies. The establishment of cinema houses in major Nigerian cities is believed to have ignited the film/cinema culture in Nigerians (Azeez, 2019).

The missionaries, who had been on evangelical mission in Nigeria, also harnessed the power of films for the indoctrination of the citizens. As noted by many scholars, including Oso, Odunlami and Adaja (2011), there is a symmetrical connection between the development of the Nigerian media and Christian evangelism in Nigeria. Thus, the evangelical films produced by these missionaries became the major platforms for spreading the message of Christianity, while subtly infusing imperialist messages (Obododinma, 2010).

From the earliest films, including *Messrs J. Walkden's Store* (1923) to those produced shortly before independence, including *Nigeria: The Making of a Nation* (1960), films made in this era fostered the interests of the imperialists; portrayed the superiority of the British Culture over that of Africa; and subtly neutralised and silenced dissenting voices (Azeez, 2019). Hence, while the colonial government physically colonised the people and their territories, they, alongside their missionary partners, used films to colonise the minds of the Nigerian people. Affirming the propaganda prowess of films in this era, Husseini & Sunday (2019) confirm that "of the 180 films produced by the Colonial Film Unit, none was without propaganda elements" (Husseini & Sunday, 2019, p. 25). More than any other government in Nigeria, the colonial government made the most use of films for projecting its ideas and policies, while providing health and educational information to Nigerians (Opubor, Nwuneli & Oreh, 1979).

Scholars are particularly critical of films made in this era for their negative and dehumanising portrayals of blacks, whilst projecting the superiority of whites (Adesanya, 2010; Azeez, 2019; Ernest-Samuel & Uduma, 2019; Obododinma, 2010). That notwithstanding, films made in the colonial era are believed to have contributed in no small measure to the development of the Nigerian film industry, because they made Africans realise the potentials of film (Ernest-Samuel & Uduma, 2019) and the opportunities in the industry.

The Independence Era

With Nigeria's independence from Great Britain in 1960, the Colonial Film Unit became the Film Division of the Federal Ministry of Information. With the creation of regions, and subsequently states from those regions, came the establishment of more film divisions within the different Ministries of Information, each serving the divergent interests of the regional and state governments (Azeez, 2019; Ernest-Samuel & Uduma, 2019).

As with the Colonial Film Unit, the Film Division also served as the propaganda arm of the Nigerian government, producing newsreels and documentaries, but unlike the Colonial Film Units, films made by the film divisions were aimed at fostering national unity, nation-building, and development (Azeez, 2019). Before Nigeria's independence, Western Nigerian Television (WNTV) had been established in the then Western Region, leading to a marriage of Television and Film Production. Even though Nigeria was said to be free from colonial rule, its cinemas were flooded with foreign films, imported into the country by foreign nationals, who had come to the country for both business and pleasure. Moved by the need to rescue the country from the cultural domination of foreign films, some Nigerians began experimenting with film production, leading to the birth of the indigenous film era (Azeez, 2019; Husseini & Sunday, 2019).

The Indigenous Film Era

Scholars have attributed the emergence, growth, and development of indigenous films in Nigeria to the inspiring activities of the Yorùbá Travelling Theatre Troops (Adesanya, 2010; Azeez, 2019; Ernest-Samuel & Uduma, 2019; Haynes & Okome, 2000).

The theatre troupes' *modus operandi* was to travel from one town to another for stage performance, thus offering premium and affordable entertainment to Nigerians, especially rural dwellers (Azeez, 2019). This continued for a long time, until, inspired by Ola Balogun's success with *Ajani Ogun* (Balogun, 1976), they abandoned stage performance for celluloid film production (Azeez, 2019). The success of *Ajani Ogun* (Balogun, 1976) was such that it "opened the floodgates, gave the much-needed impetus to local film production and led to a new career for travelling theatre troupes" (Adesanya, 2010, p. 38). Prominent among indigenous filmmakers in this era were Ola Balogun, Adeyemi Afolayan (Ade Love), Hubert Ogunde, Moses Adejumo (Baba Sala), Eddie Ugbomah, among others.

It is worthy of note here that indigenous film-making in Nigeria grew out of the need to counter the cultural and numerical domination of foreign films and foster African cultural heritage, therefore, filmmaking in this era was essentially a fight for the minds of young Nigerians (Adesanya, 2010; Azeez, 2019; Haynes & Okome, 2000). The first set of films in this era; Ola Balogun's *Black Goddess* (1978), Francis Oladele's *Kongi's Harvest* (1970) and Eddie Ugbomah's *The Mask* (1979) were essentially used to express deep anti-colonial sentiments. *The Mask* (1979), for instance, tells the story of an intelligent Nigerian (Obi) who was on a mission to London to retrieve one of Nigeria's artefacts (The Benin Ivory Mask), stolen by the British colonisers. In it, the protagonist (Obi) cleverly manoeuvred his way through the series of obstructions he faced in his attempt to break into the British Museum (Azeez, 2019; The Centenary Project, 2014). The filmmakers sought to counter British imperialism by making their stories effective for societal transformation; telling African stories, using unique African story-telling techniques; integrating them into Nigeria's social realities; and projecting Nigeria's multiple traditional cultures (Azeez, 2019).

It was, however, not a smooth ride for the filmmakers as they were constrained by many factors, prime of which was finance. It was difficult for the indigenous filmmakers to break the hold of foreign films on Nigerians when their films could not match the foreign film in terms of production quality and quantity (Azeez, 2019). Similarly, according to Aig-Imoukhuede (1979), even though most of the early indigenous films including *Moral Disarmament* (1957), *Bound for Lagos* (1962) and *Culture in Transition* (1963) had Nigerian casts, because the entire filmmaking channel (production, distribution and exhibition) was largely dominated by foreigners, the films were "foreign in philosophy and intention" (Aig-Imoukhuede, 1979, p. 41).

Apart from the problems of distribution and exhibition of films, the political upheavals and military interregnums that characterised Nigeria's polity also had their toll on the growing film industry. The situation was further worsened by economic crises and frequent changes in economic policies, which led to the death of celluloid filmmaking and a gradual decline in Nigerians' cinema culture (Ernest-Samuel & Uduma, 2019).

These challenges notwithstanding, indigenous filmmakers still made profound contributions to the rapid growth of the Nigerian film industry. Apart from inspiring other young filmmakers and showing the potentialities of the industry, films produced in this era, including *Black Goddess* (Balogun, 1978), *Kongi's Harvest* (Davis & Oladele, 1970) and *The Mask* (Ugbomah, 1979) were believed to be successful in correcting the distorted African history being portrayed in foreign films at that time (Adesanya, 2010).

The Television Era

With the demise of celluloid film production and a decline in the cinema culture, Nigeria's creatives turned their attention to television. The Western Nigeria Television (WNTV), and the states' broadcasting services, all of which have been transformed into the Nigerian Television Authority (NTA) became platforms for filmmakers to showcase their talents and nurture a new generation of filmmakers (Adesanya, 2010; Azeez, 2019; Ernest-Samuel & Uduma, 2019). And so, in place of celluloid films, the filmmakers produced and directed dramas, comedies, sitcoms, and soap serials for television.

Prominent figures in this phase of Nigeria's filmmaking development were Zeb Ejiro, Late Amaka Igwe, Tade Ogidan, Lola Fani-Kayode, Matt Dadzie, among others (Ernest-Samuel & Uduma, 2019). Soap serials such as *Mirror in the Sun* (1984–1986), *Checkmate* (1991–1994), *The Village Headmaster* (1968–1988), *Cock Crow at Dawn* (1980), *Behind the Clouds* (Mid 1980s) *Basi and Company* (1986–1990), served the entertainment need of Nigerians, as alternatives to cinema for a long while until a turn of events (Ernest-Samuel & Uduma, 2019). As highlighted by Ernest-Samuel & Uduma (2019), internal crises among producers cum directors; huge sponsorship and professional fees; as well as unfriendly regulations by the television authorities were among the challenges that diminished and crippled the success of television series in this era.

The demise of these television series notwithstanding, there is a consensus among scholars that it was indeed the fusion of television with film production in this era that set the foundation for the successful take-off of the home video industry in Nigeria, while providing it with technical and creative workforce. Apart from the fact that the earliest *Nollywood* actors and actresses (in the home videos) were those from the popular television serials, the producers of the defunct serials were also among the first set of *Nollywood* filmmakers (Adesanya, 2010; Azeez, 2019; Ernest-Samuel & Uduma, 2019).

The Home Video (Nollywood) *Era*

The phase-out of the television series gave way to the development of the Nigerian home video industry. With pioneers such as Ade Ajiboye, Alade Aromire, and Kenneth Nnebue, driving the industry in this era, the advent and subsequent boom of home videos re-awakened the interests of Nigerians in films, while resurrecting the dying film industry (Husseini & Sunday, 2019).

Driven by the need for more cost-effective ways of producing films, filmmakers, particularly those from the Yorùbá extraction, were said to have experimented with video production. Contrary to Azeez's (2019) claims of Kenneth Nnebue (an Igbo Businessman), being the pioneer of video film production with his experimental film, *Aje ni Iya mi* (1989), Alabi (2009) believes that the first person to lead the trail in this era was Ade Ajiboye, with the production of *Sonso Meji* in 1988. German-trained Nigerian filmmaker Alade Aromire shared this pioneering attribute with Ajiboye, partly because his debut video film, *Ekun* (1989) had been produced three years earlier than its screening year (1989 – two years ahead of *Sonso Meji*); and for his establishment of a Cable Television Station, *Yotomi Television* for the transmission of Yorùbá movies (Haynes, 2016; Husseini & Sunday, 2019). Also among the first set of video films were Kenneth Nnebue's experimental film, *Aje ni Iya mi* (1989), and then the popular *Asewo to re*

Mecca in 1991 (Alabi, 2019; Husseini & Sunday, 2019). This insight contradicts some claims, including that of Ismail and Ibrahim's (2019) about *Living in Bondage (1992)* being the first video film in Nigeria.

It is worth mentioning here that the tradition among Yorùbá filmmakers was for the video film to first be screened in the cinemas, and then sold in video cassettes, generating low returns (Haynes, 2016). Also, the films were not adequately publicised and did not bring about the industry's boom, neither did they make the desired impact their producers expected them to (Husseini & Sunday, 2019).

It was, however, Kenneth Nnebue, an Igbo entrepreneur, who, from his experimentation with *Aje ni Iya mi* (1989), optimised the potentialities of video film technology (Haynes, 2016). He released the first Nollywood Blockbuster *Living in Bondage* in 1992, selling about three hundred thousand (300,000) copies in less than a month of its release, with an investment of just about a hundred and fifty thousand naira (Husseini & Sunday, 2019, p. 35). Inspired by the success of *Living in Bondage*, indigenous Yorùbá filmmakers also established their own production companies and produced movies using Video Home System (VHS) cameras (Haynes & Okome, 2010). Not resting on its oars, in 1994, Kenneth came up with another blockbuster, *The Glamour Girls* (1994), following it up with a sequel – *Glamour Girls* Part 2 (1996). The other TV soap producers also found succour in the new growing film industry and were quick to follow suit, by producing their own films (Haynes & Okome, 2000). The Nigerian entertainment scene was soon inundated with video films, with huge reception among members of the public. It was also in this era that the name *Nollywood* was coined by a Japanese-Canadian reporter with the *New York Times*, Norimitsu Onishi, to represent the English-based film industry in the southern part of Nigeria (Haynes, 2016, p. xxiii).

Notwithstanding the popularity of *Nollywood*, it came under severe criticism for its negative and unrealistic portrayal of the Nigerian society. Most of early *Nollywood* films were criticised for being laden with a heavy dose of occultic and ritual activities, thus creating an image of a ritualistic society for Nigeria (Abah, 2009; Farinde, 2008). Aside from the fact that they were mostly hastily produced, poorly researched and of low production quality, one notable feature of the early *Nollywood* films is the similarity in the themes of the films. Societal ills such as witchcraft, adultery, power and oppression, poverty, inheritance scuffles, poor widowhood practices, armed robberies, and other criminal activities were so pervasive and glamorised in most of the films, that one wonders if those portrayals are a true reflection of Nigeria and Nigerians (Farinde, 2008). Most pioneer *Nollywood* films were also particularly unkind to women regarding how they portrayed them and the issues affecting them. Images of women as sex objects; weak and dependent humans, incapable of making a significant impact beyond the home front; the irrational bosses, the wicked mothers-in-law, and step-mums, etc. abound in most early *Nollywood* films (Aromona, 2016; Azeez, 2014; Okunna, 1996; Utoh-Ezeajugh & Anijah, 2018). The negative, exaggerated, and unrealistic representations of Nigeria, besides the poor production quality of the films, had telling effects on the overall perception of Nigeria on the global front (Farinde, 2008).

The developing film industry also had to grapple with several internal and external challenges that threatened its existence. One prominent challenge faced by the industry is piracy. For an industry that grew solely on independent efforts, with no significant support from the government, the problem of piracy became so challenging, that, according to veteran film producer, Tunde Kelani, (in a personal communication with Nollywood scholar Jonathan Haynes), for every legitimate copy of a produced film, there are about five to ten pirated copies (Haynes, 2014).

Scholars have however cautioned against dismissing the efforts of the early *Nollywood* filmmakers because of what they consider "teething" problems, arguing that, with every challenge, is an inherent opportunity to become better. According to Geiger (2008),

> All of the melodrama, exaggerated acting styles, loquacious scenes, rough camerawork, and untidy editing not only point to the seams or sutures that disguise most western film productions, but they also reveal loose ends, create spaces for interaction and audience engagement for Africa's "ironic chorus", as opposed to encouraging captive voyeurism.
>
> (p. 68)

The recent high penetration of information communication technologies and new online film-viewing platforms (in Nigeria), afforded by the internet, have made purchasing home videos unattractive, leading to an immense loss of revenue to film producers (Haynes, 2014). With the myriad of challenges confronting the Nigerian film industry, an alternative to *Nollywood* became quite expedient (Haynes, 2014).

The New Nollywood

Driven primarily by the need to survive and make a difference, some film producers, especially the new entrants felt the need to look inward and re-strategize, and so the *"New Nollywood"* was borne out of the existing *Nollywood* (Azeez, 2019; Ernest-Samuel & Uduma, 2019). The *"New Nollywood,"* a phrase that gained prominence around 2010, is used to describe the attempt by some young filmmakers, to produce films, that depart sharply from the old *Nollywood* films, in terms of storyline, production quality, budget, reach and professionalism (Ernest-Samuel & Uduma, 2019; Haynes, 2014). The *New Nollywood* is that section of *Nollywood* "that is trying to re-structure the industry's economy from within, practicing an innovative funding strategy and developing formal modes of distribution that imply a new role for the diasporic market" (Jedlowski, 2013, p. 38).

Unlike the typical *Nollywood* films, the *New Nollywood* films are high-budget films, which are of higher production quality; have an international and cinematic appeal; well-researched and take a longer time to produce. Their stories are more logical and relatable, while the acting is more professionally done (Azeez, 2019; Jedlowski, 2013). According to McCain (2012), the arrival of a new generation of filmmakers, including Kunle Afolayan, Chineze Anyaene, and Stephanie Linus, who had trained at international film schools, was instrumental to the establishment of a Nigerian film-making elite. As reported by Krings & Okome (2013), three films are widely considered as the pioneers of the New Nollywood Era: *The Amazing Grace* by Jeta Amata (2006), *Irapada* by Kunle Afolayan (2006), and *Through the Glass* by Stephanie Okereke (2008). The films show transformations in the Nigerian film industry in terms of production methods, audience, and settings. Despite not being a box-office hit, Amata's historical film, *The Amazing Grace* was the first internationally co-produced film targeted at an international and diaspora audience. While Afolayan's *Irapada* was one of the first set of Nigerian films to be premiered in a British cinema, Okereke's *Through the* Glass was the first Nigerian film to hit the box office, grossing about 10 Million Dollars in the first three weeks of its release while serving as inspiration to other filmmakers on the commercial possibilities of Nigerian films (Krings & Okome, 2013). Also, while *Nollywood* had grown solely from independent efforts, the New *Nollywood* emerged when the government felt the need to formalise and support the sector (Haynes, 2014). Since the launch of *Project Nollywood* in 2006, other financial support schemes such as the 2010 BOI/NEXIM's *Creative Fund* and the 2015 Bank of Industry's *Nollyfund* have been rolled out for *Nollywood* creatives to access (Azeez, 2019; Haynes, 2014). Kunle Afolayan was also one of the first set of filmmakers to access the *Nollyfund*, for his *October 1* (2014) blockbuster (Njoku, 2015). With pioneering films such as Kunle Afolayan's *Figurine* (2010) and *Phone Swap* (2012), Chineze Anyaene's *Ijé* (2010), Ali-Balogun's *Tango with me* (2010), and Box office movies such as *The Wedding Party* (Adetiba, 2016) and Funke Akindele's *Omo Ghetto: The Saga* (2020), the *New Nollywood* has undoubtedly redefined film production in Nigeria.

With the old film marketers gradually being phased out, the *New Nollywood* films offer multiple sources of revenue for film producers.

With an improvement in the cinema going culture of Nigerians, most of the films are first released into the cinemas, including to those outside the country, affording the producers the opportunity to make huge returns before releasing it on DVD for the public (Haynes, 2014; Jedlowski, 2013). This also gives them an edge over film pirates as they can make some profits before the release of the films. Other filmmakers simply sell their distribution rights to streaming companies, such as *Ibaka TV, Iroko TV*, and *Netflix*. That these *New Nollywood* films are screened at international film festivals puts *Nollywood* on a global pedestal (Adejunmobi, 2014; Haynes, 2014; Jedlowski, 2013).

With a reach that extends beyond Nigeria, to other African countries, and diaspora communities in the Global North, such as the United Kingdom, and the United States, the Nigerian film industry, has gained the global recognition that it had long coveted. *Nollywood* is currently the third most valuable film industry in the world after Hollywood and Bollywood (Azeez, 2019). In terms of production output (in numbers of production), *Nollywood* ranks second in the world, following India's Bollywood, ahead of America's Hollywood (Geiger, 2008). It has also become a significant contributor to Nigeria's Gross Domestic Product (GDP), contributing 0.25% of the country's GDP as of the fourth quarter of 2020 (National Bureau of Statistics [NBS], 2021). The re-awakening of the cinema culture among Nigerians (*albeit* elitist) and the rebound of celluloid filmmaking are among the significant contributions of the *New Nollywood* to the Nigerian film industry.

With globalisation and improved digital technologies, more and more Nigerians now tell their own stories, express opinions, and make commentaries on happenings within the country, as they deem fit (Abah, 2009; Farinde, 2008). *Nollywood* has therefore served as a pool of talents with varying degrees of expertise. That Nigerians can produce films of international standards without having to rely solely on expertise from foreign creatives has led to an improved perception of Nigerians' worth and expertise – thanks to *Nollywood* (Farinde, 2008).

Again, given its growing popularity and acceptance beyond the shores of the country, *Nollywood* has projected Nigeria as the veritable giant of Africa because it is "what is on air in Kenya, Tanzania, Ghana, Zambia and many countries in Africa" (Farinde, 2008, p. 285). This has brought about an improved global recognition for Nigeria. For scholars such as Geiger (2008), *Nollywood*'s displacement of Hollywood and Bollywood within the Nigerian space is perhaps its most notable achievement. The Nigerian film industry has thus opened up to professional and scholarly explorations (Farinde, 2008; Giwa, 2014; Haynes, 2016).

As posited by Haynes (2014), referring to a personal communication experience with former President, Directors Guild of Nigeria, Bond

Emeruwa, the *New Nollywood* might have offered a better alternative to the mainstream *Nollywood*; it is, however, unlikely to displace the latter, given the cosmopolitan and elitist nature of the former. Haynes contends, both the new and mainstream *Nollywood* will co-exist, with film producers and audiences, who cannot afford the luxuries of the *New Nollywood* films, going for the mainstream films. Even the *New Nollywood* films will eventually filter down to the masses after travelling through all of its elitist routes (Haynes, 2014).

Conclusion

The Nigerian film industry has grown in leaps and bounds, with a popularity that extends beyond the shores of the African continent. The evolution of the industry through different phases has mostly been borne out of the need for alternative and better filmmaking practices and to appeal to audiences' changing tastes and preferences. Its high level of independence, having grown with minimal support from the government but from private efforts, enhanced by a globalized economy (Adesokan, 2009), has enabled it to stimulate societal transformation because of its unofficial obligation to teach morals – a duty it inherited from the pioneering efforts of the Yoruba Travelling Theatre and the Onitsha Market literature – with ideologies that entertainment should be infused with moralizing messages and cautionary tales (Hays, cited in Abah, 2009).

References

Abah, A. L. (2009). Popular culture and social change in Africa: The case of the Nigerian video industry. *Media, Culture and Society*, *31*(5), 731–748.

Adedeji, K. O. (2014). *Representation of Women in Selected Nigerian Films and the Quest for Gender Equality: A Religious Perspective*. Unpublished Master's Dissertation, University of Lagos.

Adejunmobi, M. (2014). Evolving Nollywood templates for minor transnational film. *Black Camera: An International Film Journal*, *5*(2), 74–94.

Adesanya, A. (2010). From video to films. In *Nigerian Video Films* (pp. 37–50). Ohio University Press.

Adesokan, A. (2009). Practising "democracy" in Nigerian films. *African Affairs*, *108*(433), 599–619.

Afolayan, K. (2006). *Irapada*. Golden Effects Pictures.

Aig-Imoukhuede, F. (1979). A national film industry: Assessment of problems and suggested solutions. In A. Opubor & O. Nwuneli (eds), *The Development and Growth of the Film Industry in Nigeria* (pp. 39–60). Third Press International.

Alabi, S. (2019). Challenges of technological innovation in Nollywood film production. In B. A. Musa (ed.), *Nollywood in Glocal Perspective* (pp. 67–83). Palgrave: Macmillan.

Amata, J. (2006). *The Amazing Grace*. Jeta Amata Concepts.

Amodu, L. O., Oladotun, M. A., Oyero, O., & Ekanem, T. (2019). Portrayal of moral lesson in Nigerian movies: A study of Tunde Kelani's Maami. In L. Oso, R. Olatunji, O. Oyero, & O. Omojola (eds), *Beyond Fun: Media Entertainment, Politics and Development in Nigeria*. (pp. 263–373). Malthouse Press.

Aromona, O. (2016). Portrayal of African women in Nollywood films over a five-year period: A content analysis of traits applying the stereotype content model [East Tennessee State University]. In *Electronic Thesis and Dissertations*. https://dc.etsu.edu/etd/3166

Azeez, A. L. (2010). Audience perception of the reality in the representations of women in Nigerian films. *Journal of Media and Communication Studies*, 2(9), 200–207. https://doi.org/10.1386/jac.5.2.149_1

Azeez, A. L. (2019). History and evolution of Nollywood: A look at early and late influences. In B. A. Musa (ed.), *Nollywood in Glocal Perspective* (pp. 2–24). Palgrave: Macmillan.

Azeez, T. (2014). Identity politics, self determination and war in postcolonial african movies. *International Journal of Innovative Research and Development*, 3(7), 207–212.

Enwefah, C. (2009). Film/cinema development: From still to motion picture. In O. Onabajo & R. M'Bayo (eds), *Emergence, Growth and Challenges of Films and Home Videos in Nigeria* (pp. 53–62). African Reinaissance Books Incorporated.

Ernest-Samuel, E. C., & Uduma, N. E. (2019). From informality to "New Nollywood": Implications for the audience. In B. Musa (ed.), *Nollywood in Glocal Perspective* (pp. 45–65). Palgrave: Macmillan.

Farinde, K. O. (2008). Nollywood portrayal of the Nigerian society: Issues in question. *International Journal of Communication*, 9, 282–290.

Geiger, J. (2008). Nollywood style: Nigerian movies and "shifting perceptions of worth". *Film International*, 58–72.

George, O. (2018). Returning to Jeyifo's *The Yoruba Popular Travelling Theatre of Nigeria*. *Journal of African Literature Association*, 12(1), 14–22. https://doi.org/10.1080/21674736.2018.1433751

Giwa, E. T. (2014). *Nollywood : A Case Study of the Rising Nigerian Film Industry – Content & Production* [Southern Illinois University, Carbondale]. http://opensiuc.lib.siu.edu/gs_rp/518%0A

Haynes, J. (2012). Editorial reflections on Nollywood : Introduction to the special issue. *Journal of African Cinemas*, 4(1), 3–7.

Haynes, J. (2014). New Nollywood: Kunle Afolayan. *Black Camera*, 5(2), 53–73.

Haynes, J. (2016). *Nollywood: The Creation of Nigerian Film Genres*. The University of Chicago Press. http://repositorio.unan.edu.ni/2986/1/5624.pdf

Haynes, J., & Okome, O. (2000). Evolving popular media: Nigerian video films. In J. Haynes (ed.), *Nigerian Video Films* (pp. 51–88). Ohio University Press.

Haynes, J., & Okome, O. (2010). Evolving popular media: Nigeria video films. In *Nigerian Video Films* (pp. 51–88). Ohio University Press.

Husseini, S. H., & Sunday, O. A. (2019). From Nigerian film industry to Nollywood: Land-marking the growth of the new wave cinema. In B. Musa (ed.), *Nollywood in Glocal Perspective* (pp. 25–43). Palgrave: Macmillan.

Ismail, H., & Ibrahim, M. M. (2019). Gender demographic analysis of the audience of online Nollywood among Nigerians in diaspora. In M. O. Bhadmus (ed.), *The Nigerian Cinema: Gender and Sexuality in Nigerian Motion Picture* (pp. 192–202). Hallmark Publishing Company Ltd.

Jedlowski, A. (2011). When the Nigerian video film industry became "Nollywood": Naming, branding and the videos' transnational mobility. *Estudos Afro-Asiaticos, 33*(1–2–3), 225–251.

Jedlowski, A. (2013). From Nollywood to Nollyworld: Processes of transnationalisation in the Nigerian film industry. In *Global Nollywood: The Transnational Dimensions of an African Video Film Industry* (pp. 25–45).

Jeyifo, B. (1984). The Yoruba popular travelling theatre of Nigeria. Federal Ministry of Social Development, Youth, Sports, and Culture.

Krings, M., & Okome, O. (2013). Global Nollywood: The transnational dimensions of an African video film industry. In M. Krings & O. Okome (eds.), *Global Nollywood: The Transnational Dimensions of an African Video Film Industry.* Indiana University Press.

McCain, C. (2012). Video exposé: Metafiction and message in Nigerian films. *Journal of African Cinemas, 4*(1), 25–57.

National Bureau of Statistics. (2021). *Nigerian Gross Domestic Product Report: Q4 and full year 2020* (Issue February).

Njoku, B. (2015). *Filmmakers gather for BOI's NollyFund.* Vanguard. www.vanguardngr.com/2015/11/filmmakers-gather-for-bois-nollyfund/

Obododinma, O. (2010). The rhetoric of christian videos: The war paradigm of the great mistake. In J. Haynes (Ed.), *Nigerian Video Films* (pp. 192–199). Ohio University Press.

Okunna, C. (1996). Portrayal of women in Nigerian home video films: Empowerment or subjugation? *Africa Media Review, 10*(3), 21–36.

Okereke, S. (2008). *Through the glass.* Next Page Productions.

Onabajo, O., & Odoe, J. (2009). Film and its development in Nigeria: The neglected gap. In O. Onabajo & R. M'Bayo (eds), *Emergence, Growth and Challenges of Films and Home Videos in Nigeria.* African Reinaissance Publishers.

Onukwufor, C., & Nnebue, K. (Producer). (1994). *Glamour girls (Part 1).* NEK Video Links.

Opubor, A., Nwuneli, O., & Oreh, O. (1979). The status, role and future of the film industry in Nigeria. In A. Opubor & O. Nwuneli (eds), *The Development and Growth of the Film Industry in Nigeria* (pp. 1–22). Third Press International.

Oso, L. (2011). Press under the military: The IBB years. In L. Oso & U. Pate (eds), *Mass Media and Society in Nigeria* (2nd ed., pp. 121–140). Malthouse Press.

Oso, L., Odunlami, D., & Adaja, T. (2011). Socio-historical context of the development of Nigerian media. In L. Oso & U. Pate (eds), *Mass Media and Society in Nigeria* (2nd ed., pp. 1–24). Malthouse Press.

Sunday, O. (2009). An overview of Nigerian film industry. In O. Onabajo & R. M'Bayo (eds), *Emergence, Growth and Challenges of Films and Home Videos in Nigeria* (pp. 53–62). African Reinaissance Books Incorporated.

The Centenary Project. (2014). *Eddie Ugbomah – A Nigerian Pioneer Filmmaker Driven by Value.* The Centenary Project by Pan-Atlantic University. https://artsandculture.google.com/story/jQWhZ1nUZRbPIA

Tijani-Adenle, G. (2016). She's homely, beautiful and then, hardworking! Critiquing the representation of women leaders and managers in the Nigerian press. *Gender in Management: An International Journal, 31*(5/6), 396–410.

Ugbomah, E. (1979). *The Mask*. Edifosa Films.

Utoh-Ezeajugh, T. C., & Anijah, E. E. (2018). Gender domination and domestic violence in Nigerian video films: a paradigmatic appraisal. *UJAH: Unizik Journal of Arts and Humanities, 18*(3), 1.

Vaughn, S. (1990). Morality and Entertainment: The Origins of the Motion Picture Production Code. *The Journal of American History, 77*(1), 39–65.

Filmography

Adetiba, F. (2016). *The Wedding Party*. FilmOne Distribution.

Afolayan, K. (2010). *The Figurine*. Golden Effects.

Afolayan, K. (2012). *Phone Swap*. Golden Effects.

Ali-Balogun, M. (2010). *Tango with me*. Brickwall Communications LTD & Talking Drum Entertainment.

Anyaene, C. (2010). *Ijé – the Journey*. Xandria Productions.

Balogun, O. (1976). *Ajani Ogun*. Afrocult Foundation.

Balogun, O. (1978). *Black Goddess*. Afrocult Foundation.

Bello, A., & Akindele-Bello, F. (2020). *Omo Ghetto: The Saga*. FilmOne Distribution.

Dadzie, M., & Emema, P. [Producer] (UNKNOWN). *Behind the Clouds*. Nigerian Television Authority

Dadzie, M., & Igho, P. [Producer] (1980). *Cock Crow at Dawn*. Nigerian Television Authority.

Davis, O., & Oladele, F. [Producer]. (1970). *Kongi's Harvest*. Calpenny Nigeria.

Dejumo, L., & Olusola, O. (Executive P. (1968 - 1988). *The Village Headmaster*. Ariya Productions.

Fani-Kayode, L. (Producer). (1984 - 1986). *Mirror in the Sun (TV Series)*. Cinekraft Ltd.

Igwe, A. (Producer). (1984 - 1986). *Checkmate*. Moving Movies.

Onu, C., & Nnebue, K. (Producer). (1996). *Glamour Girls (Part 2)*. NEK Video Links.

Onungwa, U., & Saro-Wiwa, K. (1986 - 1990). *Basi and Company*. Nigeria: Nigerian Television Authority.

Part III

Identity, Representation and Media in Africa

10 Immigration, Nationalism and Political Positionalities in South Africa

Rofhiwa Felicia Mukhudwana

One may ask why immigration, nationalism, and political positionalities are included in the conservatory of communication and media studies. Even though some seminal literature on nationalism has placed the media at the heart of their work, there is still a paucity of media theory and research on the subject (Skey 2022). Studies that intersect nationalism and the media often focus on populism (Machinya 2022), reporting on xenophobia (Chiumbu & Moyo 2018), and the coverage of right-wing political parties (Green-Pedersen & Otjes 2019). The rhetoric, discursive and digital turns are starting to influence wider debates around the relationship between media and nationalism. For example, observations are made about how fake news and misinformation can fuel nativist resentment (Rone 2022) or the impact of digital technologies on social solidarities and digital mobilisation (Mathe & Motsaathebe 2022). Benedict Anderson (1982, 7) explains the four attributes that characterize the feeling of national belonging. First is that 'nations' are imagined communities that are also enacted (material). Second, a nation is *limited*, because every one of them has finite boundaries. Third, the nation is *sovereign*, because it should have self-determination, and fourthly, it is imagined as a *community* with deep comradeship. Nations are elaborate social practices enacted through time, laboriously fabricated through the media and printing press, in schools, churches, and popular culture (McClintock 1991). Therefore, nationalism is a contested representation, communication, persuasion, and myth-making system. Moreover, the new nationalism is rooted in populist politics and grass-root movements wherein marginal political actors are dependent on grassroots mobilisation and politics of spectacle to attract media and influence public opinion. Although this chapter does not focus on civil society groups such as PutSouthAfricaFirst, it explores the politicisation of immigration as campaigning rhetoric by selected political parties. The positioning of immigration resonates with agenda setting and framing of political issues as salient in public, media, and policy agendas.

DOI: 10.4324/9781003352907-13

Media discourses on immigration in South Africa

Different genres of migration discourse are political discourse, policy discourse, media discourse, and academic discourse. News reports, editorials, parliamentary debates, policies and laws, or social media and everyday conversations are among the many discourse genres that may be about migration in general (Van Dijk 2018). Looking at media discourses, Danso and McDonald (2001) analysed print media's coverage of cross-border migration in South Africa and how it may affect both public opinion and policymaking. They found that coverage of migration by the South African press reflects anti-immigration sentiments and is unanalytical. Neutral articles merely catalogue statistics on migration. Freeman (2020) concludes that media attention on migration tends to be high at times of large-scale attacks and then substantially drops. As media reporting tends to be focused on structural issues such as government failure to manage boarders, little attention is given in the media to the specific reasons for localised violence (ibid.). The majority of reporting on foreigners tends to centre on crime, depicting non-nationals as perpetrators (Freeman 2020). A similar conclusion is made by Mpofu and Matsilele (2023) who identified three themes in the framing of immigrants in South African mainstream and social media. They observe that the foreigner is framed as a criminal element and a contaminant using terms such as 'flooded' or 'overrun' and also framed as an economic threat 'who take our jobs and women.' Social media are implicated in the migration processes. Batisai and Dzimiri (2020) consider how digital technologies have empowered previously marginalised communities and provided them with a voice in alternative public spheres. Mathe and Motsaathebe (2022) found that social media participation in groups (reflected by hashtags) is determined by shared interests or grievances (mob psychology) and shaped by propaganda. Most academic work around media coverage of immigration has largely been delimited to xenophobia (Danso & McDonald, 2001; McDonald & Jacobs 2005; Ngcamu & Mantzaris 2019; Mathe & Motsaathebe 2022). One of the most damning accusations against the press in South Africa is that it perpetuates negative stereotypes about migrants that may engender xenophobia. Similarly exploring the media coverage of immigration within the context of xenophobia, Chiumbu and Moyo (2018) at least expand their focus to include media representation of immigrants around questions of identity, citizenship, and social cohesion. They base their premise on the notion that the media as a social institution has an imperative role in shaping policies on immigration. They examined thematic frames used by the selected newspapers to construct the image of immigrants during three periods of xenophobic violence, in 2008, 2015, and 2017. They concluded that the media used narrative frames that justify the exclusion of foreigners and reinforce fears of a national takeover by the foreign 'other.'

Focusing on how the xenophobic violence in South Africa in 2015 was framed in the Mozambican media, Machonisse (2020) illustrates how journalistic norms and practices were influenced by a strong sense of patriotism, culture, and national identity. Her fundamental argument is that during such key events, journalists who belong to a specific national identity are 'bound' by those identities to report as citizens belonging to that specific nation. Her study demonstrates the biopolitics around discourses on migration and xenophobia.

The media is crucial in delivering verified information, informed opinions as well as balanced and inclusive narratives. As much as the media is responsible for the representation and framing of the immigration issue, this role also falls on the prerogatives of politicians as rhetorical stakeholders in the political and public discourse that affect migration policy and its enactment. Machinya (2022) highlights the connections between populism and xenophobia. He posits that what bestows social legitimacy to xenophobia is the foregrounding of an anti-immigrant populist discourse in the mainstream discourse by political leaders. He identifies three strategies that politicians use to mobilise anti-immigrant populist rhetoric. First, politicians claim to be a voice for the people who are equally worried about illegal immigrants. Second, they elevate immigration to the level of a crisis demanding immediate and decisive action. And third, they set the enemy against the people who are looking for a culprit to blame for the crisis. While Machinya's (2022) study looks at politicians, it is still grounded on mediatisation by mainstream media. As most studies on immigration in South Africa have been written from the perspective of migrants either by migrants themselves or in response to xenophobia, shifting the focus to unmediated self-representation of the immigration issue from the perspectives of politicians could be a fresh take on the scholarship. By exploring party political positionalities of immigration as a salient political issue, we can interrogate various versions of nationalisms self-presented by political parties. This is a research gap that this chapter explores.

Theorising nationalism in the context of global immigration

The concept of nationalism proves notoriously difficult to define (Anderson 1982). The conundrum is due to the use of different analytical languages to refer to the same thing. Nationalism may be viewed as an embedded loyalty binding individual identity to an organic community. It is a political concept used to denote interactions of institutions, demographics, and individual behaviour (Mylonas & Tudor 2023). It can also be a political resource used to mobilise individuals for the rational pursuit of common interests (such as revolutions, and decolonisation). At worst, it can be an ideological myth (populism) oversimplifying complex situations with simple formulas (Brown 2000). The term 'nationalism' is even more complex because it is an umbrella for several schools of thought relating to the notion of the nation-state. One of which is *statist* nationalism. According to this type of nationalism, for states to realise political principles such as democracy, economic welfare, and distributive justice, the citizens must share a homogeneous national culture (Smith 1979). The second school is that of *cultural nationalism* where members of groups share a common history and societal culture (Gans 1998). Thus, nationalism is an instinct (primordialism), an interest (situationism), and an ideology (constructivism).

The *Primordial approach* to nationalism is associated with tribal identities. The nation is depicted as comprised of an inborn, innate, natural, organic community whose members feel an instant emotional attachment. These natural nations have the right to self-determination. From this perspective, the only authentic nationalism is ethnic nationalism and the determinant of inclusion and exclusion is only in-born (Mylonas & Tudor 2023). Primordialism also refers to the inheritance of a collective memory whereby the culture of a society is transmitted through generations, education, public channels, media, and the arts. An example of a collective memory could be the experience of apartheid in South Africa. Anthony Smith (1979) calls this a 'perennial' variant of primordialism. The awakening of the ethnic bond and its development into political nationalism is not automatic nor inevitable. It can be awakened and mobilised by creating the perception that the community's culture, cohesion, or autonomy is in some way threatened. Activists and political groups that can mobilise the grievances of the community as equally threatened often succeed in driving a nationalist agenda eliciting communal reaction as a defence. They do so by reminiscing on the authentic past, portraying a present threat, and conjuring up a future of doom. This is where the scholarship of populism comes in.

Theories of modernisation suggest that modernisation and national integration were intrinsically connected (Antonsich 2020). The general argument is that the emergence of the modern centralised state with effective and sovereign control over a demarcated territory facilitated the socioeconomic integration of the society within that territory (Brown 2003). From a modernist perspective, it is the modern state which gave birth to the nation and not the other way (Antonsich 2020; Tamir 2019). The modern nation-state thus emerges as a socio-economic, political, and cultural community supported by capitalism, industrialization, urbanization, and secularism (Antonsich 2020). A situationist approach to the study of nationalism is relatively aligned with modernism as a response to dynamic economic circumstances. Situationism sees contemporary nations as being in the process of transformation by situational changes in the structure of the global economy that relegates nation-states as less appropriate categories of national identity (Brown 2000). Global migration and economic functionalism (de-massified economy) render states weak. Situations are dynamic, changeable, and open to manipulation.

Nationalism offers individuals a sense of identity. The constructivist turn illustrates how people could be organised into a wide range of overlapping identity dimensions such as race, tribe, religion, ethnicity, and region (Mylonas & Tudor 2021). The constructivist approach to nationalism posits that a sense of identity might be neither rationally chosen nor innately given but constructed as a category of understanding (Smith 1979). It is a constructed feeling of affiliation. A nation is not a substantive entity but a form of ideological consciousness filtering the reality of unity than reflecting it. Different paradigms at least agree on their recognition of the crucial role played by élites in promoting nationalism, particularly constructivism in presenting nationalism as an ideology, invented and employed by politicians aspiring to power. 'Such élites (politicians) construct new myths of unity for the control of societies characterised by socio-economic complexity and cultural diversity' (Brown 2000, 40). Constructivism strengthens the modernist view and situationism that nations and nationalism are not inevitable but emerge out of contextual circumstances (Mylonas & Tudor 2023).

As previously mentioned, the confusion over nationalism is partly caused by the utility of different concepts meaning the same phenomena. The following concepts are similar to those described above. It is suggested that the contentious nature of nationalist politics is due to tensions between civic nationalism and ethnocultural nationalism. The origins of the distinction between civic and ethnic nationalism are to be found in the works of Hans Kohn (1944). *Ethnocultural nationalism is* denoted as ethnic or cultural nationalism. The nation is portrayed as a community, united by its ethnocultural sameness and common ancestry, sharing a common language, culture, and tradition (*Primordial approach*). Collectivism and a lack of individual choice characterize this form of nationalism (Gans 2003). Conversely, *civic nationalism* denotes a nation in terms of a shared commitment to, and pride in, the public institutions of state and civil society, which connect the people to the territory that they occupy (Tamir 2019). All that citizens need to share is loyalty to a set of political and constitutional principles irrespective of ethnic origin (Brown 2000; Gans 2003). Civic nationalism portrays a voluntaristic community committed to the common good based on rational choice, not innate consequences. New members (immigrants) are welcome if they commit themselves, as in a matrimonial contract, to the institutions and way of life in their new home.

Literature depicts *ethnocultural nationalism* as illiberal (bad) and civic nationalism as liberal (good). Civic nationalism is depicted as 'forward-looking' in the globalised village, while ethnocultural nationalism is seen as backward-looking. However, it is asserted that civic nationalism is weaker than ethnocultural nationalism. Most nationalisms combine elements of ethnocultural nationalism and elements of civic nationalism. This means that there is a potential tension within most nation-states between civic nationalist communities, and ethnocultural nationalist communities. States that are successful in providing social harmony and political stability, have done so by persuading their societies that the gap between the communities is not significant (Brown 2000). Nationalism only persists to the extent that individuals, movements, and groups choose to be nationalists (Kaldor 2004). Political leaders have tended to use nationalist and religious appeals when other tools of political mobilisation have failed. One of the most heated debates surrounding nationalism involves the ability of the nation-building state to accommodate social, cultural, and political pluralism caused by global migration in answering questions of national identity (Ndlovu-Gatsheni 2009).

Nationalism is more relevant to the politics of our time than it has been in half a century. We are seeing a global re-emergence of nationalism after decades of seeming retreat. In addition to the global economic crisis, global mobility, populism, and the upsurge of nationalist parties, this ascendance of nationalism is accentuated by the coronavirus pandemic (Mylonas & Tudor 2021). Sibanda (2022) postulates that 'the pandemic led to a silent rise in narrow, exclusionary, and extreme nationalism and deglobalisation seen through the building and fortifying of geographic borders, media nationalism, and protectionism.' The popularity of nationalism has been decried as racism, first-world supremacy, and xenophobia. However, it is not nationalism per se, but exclusionary nationalisms (also called ethnic or essentialist nationalisms) that are problematic for outcomes such as democracy, the prevention of genocide, and the provision of public goods (Mylonas & Tudor 2021). In contrast to this nationalism, there is undeniable cyber cosmopolitanism unified by technologies. These virtual ethnic and civic communities are social networks constituted by groups and individuals interacting through the internet and social media based on putative common descent or nationality (Conversi 2012). This is a complex expansion of Anderson's proverbial notion of modern nations as 'imagined communities.' Cosmopolitanism is founded on the philosophical idea that

> human beings have equal moral and political obligations to each other based solely on their humanity, without reference to state citizenship, national identity, religious affiliation, ethnicity, or place of birth. Cosmopolitanism concerns itself with the rights and responsibilities of world citizens.
>
> (Dei 2022)

But to what extent is all this new? Over the last four decades, scholars have engaged in lengthy debates about nationalism. For Antonsich (2020), nationalism is omnipresent, and its waves of manifestations are merely historical conjunctures. In this sense, there is nothing new about the current wave of nationalism. What is new is the paradox of planetary human entanglements (Moyo & Ndlovu-Gatsheni 2023) of multi-local subjects or 'missing people' that are fluid, multi-ethnic, free-flowing and not easily bounded by geographic nationalities (Mukhudwana 2022). The theorisation of nationalism is beginning to look at the implications and power dynamics in this cyber-cosmopolitan environment (Dei 2022). There is a need to theorise new cultural and civic diversities (Meer & Modood 2022).

The main thrust of the scholarship on nationalism has so far been concerned with its origins as theorists fixated on the chronological development of concepts, formations of nations, and their reproduction. But nationalism also has effects. Nationalism might implicate a wide range of substantive outcomes, including political regimes, public goods provision, citizenship and immigration laws, and different patterns of conflict (Vom Hau et al. 2023). What are the consequences of nationalism? Under what circumstances does the rise of nationalism pose a problem for outcomes such as democracy, economic development, migration policy, human rights, or global peace? (Mylonas & Tudor 2021). The consequences of nationalism resonate with issues of inclusion such as citizenship, democracy, and welfare. Nation-states are constantly confronted with the question of who belongs to them and who can become one of their members. This question is particularly relevant for immigration. The next section discusses nationalism and immigration.

Immigration as a salient political issue in immigration-receiving countries

The current wave of nationalism must be understood as a response to globalisation (Kaldor 2004; Vom Hau et al. 2023). Ernest Gellner's (1995) functionalist nationalism suggests that the modern state and modern industry require what he calls a modular man. A modular man has certain specialised skills including a shared language and can adapt to a variety of positions in modern society. A modular man is nomadic according to Braidotti (2011). Globalisation breaks down the homogeneity of the nation-state (Kaldor 2004). Nation-states which used to be considered assimilated cultural communities, integrated socio-economic communities, and sovereign political communities, are now struggling unequally with the realities of cultural pluralism, economic globalisation, and competing sovereignties (Brown 2006 39). Rustow (1967) posited that in the future, modernisation would require 'political institutions that transcend and transform the nation-state.' The same is true for the current cosmopolitan states (Dei 2022).

As global consumption and mobility know no borders, a global diaspora is emerging caused by the de-territorialisation of globalisation and systemic exodus due to civil wars, technologically mediated wars, famine, underdevelopment, indebtedness, global inequalities, terrorism, cyberterrorism, bioterrorism, and cultism for example. In addition, global mobility and capitalism produce a multi-locality of displaced and free-floating subjects. International migration has become a fundamental driver of social, economic, and political change (Cornelius & Rosenblum 2005). According to the Migration Data Portal, South Africa had a total of 2.9 million international migrants.[1] This number of migrants could be higher when adding the uncounted number of undocumented migrants. Population movements are increasing between states. Imposing considerable restrictions on immigration seems contradictory to the liberal value of freedom of movement. The increase in the global movement of people can be attributed to several factors. For example, skills are increasingly interchangeable, the abundance of information on global vocations and scholarships, travel and communication are more affordable, and international recruitment firms are much more aggressive. Capital flows and multinational corporations extend beyond national borders and have also contributed to the integration of global labour markets (Stern & Szalontai 2006). Immigration is motivated by voluntary rational factors and by involuntary structural factors. Emigration can be voluntarily motivated by economic differentials, upwards mobility, and family considerations (Cornelius & Rosenblum 2005; Meer & Modood 2022). Involuntary migration, on the other hand, refers to refugees forced from their homes by natural or human-made disasters. Immigration should not be considered a single independent variable, but a multidimensional complexity of factors that must be analysed: (1) the process of migration, (2) the characteristics and behaviours of migrants; (3) the regulatory and integration policies and the (4) the social, cultural, economic and political ramifications.

Kaushal (2019) identified seven primary drivers of public anxiety around immigration in most immigration-receiving countries. I summarise them as I generalise to South African realities. The first identified is *cultural identity*. This relates to the fear that immigrants bring with them alien cultures that threaten to disrupt the identity of host nations. However, discontent about cultural identity is expected to be less severe in countries that already have cultural pluralism such as South Africa. In the long run, immigrants tend to adopt host cultures and host communities begin to appreciate immigrants' culture, food, and music (Kaushal 2019). The second is a recession or *economic downturn*. Public dissatisfaction in general rises with declining economic prospects in the country. Economic predictions of growth are low, rising inflation, reduced financial commitments to social welfare and declining employment rates add to public anxiety that could be blamed on immigrants. Declining economic prospects often lead to third, *inequality and stagnation in living standards*. Income inequality and class disparities cause disenchantment among natives. There is also a considerable disparity of discontent between the middle class and the poor. It is primarily the poor who experience the brunt of poverty and declining living conditions. They live among undocumented immigrants who scrape for the same resources and services they do. Education has been closely associated with immigration tolerance. Those with formal education were found more tolerant (Freeman 1997). The fourth source of public anxiety around immigration is *social and demographic change*. This demographical change can be visible as the volume of immigrants settles and integrate with the communities. The proliferation of immigrant businesses and stores, and their share volume in public institutions and public health facilities may trigger anxiety. This results also in the fifth driver, the increase in refugee movements. *Escalation in refugee flows* is yet another source of intolerance toward migrants and refugees. Refugees are coming from countries embroiled in civil wars, fundamentalist terrorism, and poor economies. If the government does not respond to assisting these countries, taking in refugees is only addressing the symptom and not the cause. The majority may support strict enforcement of borders and locally conscious immigration policies, although they do not condone extreme measures (Freeman 1997). Sixth is *the diminishing confidence in governments and liberal elites*. Liberal and government elites as well as other politicians are seen as divorced from the situation on the ground, and unaffected by the upsurge of undocumented immigrants. The neo-liberal attitude of the South African economy has seen the rise of Chinese, Bangladeshi, and Pakistani immigrants. The consequence is the public alignment with political parties and civil society groups that resonate and empathise with these public discontents. The fear that government cannot monitor nor restrict immigration contributes to their illegitimacy. Last, and seventh, *international terrorism and national security*. Despite the validity of these accusations, immigrants are constantly linked with rising crime, drugs, human trafficking, terrorism, and other organised crimes (Cornelius & Rosenblum 2005; Matsilele & Mpofu 2023). Perhaps one of the most manifest indicators (or catalysts) of discontent is the rise of right-wing parties. Most of these parties advance radical restrictions or racist attitudes toward immigrants. It is vital to analyse how selected South African political parties are responding to these identified public anxieties around immigration as they position their stance on the issue. There is no denying that immigration is a politicised issue in South Africa.

The politicising of immigration: Political positionalities on immigration

Political branding is based on the principle that political parties can be managed as brands. The implication is that brands and branding are crucial elements in politics. Political parties can use positional branding to differentiate themselves, shape perception and attain competitive advantage (Mukhudwana 2021). Branding in this chapter is approached mainly from the point of positioning. Brand positioning is an organised system for finding a window in the mind. In simple words, brand positioning is about putting a brand first in a customer's (voter's) thought process against all competitive brands. Political parties construct branding through issue positioning, symbolic policies, and initiatives. In times of political uncertainties, voters tend to focus on issue positioning by political parties than on long-term party preferences. The success of a political positioning can be measured by the effectiveness to which the party is perceived as the best candidate able to respond to the immigration issue as compared to competing parties.

For immigration to be a salient issue, one or more political parties must politicize it – either as a response to pressure from voters or as an expression of their brand positionality (Alonso & Fonseca 2011). Immigration has become an issue that all parties address when faced with rising numbers of immigrants and the strengthening of radical right-wing parties (Green-Pedersen & Otjes 2019). However, it is not only right-wing parties that are *prioritising* this issue. Most parties, at the centre and the left, are pressured to respond and propagate their position. Party politics is the most vital issue of consideration when it comes to the politics of immigration. It is essential to understand how political parties have addressed the issue of immigration. Despite this growth, the saliency of immigration for political parties has received little attention. I aim to go deeper and look at how political parties are responding to this issue in terms of how they position their stances.

When do political parties pay attention to immigration? Political parties can be expected to pay more attention to public attitudes on a topical issue compared to an issue that only attracts partial party or public attention (Green-Pedersen & Otjes 2019). The politicisation of immigration is about identifying some substantial problem – such as the number of immigrants or the problems around civic integration, xenophobia, Afrophobia, refugees, or immigration regulatory policy – and setting an agenda while attempting to frame its legitimacy in public, and media and policy agendas. Radical right-wing parties have an obvious interest in immigration, but centre-right parties also hold ownership of the issue, at least compared to the centre-left. Immigration is an issue that may cause potential internal disagreement between parties. One party position may have liberal policies focused on how immigration is beneficial for the supply of labour, whereas a conservative nationalistic approach would be another (Green-Pedersen & Otjes 2019, 426). Some political parties focus on the ineffectiveness of state regulatory policies (Cornelius & Rosenblum 2005).

Literature on party positioning of immigration is predominated by a focus on radical right-wing parties (Green-Pedersen & Otjes 2019). Anti-immigration parties are defined as parties that employ the immigration issue as their main political concern in electoral campaigns. Hence, these parties not only strongly favour immigration restriction but also attach much importance to the immigration issue. Negative attitudes toward refugees, legal and illegal immigration, and multiculturalism prevail among radical right voters and are the main reason voters support these parties.

Van Spanje (2010) asks, 'Do pressures from anti-immigration parties have a "contagion" impact on other parties' immigration policy positions?' An effect is considered 'contagion' if other parties shift to more restrictive immigration policy positions after the electoral success of the anti-immigration party in their country. It seems this contagion effect involves entire party systems rather than the mainstream right only. In addition, opposition parties are more vulnerable to this contagion effect than parties in government. It is often hypothesised that anti-immigration parties cause other parties to copy these parties' rhetoric. It is assumed that when an anti-immigration party enters the political scene, the other parties may react by copying the anti-immigration stance (what is called an 'accommodative' strategy), by taking up a radically different position ('adversarial'), or by not taking any stance at all ('dismissive') (Van Spanje 2010, 568).

A distinction is generally made between the indirect and the direct influence of radical right parties. Radical right parties may have considerable indirect influence once they break through electorally. Most have entered government as coalition partners of centre-right parties in most countries including South Africa. The most basic question scholars disagree about is whether the entrance of radical right parties into parliament pushed immigration and integration policies further in a restrictive direction. Even if significant policy changes occur because they entered into government, it cannot be concluded that these changes are a result of the direct influence of radical right parties (Akkerman 2017). It is possible that gaining office makes little or no difference for policy output and implementation of those policies.

The contradictory positions that parties adopt on immigration are indicative of the challenges to understanding the changing relationship between ideology and policy positioning. What makes 'the immigration issue' so problematic is its diverse and illusive nature. Consequently, parties find it difficult to accommodate immigration within either an economic or sociocultural positionality (Odmalm 2012). Immigration messes up party classification. Parties that are supposed to be on the 'Right' may suddenly be on the 'Left' regarding immigration. This situation poses problems for understanding the role of ideology in political systems. Parties tend to be trusted on an issue or set of issues to which they have a long-standing commitment and association. Parties can become comparatively stronger on certain political issues and thus develop degrees of ownership or strategic advantage (ibid.). When it comes to immigration, it seems positioning is more related to the changing dynamics of party competition than ideology. Competition around immigration is thus expected to be around which party is 'better' at delivering this goal and how parties communicate this effectively to the electorate (ibid.).

Party manifestos are a convenient and sufficiently valid source of party positions. Ruedin and Morales (2019) identify various methods used to capture political parties' positions on specific issues. Among which are Data from the Comparative Manifesto Project (CMP) and the Chapel Hill Expert Survey (CHES). One can also follow the discourse/rhetoric/self-presentation/campaigns of political parties on their social media accounts such as Twitter or Facebook or their public discourses captured in the media. Researchers have preferences on how to measure party positions, but there are no gold standards. All methods are subject to limitations and biases.

Nationalism and political positionalities in South Africa: The cases of Action-SA and the Economic Freedom Fighters

South Africa has assumed a larger role as a home for refugees and those seeking asylum in the era Post-1994. In a once-rainbow nation opened to all, immigration has manifested as a salient issue in politicking. It is now considered a political hot potato with social, political, and economic consequences. This multi-faceted issue is taking centre stage in election campaigning by various political parties. Thabo Mbeki's devotion to African Renaissance and his 'I am an African' speech sought to define South African identity as a civic or cosmopolitan one rather than an ethnocultural one. The easing of legal and unauthorised entry into South Africa after 1994 made the country a new destination for African asylum seekers, long-distance traders, entrepreneurs, students, and professionals (Mutanda 2022). The constitution of the Republic of South Africa prescribes that South Africa belongs to all who live in it, united in our diversity. This adage has come into a challenge from civil movements groups such as PutSouthAfricaFirst. The movement has put the issue of immigration on the table suggesting that for South Africa to recover economically and socially, immigration must be managed. They argue that solving unemployment, crime, and lack of service delivery must start with the reduction of undocumented immigrants. New political parties such as ActionSA were developed around this single issue and other political parties including the ruling ANC are pressured to take a stand or state their position on the issue. The politicizing of immigration is not unique to South Africa as it gained momentum in the United States (Winders 2016), Western Europe (Grande, Schwarzbözl & Fatke 2019), and other immigration-receiving countries. South Africa is caught between the decolonial turn of solidarity with the global south and facing the socio-economic challenges of open globalisation. The closing of borders in response to the growing challenges of globalisation demonstrates protectionism. This chapter looks at the politicizing of immigration by two political parties in South Africa (the

Economic Freedom Fighters (EFF) and ActionSA). These two parties are selected because they seem to have reached some degree of ownership on the issue of immigration in South Africa. By exploring party political positionalities of immigration as a salient political issue, we can interrogate various versions of nationalisms self-presented by political parties.

Action-SA

After leaving the Democratic Movement (DA), the former Johannesburg mayor Herman Mashaba established a new political party called ActionSA. This political party was founded on 29 August 2022. The party's Senate resolved to contest all nine provinces and nationally in the upcoming 2024 General Elections. The name ActionSA is deeply rooted in the reputational brand that the party wishes to portray – to be a party of action, not words. The main goal of the party is to 'change the direction of South Africa by providing a credible alternative to a broken political system that has failed South Africans for many years.'[2] Hence, the party is a call to action, whereby 'we must act as one.' But, who is 'we' that is called into action? The party refers to 'our people.' Statements such as 'South Africans are proud, capable, and resilient' and 'South Africans recognize our collective potential' are examples. It is not clear who is the 'we' and who is the 'South African.' This position resembles the *primordial approach* of ethno-cultural nationalism by portraying an innate and unified national identity that is distinctly South African. The party's main policy issues are based on what they call solution blueprints. Eleven political issues are identified, namely: Economic prosperity, non-racialism, social justice, quality education, land reform, housing, rule of law, immigration, ethical leadership, professional public service, electoral reform climate change, and the environment. I will zone in on immigration. The feedforward statement is

> Estimates indicate that as much as 10% of all people living in South Africa are undocumented foreign nationals. The problem is not those citizens of other countries as their home, but rather that too many foreigners enter South Africa without following the legal process of immigration. The dysfunctionality at Home Affairs also results in many foreigners being unable to acquire the correct documentation for legal residency in South Africa.

This statement illustrates the framing that, there are 'insufficient immigration controls' in South Africa resulting in 'porous borders.' There is a lack of the rule of law due to the dysfunctionality of Home Affairs where it is far easier to bribe officials for faked documents than to follow the proper channels and immigration processes. This is because 'immigration laws are too strict.' In addition, 'refugees and asylum-seekers do not receive the support required to integrate into South African society.' The failure of political leadership leads to 'weak foreign policy' which no longer protects human rights internationally. ActionSA condemns all forms of xenophobia. It believes in the streamlining of the immigration process, encourages the entry of skilled immigrants and those with entrepreneurship potential, and improved border security. However, illegal immigration is said to be placing unsustainable strain on South Africa's already limited public resources. I find the immigration stance of ActionSA to be confusing and lacking a positionality. The party succeeds in placing the issue on the agenda as a salient one but does not portray a clear stance. From the above self-presentations on the website (because there is no manifesto yet), ActionSA does not oppose immigration nor call for restrictive policies, it merely advocates for efficient immigration processes with proper documentation for immigrants and their integration. This is a mild stance that is fit for all. In a press release, ActionSA delivers the following contradictory statements in terms of issue positioning[3]:

> The Republic of South Africa was built by migrants, from all walks of life, and that history continues to positively contribute to the richness of our diversity.
> We will no longer permit Home Affairs to hide their heads in the sand on this issue. Addressing this issue requires strong political will. Where we govern, we will not shy away from addressing immigration challenges faced by the city and its impact on service delivery and all residents.

Most ActionSA press release statements and self-presentations are endemic to this contradiction. It is difficult to call this positioning neutral as public statements by Mashaba can flip-flop through each side of the continuum of the immigration issue. This could be confusing to the media and the public alike. Herman Mashaba clashed with the EFF over its leader Julius Malema's remarks encouraging undocumented migrants to enter the country illegally. This is after Malema (EFF) encouraged Southern Africa Development Community (SADC) citizens to 'find a creative way' to enter South Africa in the aftermath of the momentary closure of borders by the government. The media (at a cursory analysis) seems to pit the EFF and ActionSA against each other when it comes to the issue of immigration. *News24*'s title exemplifies this: 'ActionSA, EFF square off over immigration' (18 Jan 2021). The media and some politicians mistake Mashaba's rhetorics and public discourses as indicative of right-wing political positioning around immigration. For example, EFF deputy leader Floyd Shivambu retorted on Twitter: 'Don't adopt this kind of liberal right-wing politics @ HermanMashaba. Your political life will be very difficult & your party lifespan short-lived if you adopt the ultra-right self-hating politics.' The media also insinuate ActionSA as assuming a right-wing position on immigration. For instance, Jan Gerber (*news24*, 18 Jan 2021) observes that 'Mashaba, while the DA's mayor of Johannesburg, often courted controversy and accusations of xenophobia with his hard-line stance on immigration. This issue also appears to be a central policy issue for his fledgling ActionSA.' This insinuated stance is different from the 'official' position of the party on its website. I recommend a discourse or rhetoric study on the Twitter account of ActionSA leader Herman Mashaba to evaluate his position on immigration. Also recommended is a study on how the media portrays ActionSA on the immigration issue.

The Economic Freedom Fighters

Julius Malema founded the Economic Freedom Fighters (EFF) in 2013 after being expelled from the African National Congress (ANC). Its ideology is placed on left-wing and sometimes far-left politics. The EFF positions itself as a 'radical and militant economic emancipation movement' that is anti-imperialist and leftist. Its primary mission is to rid the country of imperialist domination. Much has been written about the general ideological positioning of the EFF (Mukhudwana 2021). I will not regurgitate extant literature but only focus on the party's position on the immigration issue. The EFF identifies seven pillars of Economic Emancipation. The sixth mentions the commitment of the EFF to supporting the 'massive development of the African economy and advocating for a shift from reconciliation to justice in the entire continent.'[4] They believe that economic justice is only possible through the nationalisation of key sectors and protectionism from global neo-colonial imperialist capitalism. Key to note is the EFF's interpretation of the Freedom Charter that 'South Africa indeed belongs to all who live in it.' The EFF website does not denote much about its position on immigration. The current local government manifesto did not refer to immigration nor did the 2019 election manifesto. What is notable in both manifesto and the general language of the EFF is the reference to Africans or our black people. There is little reference to 'South Africans.' It seems the EFF has already adopted civil nationalism in line with its Pan-Africanist ideology toward a borderless Africa. This is in line with the decolonial thought that African borders are colonial constructions. For instance, in a press release statement, EFF MARKS THE 59th ANNIVERSARY OF AFRICA DAY (25 May 2022), the EFF maintains that 'the ideals of African Independence, anti-imperialism, rejection of colonial debt, a unitary African currency and promotion of intra-African trade, are the bedrock of the future of the continent.' The civic integration of Africans in a borderless continent is reinforced by another media statement, that 'all African countries and South Africa, in particular, carry a historical obligation to be home of all Africans from the diaspora because it was partly due to their efforts that apartheid was internationally condemned.' In an interview with Eusebius McKaiser, Malema mentioned that 'borders will not be there when the EFF is in government.' The EFF leader said he believes foreigners are scapegoated by frustrated South Africans. As a leftist party expected to resonate with the struggles of civil movements for social equality and egalitarianism, a spotlight was on the EFF regarding how it would relate with civil movements such as PutSouthAfricaFirst and OperationDudula, both of which could be called anti-immigration movements with ethno-nationalist tendencies. Reception studies are recommended to gauge how voters respond to each party's positioning. Srikantiah and Sinnar (2018) define white nationalism as 'the belief that national identity should be built around white ethnicity and that white people should therefore maintain both a demographic majority and dominance of the nation's culture and public life. This defines national identity in racial terms. In this context, the EFF could be said to reinforce Pan African Nationalism in South Africa which could possibly be 'black nationalism.'

Conclusion

The media is crucial in delivering verified information, informed opinions, and influencing policy on immigration. This chapter reviewed the literature on media discourses around immigration in South Africa. Most academic work around media coverage of immigration has largely been delimited to xenophobia. This means there is a gap in understanding the role of the media in broader migration and nationalism debates. As much as the media is responsible for the representation and framing of the immigration issue, this role also falls on the prerogatives of politicians as rhetorical stakeholders. This chapter focused on unmediated self-representation of the immigration issue from the perspectives of politicians.

Immigration has become an issue that all political parties address when faced with rising numbers of immigrants and the strengthening of radical right-wing parties. Both political parties present themselves as voices for the people who are equally worried about illegal immigrants – but from different positional stances. One of control (ActionSA) and the other of integrative welfare (EFF). They both elevate immigration to the level of a crisis demanding immediate and decisive action and thus succeed in positioning it as a salient political issue in the media, in public debates, and in policy discourses. Both parties succeed in placing the issue on the agenda but do not portray a clear stance (for fear of losing potential voters). The media however seems to have clearly positioned the parties, ActionSA as anti-immigration and the EFF as pro-immigration.

By exploring party political positionalities of immigration as a salient political issue, we can interrogate various versions of nationalisms self-presented by political parties. ActionSA position resembles the primordial approach of ethnocultural nationalism by portraying an innate and unified national identity that is distinctly South African. It seems the EFF has already adopted civil nationalism in line with its Pan-Africanist ideology towards a borderless Africa. There is no sufficient data to suggest a rise of nationalism in South Africa. What is noticeable is the rise of nationalist politics in the country as demonstrated by the rise of new parties (ActionSA), the electoral success of nationalist candidates such as Mashaba, or the shift of public discourse of established parties in framing immigration.

By now, Africans have become so used to the rhetoric of the 'global village' that talking about African nationalism (Africanism) sounds anachronistic and outdated. The concept of nationalism cannot be easy in Africa as the post-independence nation-states are the direct products of the Berlin Conference's mapping of African territory; cutting across nations and ethnic groups (Moloi 2020). Nonetheless, the nationalist upsurge in the post-war period in Africa was a great moment for a people that had been denied humanity by centuries of slavery and colonialism. Ideologies centred on Kwame Nkrumah's 'African Personality,' Nyerere's Ujamaa, and Leopold Senghor's 'Negritude' which expressed a common theme of African nationalism as an antidote to white supremacist rule. Concerning African nationalisms, one is compelled to rethink the direction of the national project in post-colonial Africa and the changing deployments and articulations of nationalism not only as a state ideology but also as a popular imaginary open to manipulation by both the elites and the poor (Ndlovu-Gatsheni 2009). The impression that there is a single version of African nationalism is incorrect. Such is demonstrated by these two parties, each reflecting a different take on nationalism, the EFF (Black civic nationalism that is Pan Africanist), and ActionSA reflecting ethnocultural nationalism that seeks to edify inclusion and exclusion based on global openness and classism. Regarding immigration, it seems Africanism collides with open globalisation, and political parties must straddle the two or choose one or the other.

The distinction between migrants and refugees was not consciously made in the issue position by both parties. Neither party referred to the relationship between emigration and immigration. This supports Moyo and Zanker's (2022) finding that there is a conflation between refugees and other migrants at a legislative, policy, and narrative level in South Africa. This could be due to the bifurcation of the topic into two disciplines: migration (economics and IR) and refugee (often Global South oriented and focused on conflict and security). In this chapter, I have argued for the inclusion of media studies and communication science as valid contributors to the study of international migration.

Notes

1 www.migrationdataportal.org/regional-data-overview/southern-africa
2 www.actionsa.org.za/
3 www.actionsa.org.za/
4 https://effonline.org/

References

Abdelaaty, L. & Hamlin, R. 2022. Introduction: The Politics of the Migrant/Refugee Binary. *Journal of Immigrant & Refugee Studies, 20*(2), 233–239.

Akkerman, T. 2017. Comparing radical right parties in government: Immigration and integration policies in nine countries (1996–2010). *Routledge Studies in Extremism and Democracy.*

Alonso, S. & Fonseca, S. C. D. 2012. Immigration, left and right. *Party Politics, 18*(6), 865–884.

Anderson, B. 1982. *Imagined Communities: Reflections on the Origin and Rise of Nationalism.* London.

Antonsich, M. 2020. Everyday nation in times of rising nationalism. *Sociology, 54*(6), 1230–1237.

Batisai, K. & Dzimiri, P. 2020. Not Just a Foreigner: 'Progressive' (Self-)Representations of African Migrants in the Media. In *Mediating Xenophobia in Africa: Unpacking Discourses of Migration, Belonging and Othering* (pp. 323–340). Cham: Springer International Publishing.

Braidotti, R. 2011. *Nomadic theory: The portable Rosi Braidotti.* Columbia University Press.

Brown, D. 2003. *Contemporary nationalism.* Routledge.

Chiumbu, S. H. & Moyo, D. 2018. 'South Africa belongs to all who live in it': Deconstructing media discourses of migrants during times of xenophobic attacks, from 2008 to 2017. *Communicare: Journal for Communication Sciences in Southern Africa, 37*(1), 136–152.

Conversi, D. 2012. Irresponsible radicalisation: Diasporas, globalisation and long-distance nationalism in the digital age. *Journal of Ethnic and Migration Studies, 38*(9), 1357–1379.

Cornelius, W. A. & Rosenblum, M. R. 2005. Immigration and politics. *Annu. Rev. Polit. Sci., 8*, 99–119.

Danso, R. & McDonald, D. A. 2001. Writing xenophobia: Immigration and the print media in post-apartheid South Africa. *Africa Today*, 115–137.

Dei, G. J. S. 2022. Cosmopolitanism or Multiculturalism? Towards an Anti-Colonial Reading. *International Journal for Talent Development and Creativity*, 31.

Deutsch, K. 1953. *Nationalism and Social Communication: An Inquiry into the Foundations of Nationality.* Cambridge, MA: MIT Press

Freeman, G. P. 1997. Immigration as a source of political discontent and frustration in Western democracies. *Studies in Comparative International Development, 32*(3), 42.

Freeman, L. 2020. Defying empirical and causal evidence: Busting the media's myth of Afrophobia in South Africa. In *Mediating Xenophobia in Africa: Unpacking Discourses of Migration, Belonging and Othering* (pp. 17–41). Cham: Springer International Publishing.

Gans, C. 1998. Nationalism and immigration. *Ethical Theory & Moral Practice, 1*, 159–180.

Gellner, E. 1995. *The importance of being modular.*

Grande, E., Schwarzbözl, T. & Fatke, M., 2019. Politicizing immigration in Western Europe. *Journal of European Public Policy, 26*(10), 1444–1463.

Green-Pedersen, C. & Otjes, S. 2019. A hot topic? Immigration on the agenda in Western Europe. *Party Politics*, 25(3), 424–434.

Kaldor, M. 2004. Nationalism and globalisation. *Nations and nationalism*, 10(1-2), 161–177.

Kaushal, N. 2019. *Blaming Immigrants: Nationalism and the Economics of Global Movement*. Columbia University Press.

Kohn, H. 1944. *The Idea of Nationalism: A Study of the Origins and Background*. Macmillan.

Machinya, J. 2022. Migration and Politics in South Africa: Mainstreaming Anti-Immigrant Populist Discourse. *African Human Mobility Review*, 8(1), 59–78.

Matsilele, T. & Mpofu, S. 2023. They Steal Our Jobs and Our Women and Sell Drugs to Our Youths: Hybrid-media framing of South Africa's 'Criminal Non-nationals'. In *The Paradox of Planetary Human Entanglements* (pp. 103–123). Routledge.

Machonisse, T. 2020. National Identity and Representation of Xenophobia in Mozambican Private and Public Television. In *Mediating Xenophobia in Africa: Unpacking Discourses of Migration, Belonging and Othering* (pp. 167–183).

Mathe, L. & Motsaathebe, G. 2022. Discursive Communities, Protest, Xenophobia, and Looting in South Africa: A Social Network Analysis. *Communicatio: South African Journal of Communication Theory and Research*, 48(1), 102–126.

McClintock, A. 1991. 'No longer in a future heaven': Women and nationalism in South Africa. *Transition*, 51, 104–123.

McDonald, D.A. & Jacobs, S. 2005. *Understanding press coverage of cross-border migration in southern Africa since 2000*. Migration policy series, 37. Pretoria: Idasa.

Meer, N. and Modood, T. 2022. Migration and cultural diversity challenges in the twenty-first century. In Triandafyllidou, A. (ed.), *Routledge Handbook of Immigration and Refugee Studies* (pp. 234–244). Routledge.

Moloi, L. 2020. *Towards an Afrocentric development paradigm in Africa* (Doctoral dissertation).

Moyo, I. & Ndlovu-Gatsheni, S. J. (eds) 2023. *The Paradox of Planetary Human Entanglements: Challenges of Living Together*. Taylor & Francis.

Moyo, K. & Zanker, F. 2022. No hope for the 'foreigners': The conflation of refugees and migrants in South Africa. *Journal of Immigrant & Refugee Studies*, 20(2), 253–265.

Mukhudwana, R. F. 2021. Conspicuous and performative blackness as decolonial political branding against the myth of the post-colonial society: A case of the EFF. In *Decolonising Political Communication in Africa* (pp. 26–44). Routledge.

Mukhudwana, R. F. 2022. COVID19, 'We are in this Together or are we': A decolonial crisis of locating the missing people in the post-human, South Africa. *Critical Arts*, 36(1-2), 35–52.

Mutanda, D. 2022. Economic threat, new nationalism and xenophobia in South Africa: Some reflections. *African Security Review*, 31(3), 332–350.

Mylonas, H. & Tudor, M. 2021. Nationalism: What we know and what we still need to know. *Annual Review of Political Science*, 24, 109–132.

Mylonas, H. & Tudor, M. 2023. *Varieties of Nationalism: Communities, Narratives, Identities.* Cambridge University Press.

Ndlovu-Gatsheni, S. J. 2009. Africa for Africans or Africa for 'natives' only? 'New nationalism' and nativism in Zimbabwe and South Africa. *Africa Spectrum,* 44(1), 61–78.

Ngcamu, B. S. & Mantzaris, E. 2019. Media reporting, xenophobic violence, and the 'Forgotten Dimensions': A case of selected areas in the KwaZulu-Natal Province. *International Journal of African Renaissance Studies – Multi-, Inter- and Transdisciplinarity,* 14(1), 131–146.

Odmalm, P. 2012. Party competition and positions on immigration: Strategic advantages and spatial locations. *Comparative European Politics,* 10, 1–22.

Peberdy, S. A. 2000. *Selecting Immigrants: Nationalism and National Identity in South Africa's Immigration Policies, 1910 to 1998.* Queen's University at Kingston.

Rone, J., 2022. Far-right alternative news media as 'indignation mobilization mechanisms': how the far right opposed the Global Compact for Migration. *Information, Communication & Society,* 25(9), 1333–1350.

Ruedin, D. & Morales, L. 2019. Estimating party positions on immigration: Assessing the reliability and validity of different methods. *Party Politics,* 25(3), 303–314.

Rustow, D. A., 1968. Modernization and comparative politics: Prospects in research and theory. *Comparative Politics,* 1(1), 37–51.

Sibanda, B. 2022. #Putsouthafricafirst and Afrophobic Xenophobia. In Moyo, I. & Ndlovu-Gatsheni, S. (eds.). *The paradox of planetary human entanglements.* London: Routledge.

Skey, M. 2022. Nationalism and media. *Nationalities Papers,* 50(5), pp. 839–849.

Smith, A. D. 1979. Nationalism in the twentieth century. Australian National University Press.

Srikantiah, J. & Sinnar, S., 2018. White nationalism as immigration policy. Stan. L. Rev. Online, 71, 197.

Stern, M. & Szalontai, G. 2006. Immigration policy in South Africa: does it make economic sense? *Development Southern Africa,* 23(01), 123–145.

Tamir, Y. 2019. Not so civic: Is there a difference between ethnic and civic nationalism? *Annual Review of Political Science,* 22, 419–434.

Van Dijk, T. A. 2018. Discourse and migration. *Qualitative Research in European Migration Studies,* 227–245.

Van Spanje, J. 2010. Contagious parties: Anti-immigration parties and their impact on other parties' immigration stances in contemporary Western Europe. *Party Politics,* 16(5), 563–586.

Vom Hau, M., Helbling, M., Tudor, M., Wimmer, A. and Halikiopoulou, D. 2023. The consequences of nationalism: A scholarly exchange. *Nations And Nationalism.*

Winders, J., 2016. Immigration and the 2016 Election. *Southeastern Geographer,* 56(3).291–296.

11 The Nation, the Press and Homosexuality

Framing National Identity in Uganda

Sara Namusoga-Kaale

In October 2023, Uganda will be 61 years old as an independent nation. Uganda is a small country that could fit into the Democratic Republic of Congo several times. And yet in Reid's (2017, p. xxvi) words, it "encompasses enormous diversity." This enormous diversity is both ethnic and cultural and is usually visible when government institutions, such as the Parliament, hold international events, where part of the entertainment consists of traditional dances and music from all over Uganda. The 1995 Constitution recognises over 50 ethnic groups.

When one thinks critically about the Forum for Democratic Change's (FDC) motto, "One Uganda, one people," they realise that it is one of the few times when Ugandans are deliberately called upon to unite in order to bring about democratic change. The FDC was Uganda's leading opposition party until recently when the National Unity Platform (NUP) overtook them and now leads the Opposition side in Parliament. It is fair to say, therefore, that calls for unity among Ugandans are usually associated with the politics of the country. That is, until something challenges the cultural norms around sexuality at a national level.

Traditionally, it is believed that Uganda is a heterosexual society (Nyanzi, 2013). As such, it is unacceptable for one to claim that they are homosexual. While at the International AIDS Conference in Durban in 2000, President Museveni said that homosexuals did not exist in Uganda (Nyanzi, 2013). Of course, this position has been challenged and there are several publications aimed at demonstrating that homosexuality is part of Ugandan traditional society. In fact, there is even an argument among some sections of the society that the reason Kabaka Mwanga, the King of Buganda who ordered for the death of the Uganda Martyrs, who were mostly men, did so because they refused to have same sex relations with him (Kizito, 2017). Roscoe and Murray (1998) also trace homosexuality in several African countries, including Uganda, back to the pre-colonial days. Moreover, Nyanzi (2013) interviewed some individuals in rural Uganda who identify

DOI: 10.4324/9781003352907-14

as homosexuals and yet they had never left their homes for a go at modern life in the towns. Inevitably, any discussion about homosexuality is divisive as reflected in media reports.

At the time of writing this chapter, the discussion on the immorality of homosexuality was trending on both social media and in the mainstream media. This emerged after a parent in one of the oldest and top Christian schools accused the school management of ignoring the plight of male students who she alleged were being lured into homosexuality by a male teacher (Mukhaye, 2023; *The Independent*, 2023). The school did not officially respond to the allegations but commentary from those close to management suggested that homosexuality was considered a vice in the school and those suspected of being involved in such acts were expelled.

A few weeks later, the mayor of Entebbe Municipality felt compelled to change the colours of one of the props in the newly refurbished children's park, from the rainbow colours to colours that resembled those in the national flag. This followed "public" outcry on Twitter, with people claiming that they were uncomfortable with the rainbow which culturally has come to represent the LGBTQI+ community. "What are we telling our children? That it is okay to be gay?" they asked. Homosexuality is illegal in Uganda and the Penal Code Act prescribes a life sentence for the offence of homosexuality.

From the two examples above, one can argue that the issue of homosexuality is at the heart of the discourse around Uganda's national and cultural identity. Although it would be inaccurate to say that modern Uganda is searching for a national identity, the question on national identity usually arises when the sovereignty and/or the "national culture" is under threat as in the two cases cited above. During such times, the "enormous diversity" seems to become insignificant and the question of what it means to be Ugandan takes centre stage. The discussion is usually carried in the national press, which in this case, has been found to report negatively about issues of homosexuality (Strand, 2011, 2013; Namusoga, 2017).

This chapter discusses the question of Uganda's national identity in light of how two national newspapers framed homosexuality from 2007–2011. The chapter does this by looking at frames and framing from a cultural context, and argues that when faced with a contentious issue, the media apply frames that resonate with the audience in order to remain relevant to the audience. The chapter is divided into two parts. The first part presents the concepts used in the chapter and also creates a context for the discussion. The second part applies these concepts to the issue of homosexuality.

Part 1 Concepts

Framing

Robert Entman provided one of the oldest definitions of framing when he wrote,

> to frame is to select some aspects of a perceived reality and make them more salient in a communicating text in such a way as to promote a particular problem definition, causal interpretation, moral evaluation, and/or treatment recommendation for the item described.
>
> (Entman, 1993, p. 53)

Another way to define a frame is by considering Tankard et al.'s view in which he defines a frame as, "a central organising idea for news content that supplies a context and suggests what the issue is through the use of selection, emphasis, exclusion, and elaboration" (Tankard et al., 1991, p. 11). Additionally, Gamson and Modigliani (1989, p. 3) view a frame as not only a central organising idea, but a device that helps to make sense of relevant events and suggests what the issue is. And so in a way, a frame produces meaning but also goes on to suggest which of the meanings is "truth."

All these definitions suggest that framing is a result of selection, which in turn results in emphasis. Emphasis arises when one creates a context that leads to a specific perception of an issue. Therefore, framing also defines what the issue is as well as the truth about the issue. This chapter adopts Tankard et al.'s definition of framing because it is specific to news content. Additionally, Tankard et al.'s definition emphasises the need to consider the context in which framing takes place because the context determines how members of the society understand or interpret a frame. The context, or the environment, within which a frame operates also determines why certain meanings become dominant over time (Morley, 1976).

Frames that produce a dominant idea are the ones that persist over time and end up producing patterns that organise "cognition, interpretation and presentation of selection, emphasis, and exclusion, by which symbol-handlers routinely organise discourse" (Gitlin, 1980, p. 7). It is important therefore, that frames become part of a society's way of making sense of the world, and help organise diverse information meaningfully into a structure (Reese, 2003). This idea is best demonstrated by the way the Ugandan newspapers are organised into various sections including national news, regional news, sports news and business news, among others. All the news that is reported in a day is placed into one of these categories, thus applying some logic to what is happening around Uganda. And so, it is not surprising that frames make most of what we see, or hear happening around us, intelligible. According to Tuchman (1978), most experiences or information we interact with would remain unintelligible without frames.

When it comes to news, framing is useful for providing the grounds for interconnecting facts. Specifically, a news frame defines what is possible (and therefore what is not) in the presentation of news (Durham, 1998, p. 113). Therefore, news frames play the important role of organising information into news content, especially for stories that involve controversial issues such as homosexuality. Some have even argued that frames enable the media to conceal bias when they are reporting controversies by eliminating some voices and weakening arguments (Tankard, 2003).

Another important point to note is that media frames generally organise the world for both the journalists and their audiences (Gitlin, 1980). They do this when they aid journalists to easily identify and categorise information which they then relay to the audience efficiently. For example, journalists may categorise information as hard news, published in the national news pages or on the front page of the newspaper. The information could also be categorised as health news that appears either in the health pages or in a supplement (Namusoga, 2017).

However, individual members of the audience bring their own frames to a news story and interpret the news story according to those frames. These individual frames can be defined as "mentally stored clusters of ideas that guide an individual's processing of information" (Entman, 1993, p. 53). As such, during coverage of a controversy, the media endeavour to aid the framing process of individuals in order to "help develop a particular conceptualisation of an issue or reorient their thinking about an issue" (Chong & Druckman, 2007, p. 104), and thus maintain the idea of society as "a consensus" built on ideas originating from the shared culture (Hall et al., 1978, p. 55).

In their daily work routines, journalists and other media workers also assume that society is consensual. It is another way they make meaning of social events. Journalists assume that since we all belong to the same society, we share cultural knowledge and therefore have access to the same "maps of meanings" which can be manipulated but which also form part of the common values, interests and concerns that we all endeavour to maintain. Therefore, because of everything we have in common, this view assumes that our perspective on an issue is largely provided by the culture, part of which is the media (Hall et al., 1978). This is important to remember when discussing how the press represent national identity especially during a controversy.

As cultural phenomena, frames have cultural structures, central ideas and are linked to more peripheral concepts that vary in strength and kind (Hertog & McLeod, 2003). For example, myths, narratives, and metaphors are cultural phenomena that are key to frames, and that appeal to one's inner self as a member of society who is proud to identify with the ideals, morals, stories, and definitions of culture. Again, this is crucial to how members of the Ugandan society, including journalists, view an issue like homosexuality, given that most argue against it, saying it is foreign to their culture (Strand, 2011, 2013). Because members of society easily identify the cultural frames, institutions, organisations and individuals assume that members of society share the same frame and base all communication on these shared meanings. As such, when the church pastor pronounces homosexuality unbiblical, the believers in that church easily identify with that position. Likewise, when the media get the sense that the society is opposed to homosexuality, they either reflect this position (Strand, 2011, 2013) or become ambivalent depending on other factors at play such as media ownership.

Frames and/or framing is more effective to culturally articulate individuals because such individuals will easily make the connections between the symbolism and the "myths" (Hertog & McLeod, 2003, p. 141). These cultural resonances make media content appear not only natural but also familiar (Gamson & Modigliani, 1989). These culturally constructed frames are persistent and occur over long periods of time, and with input from a variety of social actors. This means that these frames contain considerable volumes of social knowledge, which makes it almost impossible for new information to alter their meaning (Hertog & McLeod, 2003). And so, when it comes to defining the national identity in light of homosexuality, it is most likely that members of society will contend that it is impossible to be Ugandan and homosexual at the same time (Nyanzi, 2013).

Cultural frames play an important role in defining and resolving social controversies (Hertog & McLeod, 2003). This is because cultural frames define the roles of individuals, groups, organisations and institutions. A frame might also lead to the marginalisation of a group or individual as well as their views, by simply ignoring them (Hertog & McLeod, 2003). For example, part of the reason homosexuality in Uganda, and Africa in general, has met resistance is that the discussions about homosexuality take place within a cultural perspective (Van Zyl, 2011; Nyanzi, 2013); and according to the dominant view in African culture, homosexuality is a taboo (Murray & Roscoe, 1998; Dlamini, 2006; Tamale, 2009). Therefore, the idea of homosexuality as an identity is quite problematic in Africa, in comparison to most parts of the West (Tamale, 2013). From a media perspective, the result has been a near absence of homosexual or pro-homosexual voices in the African media (Muula, 2007; Strand, 2012; Namusoga, 2017), with the exception of South Africa (Cilliers, 2007), which demonstrates how frames eliminate voices and weaken arguments.

Framing, national identity and the press

It has been argued that the media play an important role in telling the national narrative (Hall, 1992). This is achieved through their flagging of the homeland daily when they call out the nation (Billig, 1995) using headlines such as, "Uganda wins gold in the UK." In so doing, the media remind the audience of the currency of the space they occupy which is home and "our" precious homeland. This kind of "language" forms part of the wider discourse of nationalism, national culture and national identity.

It is a daunting task to attempt to describe the Ugandan national culture since it has almost not been documented. However, Reid (2017) paints a picture of some of Uganda's values using the lens of the Ugandan Museum. He writes, "Culture is presented in stasis; decades of new research has (sic) failed to have much impact on the archaeological cross sections, gazed on by countless cohorts of local school children" (Reid, 2017, p. xxii). Here Reid is describing the exhibition at the Uganda Museum which consists of, "three-dimensional scenes of typical village life, and cross-sections of archaeological excavations; the first Luganda-language Bible; musical instruments, spears and bows, and cooking utensils – part of an extended display of 'tribal artefacts'" (Reid, 2017, p. xxii). One could interpret these artefacts as representatives of Uganda's cultural values, which include religion.

From a social constructivist position, the nation is a social construction. Hence, national identities are not inherent but are formed and transformed within and in relation to representation (Hall, 1992). Hall (1992, p. 292) uses the example of being English, arguing that "one knows what it is to be 'English' because of the way 'Englishness' has come to be represented as a set of meanings, by English national culture." National culture is a discourse which helps to construct meanings which influence and organise both our actions and our conceptions of ourselves as nationals of particular nations (Hall, 1992). For example, from surveys carried out by the Pew Research Centre, 99% of Ugandans are opposed to homosexuality (Pew, 2007, 2013). This reflects the Ugandan national culture with regard to the issue of homosexuality. The conceptions of ourselves have come to be naturalised through nationalism which is the ideology by which the world of nations has come to seem natural to the world making it appear as if there could be a world without nations (Billig, 1995, p. 15). As such, it has become natural for everyone to have a national identity. Hall (1992) further argues that national cultures construct identities by producing meanings about the nation with which we can identify. These meanings are contained in stories which are told about the nation, memories which connect its present with its past, and images which are constructed of it, hence the argument that in established nations, people do not generally forget their national identities and that national identity is something "banal" and imagined (Billig, 1995), and only becomes an issue when faced with a crisis (Anderson, 1983).

As special forms of social identities, national identities are produced and reproduced as well as transformed and dismantled discursively (Wodak et al., 1998) and the media play a key role in this process. Furthermore, discursive constructs of nations and national identities primarily emphasise national uniqueness and intra-national uniformity but largely ignore intra-national differences, hence the use of "we" to refer to everyone who is part of a particular identity. For example, from a cultural perspective, most African politicians and religious leaders, and in essence the media, argue that homosexuality is "un-African, a foreign imposition from the West and ungodly," (Vincent & Howell, 2014). Hence, in imagining national singularity and homogeneity, members of a national community simultaneously construct the distinctions between themselves and other nations (Wodak et al., 1998), the reason they use terms such as "us" and "them."

Whereas it appears that Uganda has a national identity (Lepp and Harris, 2008), the general perception is that the country lacks one. For example, the "Ganda ethnic nationalism" (Reid, 2017, p. xxiv) is not only a thing of the pre-independence years when Kabaka Edward Muteesa sought to guarantee Buganda's autonomy after Independence. It comes up quite often such as during the 2021 presidential elections when Buganda voted almost as a block against President Yoweri Museveni. They instead voted for Robert Kyagulanyi Ssentamu, a Muganda, and a popular Opposition leader.

Uganda's ethnic diversity could also contribute significantly to a united feeling of what the national identity is. According to Nassanga (2010) the national media have also to a large extent failed to cater for the interests of all the 53 ethnic groups in Uganda. Moreover, Nassanga contends, in an environment of globalisation and diverse ethnic and cultural identities, national media still have a role to play in the national identification process. In this chapter, national media is taken to mean media that have a national outlook, for example the *New Vision* and *Daily Monitor* newspapers. Just as Billig (1995) observes, the definition of national identity seems to revolve around "unity in diversity" with reference to ethnicity, while ignoring other forms of social identity such as religion, age, gender, social status and locality. This is characteristic of dominant positions on national identity which view the nation as the natural form of political and social organisation (Hobsbawm & Ranger, 1983).

That said, anecdotal evidence points to the likelihood of the national press rallying behind the nation (read national identity) during a controversy. In 2005, Uganda was debating the issue of lifting the constitutional presidential term limit (the so-called third term debate). A scan through the then *The Monitor* newspaper leads to two very interesting headlines: "Protestors condemn Britain, Bob Geldof" and "Calm as anti-third term supporters demonstrate." They were published three days apart on 22 and 25 March 2005 respectively. The first article is what I call the "pro-third term" article and the second one, the "anti-third term" article. What is clear is that *The Monitor* covered both sides of the debate, which is out of character for a newspaper that is largely viewed as an Opposition-leaning newspaper (Kalyegira, 2022). In this case, both articles framed the third term as a Ugandan issue that should be discussed by only Ugandans or Uganda's friends as can be seen from the first headline. In so doing, *The Monitor* decided to cleverly identify as a nationalist newspaper without necessarily abandoning its opposition to anti-democracy tendencies.

To give basis to this claim, Namusoga (2017) found that when it comes to covering controversial issues of a national nature, such as homosexuality, the *Daily Monitor* (formerly *The Monitor*) covers the issue but does so negatively. Namusoga found that while the *Daily Monitor* provided more coverage to issues of homosexuality than *New Vision*, the *Daily Monitor* had more negative stories than *New Vision*. Therefore, just like in the case of the third term scenario, the *Daily Monitor* did not ignore the issue but represented the national and cultural values regarding homosexuality. Homosexuality is illegal in Uganda. Section 145 of the Penal Code Act prescribes life imprisonment for the offence of homosexuality (Ssebaggala, 2011). The Penal Code also categorises homosexual acts as unnatural offences under the "offences against morality" chapter of the law. There was another attempt to further legislate against homosexuality, through the 2014 Anti-Homosexuality Act, but the law was repealed by the Constitutional Court which cited lack of quorum during the debate on the Bill in Parliament in 2009. During the debate on the anti-homosexuality bill, 2009 two national surveys carried out by the Pew Research Institute nearly ten years apart reported that 99% of Ugandans were opposed to homosexuality (Pew Research Centre, 2007, 2013). In May 2023, nearly ten years later, President Museveni assented to the Anti-Homosexuality Bill, 2023, which criminalises homosexuality. And so, the general sentiment is that homosexuality is unwelcome in Uganda, a sentiment that is also reproduced in the national press (Strand, 2011).

The Ugandan press

The Ugandan press is almost naturally national in outlook because the leading newspapers are the two English dailies, *Daily Monitor* and *New Vision*, and the Luganda daily, *Bukedde*, whose circulation and coverage is national. According to the Audit Bureau of Circulation, the daily circulation for the *New Vision* as at 31 March 2016 was 27,367, while that of the *Daily Monitor* was 19,793 (Audit Bureau of Circulation, 2016). The press consists of both government and privately-owned newspapers. The *Daily Monitor* has established itself as an independent newspaper, and has been pitted against *New Vision* when it comes to covering national issues that are contentious. In fact some see the two newspapers as rivals (Moehler & Singh, p. 276). That notwithstanding, a 2011 study by Moehler and Singh found that Ugandans trusted news from government-owned media more than news from private media. *Daily Monitor* is also viewed as very critical to the Government and on several occasions, President Museveni has called *Daily Monitor*, "A very bad newspaper" (Orikunda, 2022).

Additionally, the Ugandan press is influential in many social aspects especially politics (Friedrich-Ebert Stiftung, 2012). In fact "mainstream newspapers in Uganda are [...] the conscience of the political elite" (Lugalambi, 2006, p. 173). It is worth noting that radio is the dominant medium in Uganda. However, it is the same political voices that both print and radio carry (Mwesige, 2004).

New Vision

New Vision was established by the National Resistance Movement government in 1986 as a state-owned newspaper. It is published by the New Vision Printing and Publishing Corporation (or Vision Group), which has since evolved into a multimedia company whose staple includes newspaper, magazine and internet publishing as well as television and radio broadcasting. Vision Group is a publicly listed company and the government is the majority shareholder (The Open Society Initiative for East Africa, 2010). In the earlier years, *New Vision's* journalism was respected, even though it was government-owned (Lugalambi, 2006; Moehler & Singh, 2011), but public opinion seems to be changing lately.

Vision Group also used to publish three other vernacular newspapers, namely, Rupiny (Luo), Etop (Ateso) and Orumuri (Runyankole-Rukiga). However, their publication ceased in the early days of the COVID-19 pandemic, citing unprofitability of the papers (Muhindo, 2022).

Daily Monitor

The Monitor was established in 1992 by a group of six journalists at the now defunct *Weekly Topic*, which was owned by three cabinet ministers at the time. *The Monitor* was bought by the Nation Media Group (NMG) which is based in Nairobi and is listed on the Nairobi Stock Exchange, making it part of a big media empire whose majority shareholder is the Aga Khan Foundation for Economic Development (The Open Society Initiative for East Africa, 2010). The paper was renamed *Daily Monitor* in June 2005. Nation Media Group also owns radio and television stations in Uganda.

Part 2 Application

The press, homosexuality and the Ugandan national identity

In many ways, national identity is considered one of several identities that an individual can assume at any moment. In fact it is often mundane, and probably unnecessarily until one is faced with a challenge to their national identity. To a Ugandan, being Ugandan is something they hardly think about, because of the way Ugandanness has been constructed. For example, an ordinary Ugandan would most likely tell another Ugandan's ethnicity simply using their surname. The name Bukenya suggests that one is a Muganda, while Achan would mean that that person is from one of the Luo ethnic groups. An English name would mean that one is most likely a Christian. All this is not obvious when one travels to Europe or the United States of America. It is at such a time that one's national identity comes to the fore and suddenly they might have to explain what their surname signifies and why they have an English first name. They find themselves having to defend their national identity, so to speak. But that is because ideally, normally, we take so much for granted until something challenges our understanding of an issue.

Likewise, in Africa, the discussion of homosexuality usually takes place in the cultural realm where the debate is about whether homosexuality is un-African and a Western imposition (Cock, 2003; Van Zyl, 2011; Nyanzi, 2013). Political and religious leaders are the main drivers of this cultural view (Reddy, 2002; Stobie, 2003). In addition, most of the legislation against homosexuality in Africa is informed by this view (Nagadya & Morgan, 2005). As such, homosexuality is viewed as unnatural, un-African and ungodly (Vincent & Howell, 2014).

To support their arguments, proponents of this view contend that Africans are heterosexual by nature (Dlamini, 2006; Epprecht, 2008; Nyanzi, 2013), which implies that they are productive just as an African marriage is expected to be, while homosexual couples are not productive (Lewis, 2011; Sadgrove et al., 2012). According to Nyanzi (2013, p. 954) this is because the traditional African family as imagined culturally is "identified and named as characteristically heterosexual."

On their part those opposed to the cultural view question the criteria used to homogenise the African traditional family, in view of the ethnic, religious and cultural diversity in most African societies (Nyanzi, 2013, p. 953). Others even argue that there are multiple African sexualities and homosexuality is just one of them, making it a futile attempt to bunch all sexual practices in Africa as one (Tamale, 2011).

Closely related to the cultural view is the religious perspective especially when it comes to Africa (Ward, 2015). Religion is a key determinant of individuals' attitudes towards homosexuality (Olson et al., 2006; Rowatt et al., 2006). Most religions condemn homosexuality and consider it unnatural, ungodly, and impure (Yip, 2005).

According to Ward (2013), the Bible is the most cited religious book when discussing homosexuality issues. This is because the Old Testament Bible teachings, which prescribe death for homosexuality in Leviticus 20:13, are some of the oldest taboos on homosexuality (Sullivan, 2003). In fact, some studies found that newspaper readers on either side of the debate, supported or rejected homosexuality while using the Bible to emphasise their point (Muula, 2007; Rojas-Lizana, 2011).

Nonetheless, Ward (2013) argues that African traditional religion plays a critical role in the socialisation process, including sexuality issues. He attributes the current hostility to homosexuality in Uganda to politicians, religious leaders and the press who are the public opinion influencers. Worth noting is that the religious leaders in Uganda supported the 2009 anti-homosexuality bill, hence contributing to the negative perceptions of homosexuality in Uganda (Kaoma, 2009; Englander, 2011). Ward (2013) further argues that historically, the Uganda society was tolerant towards homosexuality.

It is this last point that links the idea of homosexuality to the Uganda national identity. Previous historical studies such as Murray and Roscoe (1998) have laboured to demonstrate that contrary to popular opinion that homosexuality was imported into Africa by the colonialists, it already existed in society prior to the coming of the colonialists. Moreover, a 2013 ethnographic study by Stella Nyanzi also found that some women who lived in rural Uganda and had never travelled abroad (locally or internationally) identified as lesbians. Nyanzi argues that that is proof that homosexuality is indigenous to Uganda.

As such, the question becomes, to be or not to be Ugandan? The foregoing discussion suggests that there is opposition to people who identify as both African/Ugandan and homosexual. From the perspective of most politicians and religious leaders, one cannot be both because it is taboo, un-African, unnatural and ungodly. It is important therefore to see how these perspectives play(ed) out in Uganda's press.

Namusoga (2017) examined how *New Vision* and the *Daily Monitor* framed homosexuality before the introduction of the anti-homosexuality bill, at the discussion of the bill, and after the introduction of the bill, a period that spanned the years 2007–2011. She identified the frames that the two newspapers used in their coverage of homosexuality, as well as the changing patterns in reporting homosexuality. Her frame analysis also studied, among other variables, the placement of the news stories in the newspaper pages. Placement meant the various sections in which the two newspapers are divided, namely, the front page, national news, regional news, international/foreign news, sports, business, supplements, opinion and editorial and letter to the editor. Namusoga's (2017) analysis described above shows that *New Vision* and the *Daily Monitor* framed homosexuality firstly as a human rights issue and secondly as a culture/religion issue as seen in Tables 11.1 and 11.2.

The analysis in this chapter focuses on the culture/religion frames. This is important when one considers that regardless of the topic at hand (for example, the anti-homosexuality bill or homosexual marriage), the culture and religious frames dominate press coverage, alongside the human rights frame (see Table 11.3). This shows how deep the Ugandan cultural and religious values are, and most likely the extent to which they influence the perceptions towards homosexuality.

Furthermore, the two newspapers placed the majority of their stories on homosexuality in their national pages as seen in Table 11.3. This means that the two newspapers considered homosexuality a national issue as opposed to a regional or even international issue. According to Namusoga (2017), this also meant that by framing homosexuality as a national issue, *New Vision* and the *Daily Monitor* opened it up to the national level, and as a result, distanced the rural Ugandan at the grassroots from the discussion. This points to the argument by those opposed to homosexuality that homosexuality as it is today is an elite lifestyle that the Anglican man or woman in the village knows nothing about, and therefore has little to contribute in a debate such as this (Nyanzi, 2013; Tamale, 2013).

So far, it is possible to see that the framing by *New Vision* and the *Daily Monitor* has set the boundaries for the discussion on homosexuality. These boundaries are that homosexuality is a cultural issue that is to be discussed at the national level. The framing also indicates that by viewing homosexuality from a cultural perspective, which in Africa and Uganda is generally opposed to homosexuality, the Ugandan national identity does not include homosexuality. This is even more evident when one considers that during the period

Table 11.1 Frequency of frames used by *New Vision* and *Daily Monitor*

Frames	Frequency	%
Human Rights	104	31.7
Crime	55	16.8
Culture	53	16.2
Religion	42	12.8
Legislation	39	11.9
Medicine	34	10.4
Total	328	100

Source: Namusoga (2017)

Table 11.2 The placement of items

Placement of the item	Count	%
Front page	25	7.6
National news	115	35.1
Regional news	34	10.4
International news/Africa	39	11.9
Sports page	4	1.2
Business page	1	0.3
Supplements	26	7.9
Opinion & Editorial (OpEd)	51	15.5
Letter to the editor	33	10.1
Total	328	100

Source: Namusoga (2017)

Table 11.3 Frames before and after the introduction of the bill

	Before the bill		Introduction of the bill		After the bill		
	(2007 & 2008)		(2009)		(2010 & 2011)		
Frames	Count	%	Count	%	Count	%	Total
Human rights	60	34.5	27	27.6	18	32.7	105
Culture	34	19.5	11	11.2	6	10.9	51
Religion	29	16.7	10	10.2	3	5.5	42
Crime	22	12.6	23	23.5	10	18.2	55
Medicine	18	10.3	13	13.3	4	7.3	35
Legislation	11	6.3	14	14.3	14	25.5	40
Total	174	100	98	100	55	100	328

Source: Namusoga (2017)

under consideration, the majority of the sources used in both newspapers were Ugandan, not even African (Namusoga, 2017) (see Table 11.4). Furthermore, homosexuals hardly featured as sources (Namusoga, 2017). In other words, they have no business being Ugandan.

This framing also demonstrates the consensual nature of society that the media assume when reporting a controversial issue such as homosexuality. This is because the reporting as described above reflects the Ugandan society's opposition to homosexuality as reported in the national surveys. And so, I argue that *New Vision* and the *Daily Monitor* constructed the Ugandan national identity as one that excludes homosexuals. By relying mostly on Ugandan sources, and generally excluding homosexuals in their

Table 11.4 Combined distribution of sources (geographically) for both *New Vision* and the *Daily Monitor*

Source	Count	%
Ugandan	241	73.6
Other	67	20.4
African	20	6.0
Total	328	100

Source: Namusoga (2017)

reports, while at the same time framing this as a cultural and national issue, the media seem to be saying, "it is Ugandans who speak for and about Uganda, and you, homosexuals, are not Ugandans since our national culture does not include you."

Conclusion

National identity is one of many identities that one assumes as a citizen of a country. This identity is constructed by the national culture, which is responsible for setting the terms for identifying as a national of a given country. The media, specifically the press, play a critical role in constructing this national identity. In the context of the Ugandan national culture, national identity does not include being a homosexual as reflected in the country's laws, the citizens' attitudes and the media coverage of homosexuality. Coverage shows the prominence of the cultural/religion frames, which reflect a negative attitude to homosexuality in Uganda. Furthermore, homosexuals are rarely sources, and coverage frames homosexuality as a national issue by placing it on the national pages. Therefore, to discuss homosexuality in the Ugandan context is to discuss the issue of national identity.

References

Anderson, B. 1983. *Imagined Communities*. London: Verso
Audit Bureau of Circulation Figures. 2016. Circulation figures for January to March 2016.
Billig, M. 1995. *Banal Nationalism*. London: Sage
Chong, D., & Druckman, J.N. 2007. A theory of framing and opinion formation in competitive elite environments. *Journal of Communication*, 57, 99–118.
Cilliers, C. 2007. Media and sexual orientation: The portrayal of gays and lesbians. In P.J. Fourie (ed.) *Media Studies volume 2: Policy, Management and Media Representation*. Cape Town: Juta.
Cock, J. 2003. Engendering gay and lesbian rights: The equality clause in the South African Constitution. *Women's Studies International Forum*, 26(1), 35–45.

Dlamini, B. 2006. Homosexuality in the African context. *Agenda: Empowering Women for Gender Equity*, 2(3), 128–136.

Durham, F.D. 1998. News frames as social narratives: TWA flight 800. *Journal of Communication*, 48, 101–117.

Englander, D. 2011. Protecting the human rights of LGBT people in Uganda in the wake of Uganda's anti-homosexuality bill, 2009. *Emory International Law Review*, 25(3), 1263–1316.

Entman, R. 1993. Framing: Toward clarification of a fractured paradigm. *Journal of Communication*, 43(4), 51–58.

Epprecht, M. 2008. *Heterosexual Africa? The History of an Idea from the Age of Exploration to the Age of AIDS*. Athens, Ohio: Ohio University Press.

Freidrich-Ebert-Stiftung. 2012. African media barometer: The first home-grown analysis of the media landscape in Africa, Uganda 2012. [Online]. Available from: http://library.fes.de/pdf-files/bueros/africa-media/09427.pdf [Accessed 14 June 2014].

Gamson, W.A., & Modigliani, A. 1989. Media discourse and public opinion on nuclear power: A constructionist approach. *American Journal of Sociology*, 95, 1–37.

Gitlin, T. 1980. *The Whole World Is Watching: Mass Media in The Making and Unmaking of the New Left*. Berkeley: University of California Press.

Hall, S., Critcher, C., Jefferson, T., Clarke, J., & Roberts, B. 1978. *Policing the Crisis: Mugging, the State and Law and Order*. London: Palgrave Macmillan.

Hall, S. 1992. The question of cultural identity. In S. Hall, et al. (eds), *Modernity and its Features* (pp. 274–325). Cambridge: Polity Press.

Hertog, J.K., & McLeod, D.M. 2003. A multi-perspectival approach to framing analysis: A field guide. In S. Reese, O.H. Gandy, & A.E. Grant (eds), *Framing Public Life: Perspectives on Media and our Understanding of the Social World*. Mahwah, New Jersey: Lawrence Erlbaum Associates.

Hobsbawm, E., & Ranger, T. (eds) 1983. *The Invention of Tradition*. New York: Cambridge University Press.

Kalyegira, T. 2022. Monitor at 30: A journey of endurance, innovation and bold news reporting. *Daily Monitor*.

Kaoma, K. 2009. *Globalising the Culture Wars: American Conservatives, African Churches and Homophobia*. Somerville: Political Research Associates.

Kizito, K. 2017. Bequeathed legacies: Colonialism and state-led homophobia in Uganda. *Surveillance & Society*, 15(3/4), 567–572.

Lepp, A., & Harris, J. 2008. Tourism and national identity in Uganda. *International Journal of Tourism Research*, 10(6), 525–536.

Lewis, D. 2011. Representing African sexualities. In S. Tamale (ed.), *African Sexualities: A Reader*. Cape Town: Pambazuka.

Lugalambi, G.W. 2006. An assessment of democratic deliberation in Uganda: A case study of the framing of key political issues in the press. Unpublished PhD thesis. Pennsylvania State University.

Moehler, D.C., & Singh, N. 2011. Whose news do you trust? Explaining trust in private versus public media in Africa. *Political Research Quarterly*, 64(2), 276–292.

Morley, D. 1976. Industrial conflict and the mass media. *Sociological Review*, 24, 245–268.

Muhindo, C. 2020. Covid-19 sounds the death knell for local language newspapers. ACME. [Online]. Available from https://acme-ug.org/2020/06/02/covid-19-sounds-the-death-knell-for-local-language-newspapers/ [Accessed 6 February 2023].

Mukhaye, D. 2023, February 16. Ministry probes sexual misconduct in schools. *Daily Monitor*. Available from www.monitor.co.ug/uganda/news/national/ministry-probes-sexual-misconduct-in-schools-4125876 [Accessed 28 June 2023].

Murray, S.O., & Roscoe, W. 1998. Africa and African homosexualities: An introduction. In S.O. Murray & W. Roscoe (eds), *Boy Wives and Female Husbands: Studies of African Homosexualities*. New York: St Martin's Press.

Muula, A.S. 2007. Perceptions about men having sex with men in southern Africa. *Croat Med*, 48, 398–404.

Mwesige, P. 2014. Museveni, NRM misread, distorted scientific report on homosexuality. [Online] available from www.acme-ug.org/index.php/museveni-nrm-misread-distorted-scientific-report-homosexuality/ [Accessed 30 May 2014].

Nagadya, M. and Morgan, R. 2005. "Some Say I am a hermaphrodite just because I put on Trousers": Lesbians and tommy boys in Kampala, Uganda. In R. Morgan, & S. Wieringa (eds.) *Tommy boys, lesbian wives and ancestral wives: Female same-sex practices in Africa*. Johannesburg: Jacana Media.

Namusoga, S. 2017. The Framing of Homosexuality by Two Ugandan Newspapers: An Analysis of the New Vision and Daily Monitor, PhD thesis, University of KwaZulu-Natal.

Nassanga, L.G. 2010. Media and national identity: Should national media be relegated to the backseat? In K. Njogu, K. Ngeta, & M. Wanjau (eds), *Ethnic Diversity in Eastern Africa: Opportunities and Challenges* (pp. 141–160). Twaweza Communications. https://doi.org/10.2307/j.ctvk3gp8v.14

Nyanzi, S. 2013. Dismantling reified African culture through localised homosexualities in Uganda. *Culture, Health and Sexuality: An International Journal for Research, Intervention and Care*, 15(8), 952–967.

Olson, R.R., Cadge, W., & Harrison, J.T. 2006. Religion and public opinion about same-sex marriage. *Social Science Quarterly*, 87, 340–360.

Orikunda, S.E. 2022. Daily Monitor's 30 years of negativity against govt. *The Observer* [Online]. Available from: https://observer.ug/viewpoint/74608-daily-monitor-s-30-years-of-negativity-against-govt [Accessed 6 February 2023].

Pew Research Centre. 2007. World publics welcome global trade – But not immigration. [Online]. Available from www.pewglobal.org/2007/10/04/world-publics-welcome-global-trade-but-not-immigration/ [Accessed 19 May 2015].

Pew Research Centre. 2013. The global divide on homosexuality: Greater acceptance in more secular and affluent countries. [Online]. Available from www.pewglobal.org/files/2013/06/Pew-Global-Attitudes-Homosexuality-Report-FINAL-JUNE-4-2013.pdf [Accessed 30 May 2014].

Reddy, V. 2002. Perverts and sodomites: Homophobia as hate speech in Africa. *Southern African Linguistics Applied Language Studies*, 20(3), 163–175.

Reese, S. 2003. Prologue: Framing public life. A bridging model for media research. In S. Reese, O.H. Gandy & A. Grant (eds), *Framing Public Life: Perspectives on*

Media and Our Understanding of the Social World. Mahwah, New Jersey: Lawrence Erlbaum Associates.

Reid, R.J. 2017. *A History of Modern Uganda.* Cambridge: Cambridge University Press.

Rojas-Lizana, I. 2011. Justifying and condemning sexual discrimination in everyday discourse: Letters to the editor in the Australian press. *Journal of Pragmatics,* 43(2011), 663–676.

Rowatt, W., Tsang, J.A., Kelly, J., La Martina, B., McCullers, M., & McKinley, A. 2006. Associations between religious personality dimensions and implicit homosexual prejudice. *Journal for the Scientific Study of Religion,* 3, 397–406.

Sadgrove, J., Vanderbeck, R.M., Andersson, J., Valentine, G., & Ward, K. 2012. Morality plays and money matters: Towards a situated understanding of the politics of homosexuality in Uganda. *The Journal of Modern African Studies,* 50(1), 103–129.

Ssebaggala, R. 2011. Straight talk on the gay question in Uganda. *Transition: An international Review,* 106, B-44–B-57.

Stobie, C. 2003. Reading bisexualities from a South African perspective. *Journal of Bisexuality,* 3(1), 33–52.

Strand, C. 2011. Kill Bill! Ugandan human rights organisations' attempts to influence the media's coverage of the Anti-Homosexuality Bill. *Culture, Health and Sexuality,* 13(8), 917–931.

Strand, C. 2012. Homophobia as a barrier to comprehensive media coverage of the Uganda Anti-Homosexual Bill. *Journal of Homosexuality,* 59(4), 564–579.

Strand, C. 2013. The rise and fall of a contentious social policy option – narratives around the Ugandan Anti-Homosexuality Bill in the domestic press. *Journal of African Media Studies,* 5(3), 275–294

Sullivan, M.K. 2003. Homophobia, history and homosexuality: Trends for sexual minorities. *Journal of Human Behaviour in the Social Environment,* 8(2–3), 1–13.

Tamale, S. 2009. A human rights impact assessment of the Ugandan anti-homosexuality bill, 2009. *The Equal Rights Review,* 4, 49–57.

Tamale, S. 2011. Introduction. In S. Tamale (ed.) *African Sexualities: A Reader.* Cape Town: Pambazuka.

Tamale, S. 2013. Confronting the politics of nonconforming sexualities in Africa. *African Studies Review,* 56(2), 31–45. doi:10.1017/asr.2013.40

Tankard, J.W., Hendrickson, L., Silberman, J., Bliss, K., & Ghanem, S. (1991). Media frames: Approaches to conceptualisation and measurement. Paper presented to *the Association for Education in Journalism and Mass Communication,* Boston.

Tankard, J.W. 2003. The empirical approach to the study of media framing. In. S. Reese; O.H. Gandy; and A.E. Grant (eds.) *Framing Public Life: Perspectives on Media and Our Understanding of the Social World.* Mahwah, New Jersey: Lawrence Erlbaum Associates.

The Independent. 2023. Namirembe probe homosexuality claims at King's College Budo. Available from www.independent.co.ug/namirembe-probe-homosexuality-claims-at-kings-college-budo/ [Accessed 28 June 2023].

The Open Society Initiative for East Africa. 2010. *On Air: Uganda.* Nairobi, Kenya: The open society initiative for East Africa.

Tuchman, G. 1978. Making news: A study in the construction of reality. New York: Free Press.

Van Zyl, M. 2011. Are same-sex marriages unAfrican? Same-sex relationships and belonging in post-apartheid South Africa. *Journal of Social Issues*, 67(2), 335–357.

Vincent, L., & Howell, S. 2014. 'Unnatural', 'Un-African' and 'Ungodly': Homophobic discourse in democratic South Africa. *Sexualities*, 17(4), 472–483.

Ward, K. 2013. Religious institutions and actors and religious attitudes to homosexual rights: South Africa and Uganda. *Human Rights, Sexual Orientation and Gender Identity in the Commonwealth: Struggles for decriminalisation and change*, 2013, 409–427.

Ward, K. 2015. The role of the Anglican and Catholic Churches in Uganda in public discourse on homosexuality and ethics. *Journal of Eastern African Studies*, 9(1), 127–144.

Wodak, R. et al. 1998. *The Discursive Construction of National Identity*. Edinburgh: Edinburgh University Press.

Yip, A. 2005. Queering religious texts: An exploration of British non-heterosexual Christians' and Muslims' strategy of constructing sexuality affirming hermeneutics. *Sociology BSA Publications Ltd.*, 39(1), 47–65.

12 Queering the Game

Policy, Power and the Mediation of Intersex Athletes in Sub-Saharan Africa

Tammy Rae Matthews

Foucault (1978) dissects the specific historical dynamics of power and its social significance. He writes that analyzing power relations is central to critiquing patriarchal social structures that result in marginalized groups' subordination, repression, and othering (Foucault, 1978). Foucault's treatment of the relations of power and body stimulated extensive activist interest. Queer theory epitomizes fluidity reminiscent of Foucault's (1982) conceptual journey classifying power (Foucault, 1982) and supplies a framework to queer the most organizing aspect of sports: sex.

Media can contradict or reinforce social structures. Media outlets bestow power onto athletic figures by prominently featuring them. This power acquisition is vital for representation and self-efficacy. Sport media could formulate attitudes or judgments about intersex athletes. Thus, media should ethically cover the intersex community.

Sub-Saharan African countries are at the forefront of the debate on intersex athletes. At the summer Tokyo 2020 Olympics, held in 2021 due to COVID-19, World Athletics disqualified two Namibian track and field runners – Christine Mboma and Beatrice Masilingi – due to naturally high testosterone levels and banned them from running in the 400-meter to 1,600-meter races. Their story forged a gateway for the global press to deliberate the controversy surrounding intersex athletes. Traditionally, sport organizations exploit sex-based distinctions to justify forced segregation in a biopolitical attempt to assert power over athletes (Carlson, 2005).

High testosterone testing occurrences disproportionately affect women from Africa and South Asia (Adom-Aboagye, 2021). The appearance of women with high testosterone coming from these areas is likely due to more women from these regions being identified for sex testing by athletics officials (Karkazis & Jordan-Young, 2018). This issue raises two points that lack clarity and have not been adequately explored (Adom-Aboagye, 2021). First, why do many people believe testosterone levels seemingly differ among women of color from specific geographic regions? Second, "What this has led to, is the appearance of World Athletics 'targeting'

DOI: 10.4324/9781003352907-15

African women, based on their supposed masculine features, once they start excelling on the global stage" (Adom-Aboagye, 2021). This targeting increases if the athletes are from marginalized backgrounds.

Media platforms can be a space for activism and social change. Sport media can help queer the social and scientific justifications engrained in the sex-binary structure. African media have power to reconstruct ideas about identity by telling the continent's stories about intersexuality in sport. This chapter addresses how voices in Namibia media report on or perhaps challenge the hegemonic governing order of intersexual discrimination in sport. African media could use signs (Saussure, 1916) to frame (Entman, 1993) conversations about intersex athletes in ways that generate an increasingly inclusive media environment. In addition, this exploratory oral history study, facilitated by semi-structured interviews from two field visits: June–July 2017 and April–May 2021, addresses Namibian media's assessment of intersexuality in sport. Oral history, the archeology of storytelling, documents lived experience. Recalling a memory is an amorous gesture (Rodríguez, 2014) toward history.

Language, Intersexuality, and Sovereignty

Linguistic signs (Saussure, 1916) function as representations and connect to culture. Saussure (1916) says that signs are arbitrary, which is "a radical concept because it proposes the autonomy of language in relation to reality" (Chandler, 2016, p. 27). A sign has a two-part model: signifier (sign's form, such as spoken or written) and signified (a concept the sign represents) (Saussure, 1916).

Language not only has power; it also dictates experience. Language is a cultural resource (Duranti, 1997). Linguistic determinism (Hickmann, 2000) explains the social significance of changing language. It postulates that language sways thinking and suggests that thinking outside language's boundaries is unfeasible. For example, if a language does not have a word for "love," then the concept of love does not exist for those who speak the language. Similarly, if a language does not have a word for "intersex," then "intersex" appears to not exist to that population that speaks the language. Linguistic determinism endorses that language might codetermine or fully determine nonlinguistic behavior such as memory, perception, categorization, and thinking (Hickmann, 2000).

English is Namibia's official language, and its institutionalization is rooted in a colonial past (Frydman, 2011). I conducted interviews in English. Some narrators spoke fluent English. Other interviews highlighted my language barrier. Oral historians and journalists who speak multiple languages can intimately connect with more people. African media practitioners should capitalize on this privilege by interviewing and documenting oral histories from non-English-speaking, especially Indigenous, peoples. Academic research needs these documented viewpoints, and progressive scholarly journals prioritize these perspectives. Recording perspectives on gender and sex – specifically intersexuality – in athletics from all African communities would exceedingly benefit sports research, public-facing knowledge, and inclusion.

The words "sex" and "gender" have discrete definitions despite often used interchangeably (Nordqvist, 2015). Gender refers to socially constructed roles, behaviors, activities, and attributes that a given society considers appropriate for a particular sex (Butler, 1988). Gender is a construct. Gender and sexuality are fluid (Butler, 1990). Alternatively, sex is a biological status signifying an individual's physical, physiological, chromosomal, genetic, and anatomical composition used to classify bodies based on socio-cultural concepts of physiology (Beauvoir, 1949). A person could be one of three sexes: intersex, female, or male.

> Nature presents us with sex anatomy spectrums. Breasts, penises, clitorises, scrotums, labia, gonads – all of these vary in size and shape and morphology. So-called "sex" chromosomes can vary quite a bit, too. But in human cultures, sex categories get simplified into male, female, and sometimes intersex, in order to simplify social interactions, express what we know and feel, and maintain order.
>
> (Intersex Society of North America, 2008)

Multifarious sequences of physiological and genetic structures – including hormones, chromosomes, internal and external reproduction organs, and secondary sex characteristics – manifest in bodies (Lucas-Carr & Krane, 2011; interACT: Advocates for Intersex Youth, 2021). People are born intersex or develop characteristics at an early age, and many might never know they are intersex. Intersex traits generally do not impact a person's daily life. Traits can be revealed and contested in highly competitive sporting spaces.

The fundamental question is thus: Who prescribes the parameters of the sex spectrum? Who decides the boundaries of what is "intersex," "female," and "male" biologically? The answer is humans. "Humans decide whether a person with XXY chromosomes or XY chromosomes and androgen insensitivity will count as intersex" (Intersex Society of North America, 2008). No ancient sea scrolls outline testosterone tiers for the "intersex," "female," and "male" categorizations. As the Intersex Society of North America wrote more than 20 years ago: "Nature doesn't decide where the category of 'male' ends and the category of 'intersex' begins, or where the category of 'intersex' ends and the category of 'female' begins. Humans decide" (Intersex Society of North America, 2008). Who, among the humans, is the decisive authority? Medical providers have authority, and many people privilege doctors' opinions.

As mentioned, not all intersex people have traits in organs, and also queer theory endorses the beauty intrinsically in body diversity. Historically, medical providers often favor surgery when intersex traits physically manifest in organs (interACT: Advocates for Intersex Youth, 2021). Parents have legal agency and power, too. Either way, infants lose future agency when someone publicly imposes a sexual identity and life-altering surgery on them without consent. Doctors or parents might declare that an infant is one of the three sexes that does not match the child's reality. "As these children are usually in the first year of life when these interventions take place, there is no possibility of them understanding the decisions being made about their attributed identities and bodies" (Paechter, 2021, p. 847). Infants cannot legally consent, so allowing children to declare their sex and gender when emotionally and developmentally ready is moral, ethical, and just.

A further concern arises for children with intersex traits assigned as females. "Girls are generally expected to be protected from female genital mutilation (FGM), which means that it is banned in most jurisdictions" (Paechter, 2021, p. 847). The United Nations Convention on the Rights of the Child (UNCRC) and the UN Convention on the Elimination of All Forms of Discrimination Against Women focus on girls' rights. "Intersex operations on babies assigned female, however, while similar in character, involving such treatment as partial or entire excision of the clitoris, are not usually considered to be FGM, and are not usually covered by anti-FGM legislation" (Paechter, 2021, p. 847).

> For rhetorical and legal purposes, this framing serves a point: intersex children's bodies are constructed as female – literally – on the operating table, but not as female for the purposes of FGM law. The same doctor should not be allowed to assign a child female to claim the too-large clitoris must be reduced to a more "feminine" size, and then be insulated from prosecution under a law designed to prevent clitoral cutting for social reasons.
>
> (Fraser, 2016, p. 69)

Fraser (2016) further says that these types of surgeries cause the type of harm that the FGM laws strive to prevent. "It therefore appears that, even as many intersex children are assigned female, they are at the same time refused the health protections that should be afforded to them as females. Such contradictions are clearly problematic" (Paechter, 2021, p. 847). Sandberg (2015) argues that current medical practice constitutes an intervention into the physical integrity of the child, from which the child has a right to be protected unless such intervention is medically necessary. Since it has been established that this treatment is not medically necessary, at least at the early stages of a child's life, the parents have no right to consent to it.

(Sandberg, 2015, p. 349)

Therefore, doctors "should not carry out any interventions on intersex children, whether surgical or endocrinal, that are not focused solely on addressing medical rather than social needs" (Paechter, 2021, p. 850). Doctors should postpone any unnecessary medical intervention until the child can consent. The child should be at an age to understand what is involved and have a say about what is happening to their body; the treatment is serious and personal, and performing the surgery without their consent violates the child's right to self-determination (Sandberg, 2015). Many intersex adults are displeased about their childhood surgery (Fraser, 2016). "Early surgical intervention forecloses such decisions by removing the flesh that could be used to make them happen, as well as preventing the child from exploring and understanding their body as it is" (Paechter, 2021, p. 850). Researchers promote "training of professionals as well as the need for investigation of violations and redress for the victims" (Sandberg, 2015, p. 352). Discourse on intersexuality allows journalists and academics to question these intricacies in conversations about body sovereignty, autonomy, and self-determination.

Foucault considers how non-discursive practices influence discourse (Rabinow, 1984) through a sign's signifier and what it signified (Saussure, 1916). Discourse is not isolated from the social and cultural practices surrounding it (Rabinow, 1984). Repeated sign exposure can etch framed messages in semantic memory (Rada & Wulfemeyer, 2005), which is "general knowledge about the world" (Squire, Knowlton, & Musen, 1993, p. 459). Topics media ignore, thus, do not ingrain in memory (Entman, 1993). Journalists must consider their coverage of the intersex population because language and media exude power. Operations of intersex discourses could formulate knowledge. A media guide published by interACT, an intersex youth activism organization, helps reporters cover the intersex community. All media practitioners and consumers should download this guide at: https://secureservercdn.net/198.71.233.216/7np.6b9. myftpupload.com/wp-content/uploads/2017/01/INTERSEX-MEDIAGUIDE-interACT.pdf. It details how, for example, the word "hermaphrodite" is "outdated," "medically inaccurate," and "derogatory" (interACT: Advocates for Intersex Youth, 2022). Instead, use the following phrases: "Susan is an intersex person," "Susan is intersex," "Intersex people are …," and

"People who are intersex ..." (interACT: Advocates for Intersex Youth, 2022). In addition, do not use the phrase "Disorders of Sex Development (DSD)." Some advocates opt to replace "disorders" with "differences," but the guide says the intersex community gravitates toward the exclusive use of "intersex." In any instance, honor an individual's self-determined terminology choice (interACT: Advocates for Intersex Youth, 2022) to foster the erotics of sovereignty (Rifkin, 2011). Media using improper language in self-formation is a gesture away from social justice.

Homonationalism (Puar, 2007) and trans(homo)nationalism (Puar, 2015) is the naming of how neoliberal nation-states engage in institutional policies and how the public performs them. Their agendas reinforce heteronormativity, social order, and nationalism. Honoring the erotics of sovereignty (Rifkin, 2011) is a tool for decolonization. Decolonization "partially entails a changed understanding of the relation between *sexuality* and *sovereignty*, in which the former does not serve as a basis for exiling people from inclusion in the latter" (Rifkin, 2011, p. 174). Healing Native sexual desires after a long history of suppression and the institution of trans(homo)nationalism (Puar, 2015) is erotic (Rifkin, 2011). Embracing identity fluidity found within many Indigenous populations supports sovereignty. Foucault's chief concern focuses on how humans induce active self-formation (Rabinow, 1984), a dynamic and complicated genealogy situated through bodies and gestures (Rodríguez, 2014). Foucault asks scholars to search for the "margins, gaps, and locations on and through the body where agency can be found" (hooks, 1992, p. 116), and sport is all about mastering body agency. Humans should be able to self-determine their existence without fear of social or political prosecution.

Media on Namibian Intersex Athletes

Time and place structure identities (Halberstam, 2005). As assemblage (Puar, 2007) illustrates, spaces in time impact identity marginalization. Despite existing during the same time in history, the experiences of LGBTQI+ athletes from Africa and Namibia specifically vastly differ from the experience of LGBTQI+ athletes from other continents and countries. Namibia is in southwestern Africa. Angola and Zambia border it on the north, Botswana on the east, South Africa on the south, and the Atlantic Ocean on the west. Namibia's vast terrain, covering approximately 318,695 square miles, moves from semi-arid mountains and plateaus to coastal deserts (Frydman, 2011). Namibia has a prominent media system "conducive to the free exercise of journalism" due to the "political and legislative environment" (Reporters Without Borders, 2023). In 2022,

Reporters Without Borders (2023) – (Reporters Sans Frontières in French or RSF) – ranked Namibia 18th out of 180 countries on the World Press Freedom Index. Namibia's largest city and capital is Windhoek, and the anniversary of the Declaration of Windhoek, May 3, is World Press Freedom Day. "Freedom of the press is firmly anchored in Namibia" (Reporters Without Borders, 2023).

The oral history methodology is in line with many ideals of journalism. Researchers intertwine theory and practice in oral history. Indeed, it was feminist oral historians – by a framework of reflexivity, inclusivity, and an analysis of social inter-relations – who embraced the shared authority (Frisch, 1990). "Oral history's sharing of authority places the narrator on equal footing within storytelling and interpretation with the oral historian" (Ryan, 2020, p. 58). I adhere to the OHA Principles and Best Practices for engaging in oral history. The code outlines the principles of rigorous oral history research (Oral History Association, 2018), which includes engaging in thoughtful and productive conversations designed not to harm but rather work to secure responses that are beyond the superficial while encouraging the subjects to respond to questions in their own ways and openly reflect their concerns. In 2017 and 2021, I interviewed a Namibian sports reporter and editor, Emmanuel Johannes[1] (EJ), based in Windhoek. On May 7, 2021, I asked him about the prominence of conversations about LGBTQI+ people in sport.

EJ: It hasn't flared up, so to speak, in sports yet. It might in the future. I-I-I haven't come across anyone who wants to come out and they are afraid or any story relating to that. Um, at the moment, it's still a bit hush-hush. I don't think a lot of, ah, guys or girls really, um, feel as if they're being discriminated against because of their preferences.

Johannes could not have known that, just a few months later, the conversation about Namibian intersex athletes would flare internationally. In our interview, he continued.

EJ: I think the more, the more exposure people get and the more they want people to know them for who they are, that's when it comes out, and you, you are most likely to say, "Look, I identify as so-and-so, so please treat me as such."

Foucault says discourse (archaeology) and practices (genealogy) disseminate power (Dreyfus & Rabinow, 1982). Sport is a practice. Genealogy claims to be descriptive, rather than critical, about practices. It shows how the sovereign, such as media and coaches, instill power into athletes through the practice of sport participation. The power of self-formation has an active genealogy situated through bodies, and sport can help manifest further power. Discursive representations organize the athletes' experience and the audience's knowledge. Circulating strong opinions based on history and positionality has fervent consequences as well.

EJ: What's interesting, though, is you still find people making silly comments, like of the girls who are, those two girls I mentioned earlier, they are really very athletically built, so ...

TM: They're athletes.

"Those two" are the runners Mboma and Masilingi, whose story became a worldwide intersex controversy during the summer 2020 Tokyo Olympics. On May 7, 2021, Johannes said:

EJ: We have two girls who are really doing very well in athletics. At some point, they were the world leaders with their times: two teenagers.

TM: Is it?

EJ: They are 400-meter runners. One is Beatrice, and the other is, um, what's her name? Christine.

I use "gesture" (Rodríguez, 2014) to frame the experience of Masilingi and Mboma in their literal gesture of physical movements and also a gesture toward social justice as they became Olympians despite regulations on their bodies. "'Gesture' can signal both those defined movements that we make with our bodies and to which we assign meaning, and an action that extends beyond itself, that reaches, suggests, motions; an action that signals its desire to act, perhaps to touch" (Rodríguez, 2014, p. 2). The athletes tendered four of the world's top five women's 400-meter times in 2021 (Granville, 2021).

EJ: They broke the national record three times this year.

Therefore, in "an action that signals its desire to act" (Rodríguez, 2014, p. 2), the runners targeted the 400-meter races in the summer 2020 Tokyo Olympics and were serious medal contenders. Mboma "clocked 48.54 for the 400m at a meet in Poland in June, the fastest time of the season" (AFP, 2021) and set the world's under-age-20 record. Masilingi ranked third in 2021 (Shapiro, 2021) behind Mboma and second-place Olympic race champion Shaunae Miller-Uibo from the Bahamas.

EJ: *They qualified for the Olympics.*

"Gestures emphasize the mobile spaces of interpretation between actions and meaning" (Rodríguez, 2014, p. 2). The meaning of Olympic qualification is a gesture of transnational empowerment.

EJ: So, what we've done is we've tried to, to really push their story and their narrative to say, "Look; look at these girls; they're doing really well; help them prepare for the Olympics."

Johannes continued praising their ability. His assertion about their accomplishments demonstrates how impactful these runners were on Namibian sport and media. Masilingi and Mboma became exemplars of transnational success stories. Johannes seemed aware of his impact as a media arbitrator and curator of the sport pages.

EJ: They've been on the front pages and, and the back pages on the regular.

Describing the athletes' success instigates audiences to think about them as success stories.

EJ: They're shining. So, it's not, like, "Oh, we're feeling sorry for them." No. They're earning this, this space. They are earning that, that space on the front and the back page. They, they earned it through their hard work and, obviously, their achievements.

Unfortunately, Mboma and Masilingi's trajectory was rerouted. On July 2, 2021, in a statement posted on Facebook, the Namibia National Olympic Committee (NNOC) and Commonwealth Games Association reported that World Athletics, the international sports governing body, required the two Namibians to undergo medical assessments per procedures outlined the "Athletes with Differences of Sex Development" policy (Namibia National Olympic Committee, 2021). The evaluation, conducted at a training camp in Italy, concluded that Mboma and Masilingi have "naturally high testosterone levels" (Namibia National Olympic Committee, 2021). The Facebook statement indicated: "It is important to understand that both our athletes were not aware of this condition, neither did any family member, their coach or the NNOC-CGA" (Namibia National Olympic Committee, 2021). The pair had never evaluated their testosterone levels before; "they had no reason to think their hormone levels were not within the typical range" (Granville, 2021). Both athletes reported "shock" (Granville, 2021) at the assessment's results. In its statement, the NNOC said:

> We will analyse all information and apply it in the best interest of those two young girls. We are positive on their future as elite athletes. This should not be viewed negatively but rather as a new challenge and opportunity. Both Christine and Beatrice will be able to compete in the 100m and 200m events. Henk Botha, their coach is positive to continue working with the girls on those events while we are consolidating on the way forward.
>
> (Namibia National Olympic Committee, 2021)

Thus, their track to Olympic medals in the 400-meter abruptly halted. World Athletics banned them from running in 400-meter to 1,600-meter races, including the 400-meter races, 400-meter hurdles races, 800-meter races, 1500-meter races, one-mile races, and all other track events with distances between 400 meters and one mile. Mboma was with her and Masilingi's coach, Botha, traveling back to Italy when Botha told Mboma the news after the NNOC called him. By the time the coach called Masilingi, she had already learned about the ruling on social media (Granville, 2021).

Therefore, World Athletics disqualified Mboma and Masilingi from running in their preferred event due to their naturally high testosterone levels. While they could still compete in the 100-meter and 200-meter races, they would have had to take testosterone-suppressing measures to stay in the other events. "These athletes are banned from competing at certain events unless they agree to artificially lower their testosterone through medication or surgery, an option for which there is currently no scientific data on the long-term effects" (Adom-Aboagye, 2021). Asking athletes to take medication to alter a body they are happy with is arguably unjust. "I would ruin the way my body develops because that'll be something that rearranges everything – how my body functions and everything," Masilingi said in an interview (Granville, 2021). "I wouldn't want to involve any other things because this is the way my body functions in its normal way. And if I try something else, I might get caught somewhere else, and something might go wrong with my body" (Granville, 2021).

As the media described, the presence of both women "reopened debate about track and field's complex rules regarding women born with elevated testosterone" (AFP, 2021). Headlines like "Namibian medallist reopens athletics' intersex' debate" (AFP, 2021) puts the athletes' bodies as back-page news above the fold in the Sports section in full color. As a case study, I consider the news source *The Guardian*, published in Isolo, Nigeria. I selected this piece as an example of inclusive language reform and nuanced media coverage. The article systematically reflected on dubious athletic inclusion policies. "I would love to compete in the 400m as well," Masilingi was quoted to have said in *The Guardian* interview (AFP, 2021). She continued, "It is very strange. I don't really understand it. For me, it doesn't make any sense at the moment. I hope there will be changes in the future" (AFP, 2021). Despite the ruling, Mboma and Masilingi excelled at the 2020 Tokyo Olympics. The media described Mboma as producing one of the games' most "eye-catching performances" (AFP, 2021). As she moved up from the fifth place in the home stretch, "she began screaming in what appeared to be a mix of exertion and elation" (Cacciola & Longman, 2021). She surged through the women's 200-meter field to claim the silver medal in 21.81 seconds (AFP, 2021), which became the world record for the fastest time run by an under-20-year-old woman (Cacciola & Longman, 2021). Mboma finished the race second after Elaine Thompson-Herah of Jamaica. Masilingi finished sixth and earned a spot in the 200m final in her first major championships. "Gesture" (Rodríguez, 2014) can frame athletes' experience in literal body movements and a gesture toward social justice. Mboma and Masilingi are indeed flourishing despite sovereign regulations on intersex people. They became national treasures in Namibia and continued to rise in popularity transnationally. The BBC voted Mboma as African Sports Personality of the Year for 2021. She became the first woman to win the accolade.

International media, mixed in with celebrating their achievements, ruminated on a question like one previously posed in this chapter: Who prescribes the parameters of the intersex spectrum in sport?

> Mboma's silver medal raised a question: Does the supposed significant physiological advantage gained by intersex athletes begin after 399 meters? Or is the science relied on by World Athletics to institute its restrictions flawed and in need of re-evaluation or expansion to include other running events?
>
> (Cacciola & Longman, 2021)

A governing body decided that Mboma and Masilingi had intersex conditions even though they had never previously identified as intersex.

The 2020 Tokyo Olympics became the first Olympics where openly transgender and nonbinary athletes competed. However, the profusely criticized sex-gender testing model still regulated those summer games. On November 16, 2021, the International Olympic Committee (IOC) released the "IOC Framework on Fairness, Inclusion and Non-Discrimination on the Basis of Gender Identity and Sex Variations" (International Olympic Committee, 2021) report to fortify equitable athletic inclusion. The IOC endorsed an inclusion policy that promotes bodily autonomy. It states that international federations, sports organizations, or any other entity should not pressure or coerce athletes to undergo medically unnecessary procedures or treatments to meet eligibility requirements. It also declares that eligibility criteria for gender categories should not encompass gynecological examinations or invasive physical examinations deployed to ascertain an athlete's sex or gender. The policy also promotes intersex education and training for sport organizations, coaches, managers, and other affiliated individuals to impart comprehensive knowledge, prevent harmful interpretations of eligibility criteria, and lead to a more inclusive and welcoming sports environment for intersex athletes.

Then, in a press release published on March 23, 2023, World Athletics announced a new policy to be implemented on March 31, 2023, which would stipulate that, to participate in the female category, intersex athletes must maintain a testosterone concentration below the threshold of 2.5 nanomoles per liter (nmol/L) for a minimum period of 24 months prior to engaging in international competitions "in any event, not just the events that were restricted (400m to one mile) under the previous regulations" (World Athletics, 2023). Some researchers say the discriminatory policy is not evidence-based (Ortega, 2023). A CNN article quoted the founder and executive director of advocacy group Athlete Ally, Hudson Taylor, to have said: "We are beyond devastated to see World Athletics succumbing to political pressure instead of core principles of inclusion, fairness and nondiscrimination for transgender athletes and athletes with intersex variations" (Morse, 2023). He said the new directives "do nothing to address what we know to be the actual, proven threats to women's sports: unequal pay, rampant sexual abuse and harassment, lack of women in leadership and inequities in resources for women athletes" (Morse, 2023). Further, the decision could thwart research on the topic because athletes who are intersex "who wish to compete will have to manipulate their hormone levels by lowering them, thereby complicating research endeavors" (Ortega, 2023).

Namibian Oral Histories on Caster Semenya

The most internationally recognized intersex athlete is Caster Semenya, the South African runner and two-time Olympic 800-meter champion. Her biological body elicits scrutiny because of her testosterone levels (Longman & Macur, 2019). Semenya failed twice in legal bids to overturn the World Athletics rules (AFP, 2021). In 2018, the year after I completed my first field visit, World Athletics banned Semenya from competing after it ruled that "to ensure fair competition, women with high natural testosterone levels must take medication to reduce them to compete in middle-distance races" (Granville, 2021). She took her case to the European Court of Human Rights in a final attempt to reverse the regulations (AFP, 2021). In 2019, the Court of Arbitration for Sport (CAS) ruled that Semenya would still have to take a supplement to decrease the natural testosterone levels in her body. In a 2-to-1 decision, CAS ruled that restrictions on permitted levels of naturally occurring testosterone were discriminatory. However, it also ruled that such discrimination was a "necessary, reasonable and proportionate means" to preserve the "integrity of female competition" (Longman & Macur, 2019). Semenya could not defend her middle-distance title in her signature 800-meter event at the summer 2020 Tokyo Olympics because she refused medication to reduce her naturally occurring testosterone (AFP, 2021).

Namibia and South Africa's histories deeply connect. South Africa enacted its apartheid regime in Namibia after the Union of South Africa, which was part of the British Empire, took over its administration (Chappell, 2005). After a struggle beginning in 1966, Namibia finally earned independence on March 21, 1990. During my first field visit in 2017, I learned about Namibia's stance on intersex athletes. I asked journalism professionals and members of the LGBTQI+ community about Semenya. On July 18, 2017, at an LGBTQI+ safehouse, I asked Randy, a youth athlete and transgender man, if he was familiar with Semenya.

R: I know her!
TM: Oh, okay!
R: I watch her every day on sports.

Randy and I meaningfully connected despite a partial language barrier. I asked Randy to describe his perspective on Semenya.

R: Me, myself, think about that person. She is a very courageous person; that I know.

He continued:

R: Ya, she is a good person.

Namibian support for Semenya consistently resurfaced in my interviews. On July 17, 2017, I asked Charles Shikongo, a newspaper managing editor who later became editor-in-chief for another daily, how Namibia regarded Semenya and her quandary.

CS: That was a, a couple of years ago now, especially when it first made its prominence, but, um, I think, being a Black majority country, it was a lot of support here for her. People believing that, uh, right-rightly or wrongly, that she was a victim of, of racism, basically.

By encouraging the publics to explore a radicalized intersex body in a sporting space, media outlets who feature her are critically engaging with audiences to decolonize uncivilized views of the Black body (Johnson & Rivera-Servera, 2016).

CS: We had people especially the, the, the, the right activists who were saying, but maybe – because of eventually she married, she married eh, eh, a woman. And, uh, well, I say, but, you know, the right activist were saying, "But, you know, since when is being homosexual a crime?" Of course, in Namibia, it's not recognized. Homosexuality: it is not, is not recognized in Namibia. That's why people go and marry, marry in Cape Town, where it is recognized, and they come back with their spouses here.

Semenya's performance of Black intersex lesbianism in sport regulatory spaces illustrates her striving for self-determination sovereignty while challenging hegemonic masculinity and trans(homo)nationalism (Puar, 2015). Semenya extends her positions on identity and body by focusing on the body in performance (Johnson & Rivera-Servera, 2016).

CS: She is discriminated because she is African. She is being discriminated because she's uh, she's Black, uh, and if, if she's homosexual, I mean, what she does in her bedroom is entirely up to her. Uh, that was the, the dominant theme really around here. Um, people are just proud of her. Maybe voices of descent once, once in a while, but I think the, the dominant view was that, a, that there was a lot of support.

This framing exhibits Semenya's status as an exemplar: the "dominant theme," he said, is that "people are just proud of her." Exemplars function as representatives of a larger group (Gamson & Lasch, 1981) who could contribute to the publics' semantic memories of intersex people. Coupled with escalated salience, a memory of Semenya as a primary exemplar in media for intersex inclusion in sport will increase the likelihood that viewers will store a frame about her in their semantic memory (Nicely, 2007; Scheufele, 2000; Entman, 1993). During our July 17, 2017, interview, I also asked Johannes about the dialogue and reaction to Semenya.

EJ: It was small (exaggerates this word). It was; people didn't really take it as serious as other places.
TM: Oh, okay.
EJ: It was more the... humor factor.
TM: Really?

EJ: You would find the people who were concerned, and who: one or two spoke out publicly about it, saying, "Look, that person should be, shouldn't be subjected to such treatment; it's not of their own doing." You know?

TM: Right.

EJ: But above and beyond, um, no. There wasn't much interest in whether Caster is a woman or a man. It was just the humor, you know, that came with it.

I revisited the conversation with Johannes on May 7, 2021. I asked him to detail the general impression of and support for Semenya at that time.

EJ: You have, uh, the, the people who say the positive stuff where they understand where she's coming from and that it's none of her doing, really. She didn't choose to be the way she is. Then, you find the idiots who constantly happen about, "yeah, that she is more man than she is female," what, what, what, you know? It's, so, it's, it's … uh, it's not really 50–50. They're more of the naysayers than the people who understand what's going on. I think that's a, a lack of understanding that these people to make those sort of comments. I think if someone really sits down or if they take the time to get to know what the issue is, maybe they'll also understand that what Caster is fighting for.

A shift transpired from 2017, when Johannes reported that a "humor factor" led the narrative about Semenya, to 2021 when he called the "naysayers" "idiots" who have a "lack of understanding." This move illustrates how African sport media could function as social justice warriors and champions for intersex athletes by circulating ethical and factual education. Later, he said:

EJ: I think if you're identifying as a woman, then you know, or female, they may this way, case closed, really.

We also talked a bit about diverse ways to categorize bodies in sport.

EJ: Then you find some people having the conversation about … even here, they started talking about having, uh, races for people who don't conform to either male or female.

TM: Yeah.

EJ: But then that's going to make it a bit more complex again.

TM: Oh yeah.

EJ:　Then you still have someone who has a bit too much of this and a bit too little of this.

TM:　Yeah.

EJ:　I think if you're identifying as a woman then, you know, or female, they are made this way. Case closed, really. [Returning to Semenya] I just feel if, if you took anything other than your natural ability to enhance your ability, then, then it's an issue. If you did not, then I don't see why it should be an issue.

Yet, the debate still exists. On June 29, 2017, activist and transgender women Celine said in, "our neighboring country, South Africa, Caster Semenya had issues." She said that Namibia "wouldn't deal with it the way South Africa did" if a Namibian athlete were in Semenya's position. "They would have issues with it here, and, yeah, I, I think it would be a challenge for them."

In a July 17, 2017, interview, a then-graduate student at the University of Namibia and former sports journalist Bella Paulus said she discussed Semenya "with my male counterparts."

BP:　It's such an unfortunate, like the commissioner said, that it, that she is now being, sort of, disadvantaged because of her muscles.

She referenced our chat with the Namibian Sports Commission (NSC) chief administrator, whom I interviewed earlier that day. Paulus sat in on the interview. After the chief administrator told me that he did not know of any intersex athletes in Namibia, I asked him what would happen if an intersex athlete participated in Namibian sport.

CAM:　It was very much unfortunate, you know, because if you just look at, eh, God created the human being, and you look at the face, then you all the sudden when a person, eh, with muscles who, who must now try to descr – to give a description about a, a woman with a lot of muscles. I mean, that description, I mean, it's only God Himself who must make that description. Yes.

The chief administrator relied on the Christian narrative that was traditionally oppressive to the LGBTQI+ population. Most often, my narrators, even when more ambiguous, predominantly supported Semenya, who has not taken any measures to change her body. I wonder if his sentiments would diverge now that Namibia has two prominent athletes with intersex variations.

On July 17, 2017, I met with Geoffrey Petrus, a sports journalist at another newspaper, and asked him to describe the consensuses of Semenya.

GP: They talking about, they want him to reduce some of his hormones, sort of. I don't know how, but. Okay, with Caster, it's ... I don't know; I don't know if it's a "she" or a "he."

TM: She's a "she."

GP: Okay, that's, a, correct because other South Africans. But, if the person is born like that, I don't see. And the reason for somebody really to become a, a debatable issue if the person is born as a female. So, it is all about political leaning for me, just a politic thing. Because if the person is a "she," she is a "she." Whatever she uses or she go to the gym to ... or whatever. As long as she, she is not using any substances that bends or, or medication or whatever they use to increase whatever. But if the person is doing the right thing. I don't really follow South African, ya.

He continued.

GP: And that also discourage other women who are, like, in Caster's situation, that will look at, "No, man, I can't take up sport," although that person is talented. So, with all these issues that is ongoing, I think it's just tarnishing the image of those that wants to come into the sport who are in that situation. You never know; there may be someone like Caster again in South Africa.

We chatted about the prospect of Namibian athletes having a similar experience to Semenya.

GP: Ya, because in Namibia, we, we have not really experienced such a person. Na, not that I know of. Ya, not yet.

Other narrators also disclosed that the country had not witnessed a prominent, publicized case about intersex athletes from Namibia. As we now know, later, such a circumstance transpired.

Fueling the Conversation

Power domination reproduces in various locations using recognizable apparatuses and mechanisms of control (hooks, 1992). Media is a subject with power (Foucault, 1982). A newspaper is a recognizable apparatus that disseminates power. Sport is the location. Media can influence the salience of topics on the public agenda (McCombs & Shaw, 1972). Audiences regard prominently covered issues as significant and consider minimized frames as insignificant. Stories of female athletes found to have unusually high testosterone levels are prolific (AFP, 2021; Cacciola &

Longman, 2021; Granville, 2021). Media power narratives should highlight that World Athletics only tested athletes when someone questioned their testosterone levels, which is a fact that requires further deconstruction and critique in media. The media need to question what this policy means in terms of feminist activism and fairness.

Borrowing from Mbembe, I considered, "what is at stake in writing about Africa" (Shipley, 2010, p. 656) and intersex athletes while writing this chapter on African media representation and identities. Mbembe says, "to write the world from Africa or to write Africa into the world or as a fragment thereof is a compelling, exhilarating, and, most of the time, perplexing task" (Shipley, 2010, p. 656). Namibian sport media can shape social change and developments in Africa by reporting on underrepresented athletic populations. On May 7, 2021, Johannes said that the media's role in promoting women's sport is a prerequisite.

EJ: Our job is to highlight, um, every time there is an event involving the girl child, we have to shine a spotlight on it. We have to bring it out, and people must see it. It must be in people's faces every other day. That way, they get accustomed to the idea that, "Oh, girls are also really cool when it comes to sports," or "Let's go check them out; let's support them," that kind of thing. Otherwise, if we keep ignoring them and, you know, we don't give them as much attention as the guys do. Like, say, on the back page, you keep putting them in the inside pages and all that small little story to say, "Oh, yeah, by the way, Emily did well yesterday." No, you must put Emily on the back or the front.

He asserts that the media's job is "to shine a spotlight on" women athletes. Hence, readers "get accustomed to the idea that" women's sport is formidable. As linguistic determinism postulates, language could influence non-linguistic behavior, such as memory, perception, categorization, and thinking (Hickmann, 2000). Media consumers could be, for example, business professionals who can grant sponsorships or fund athletes so they can afford to continue their sport.

EJ: That's the only way we can help other people understand that the girls also need attention.

The operation of discourse formulates knowledge. Mboma, Masilingi, and Semenya bestow media the opportunity to confront conversations about sex disparity in sport. African media has a front seat in this international debate. Having well-trained and knowledgeable media would help audiences navigate their thoughts, feelings, and actions more clearly and ethically.

The more education African media practitioners have on intersexuality in sport, the more honorably they can report on it. In Namibia, knowledge about the issue marginally shifted between 2017 and 2021. Activists exercising their voices and platforms, researchers studying media power and gender relations, and media producers focusing on equitable athletic inclusion facilitated increasingly socially just mindsets. Knowledge about intersexuality in sport is still evolving. Further multidisciplinary research is obligatory. However, inclusive dialogue that once only lived in feminist scholarship has now extended into many disciplines and discourses.

Queering, decolonizing, and dismantling binary language in sports and journalism could help undo pervasive stereotypes. Queering media and sport media studies help question the social and scientific justification engrained in the traditional athletic sex-binary structure. Queer scholars argue that gender is an arbitrary arrangement (Halberstam, 2005). Gender suggests socially constructed attributes (Butler, 1988). Decolonizing the relationship between gender and sport imagines alternatives to the antiquated two-sex system and challenges archaically established norms of sex segregation. Researchers suggest genitalia are unrelated to athletic performance (Griffin & Carroll, 2010), gender identities are fluid (Halberstam, 2005) and the sex-segregation in sport is socially exclusionary (Travers, 2014). They also argue that a sex dichotomy in sport is scientifically problematic. It sets up perceived variance between women and men that is not biological or natural (West & Zimmerman, 1987). "Any attempt to separate the sexes for sport by use of black and white constructs of maleness/femaleness creates more problems than it solves. Chromosome screens imposed these cut and dried distinctions, which simply do not exist biologically" (Carlson, 2005, p. s40).

According to Foucault, power is a network of relations that operate in ordering institutions, normalizing procedures, disciplining practices, and positioning bodies in space. Researchers find "a widening discursive gap within and between the biomedical discourse and the subjective psychosocial discourse on the meaning of intersex bodies and body–gender relations" (Danon, 2022, p. 220). On the one hand, "biomedical discourse assumes that human bodies evolve into two sexes, male or female, and two genders, woman or man, and that the essence of masculinity and femininity is explained and manifested through genes and hormones" (Danon, 2022, p. 220). On the other side, subjective psychosocial discourse says that biological sex (Fausto-Sterling, 2000) and gender identities (Butler, 1990) are dynamically fluid and established through social power relations (Foucault, 1978), interactions, and political interests (Danon, 2022). The true turmoil is when these scientific facts and ideas of social inclusion strive to dismantle a high-engrained and colonized, capitalistic, and religious-based two-sex system that infiltrates our daily lives and the basketball court. Binary sex segregation is pervasive. "Intersex traits show that trying to sort all human bodies into two categories is not simple" (interACT: Advocates for Intersex Youth, 2021). As Dannon (2022) notes, researchers conducted studies about "sex hormones" and "sex chromosomes," or karyotypes, not on humans but on animals. "Although intersex bodies signify how biological sex can exist in multiple and varied ways, they continued to be studied and perceived as nature's 'error,' an approach that reinforces the binary of human biological sex" (Danon, 2022, p. 222). Intersexuality is not an error. It is a naturally occurring biological normality. Traditionally, sport organizations have exploited sex-based distinctions to justify forced segregation in a biopolitical attempt to assert power over athletes (Carlson, 2005). Now, we see the potential for movement toward change.

Note

1 The names of all the interviewees in this chapter were changed to preserve their anonymity.

References

Adom-Aboagye, N. (2021, August 6). Olympics: Namibia's sprinters highlight a flawed testosterone testing system. Retrieved from *The Conversation*: https://theconversation.com/olympics-namibias-sprinters-highlight-a-flawed-testosterone-testing-system-165676

AFP (2021, August 4). Namibian medallist reopens athletics "intersex" debate. Retrieved from *The Guardian*: https://guardian.ng/sport/namibian-medallist-reopens-athletics-intersex-debate/

Beauvoir, S. (1949). *The second sex* (T. C. Malovany-Chevallier, Trans.). Paris: Éditions Gallimard.

Butler, J. (1988). Performative acts and gender constitution: An essay in phenomenology and feminist theory. *Theatre Journal*, 40(4), 519–531.

Butler, J. (1990). *Gender trouble: Feminism and the subversion of identity*. New York, New York: Routledge.

Cacciola, S., & Longman, J. (2021, August 3). Barred From 400 Meters, Namibia's Mboma Wins Silver in the 200. Retrieved from *The New York Times*: www.nytimes.com/2021/08/03/sports/olympics/olympics-testosterone-namibia.html

Carlson, A. (2005, December). Suspect sex. *The Lancet: Special Issue: Medicine and Sport*, 366, s39–s40.

Chandler, D. (2016). *Semiotics for Beginners*. Retrieved from https://visual-memory.co.uk/daniel/Documents/S4B

Chappell, R. (2005). Sport in Namibia: Conflicts, Negotiations and Struggles since Independence. *International Review for the Sociology of Sport*, 4(2), 241–254.

Danon, L. M. (2022). The geneticisation of intersex bodies in Israel. In M. Walker (ed.), *Interdisciplinary and Global Perspectives on Intersex* (pp. 219–239). Cham, Switzerland: Palgrave Macmillan.

Dreyfus, H. L., & Rabinow, P. (1982). *Michel Foucault: Beyond structuralism and hermeneutics.* Chicago: The University of Chicago Press.

Duranti, A. (1997). *Linguistic anthropology.* West Nyack, GB: Cambridge University Press.

Entman, R. M. (1993). Framing: Toward clarification of a fractured paradigm. *Journal of Communication, 43*(4), 51–58.

Fausto-Sterling, A. (2000). *Sexing the body: Gender politics and the construction of sexuality.* New York: Basic Books.

Foucault, M. (1978). *The history of sexuality,* vol. I: *An introduction.* New York: Pantheon Books.

Foucault, M. (1982, Summer). The subject and power. *Critical Inquiry, 8*(4), 777–795.

Fraser, S. (2016). Constructing the female body: Using female genital mutilation law to address genital-normalizing surgery on intersex children in the United States. *International Journal of Human Rights in Healthcare, 9*(1), 62–72.

Frisch, M. H. (1990). *A shared authority: Essays on the craft and meaning of oral and public history.* Albany: State University of New York Press.

Frydman, J. (2011). A critical analysis of Namibia's English-only language policy. *Selected Proceedings of the 40th Annual Conference on African Linguistics* (pp. 178–189). Somerville, MA: Cascadilla Proceedings Project.

Gamson, W. A., & Lasch, K. E. (1981). *The political culture of social welfare policy.* University of Michigan, Center for Research on Social Organization.

Granville, S. (2021, July 7). Namibian teens vow to fight Olympics testosterone ban. Retrieved from BBC: www.bbc.com/news/world-africa-57748135

Griffin, P., & Carroll, H. J. (2010). *On the team: Equal opportunities for transgender student athletes.* National Center of Lesbian Right and Women's Sports Foundation.

Halberstam, J. (2005). *Queer time and place: Transgender bodies, subcultural lives.* New York University Press.

Hickmann, M. (2000). Linguistic relativity and linguistic determinism: Some new directions. *Linguistics, 38*(2), 409–434.

Hooks, B. (1992). The Oppositional Gaze: Black Female Spectators. In *Black looks: Race and representation* (pp. 115–131). Boston, MA: South End Press.

interACT: Advocates for Intersex Youth (2021, January 26). *FAQ: What is intersex?* Retrieved from interACT: Advocates for Intersex Youth: https://interactadvocates.org/faq/

interACT: Advocates for Intersex Youth (2022, March 13). *Media guide: Covering the intersex community.* Retrieved from interAct: Advocates for Intersex Youth: https://secureservercdn.net/198.71.233.216/7np.6b9.myftpupload.com/wp-content/uploads/2017/01/INTERSEX-MEDIAGUIDE-interACT.pdf

International Olympic Committee (2021, November 16). IOC releases Framework on Fairness, Inclusion and Non-discrimination on the basis of gender identity and sex variations. Retrieved from International Olympic Committee: olympics.com/ioc/news/ioc-releases-framework-on-fairness-inclusion-and-non-discrimination-on-the-basis-of-gender-identity-and-sex-variations

Intersex Society of North America (2008). *What is intersex?.* Retrieved from Intersex Society of North America: https://isna.org/faq/what_is_intersex

Johnson, E. P., & Rivera-Servera, R. H. (eds) (2016). *Blacktino queer performance.* Durham: Duke University Press.

Karkazis, K., & Jordan-Young, R. M. (2018). The powers of testosterone: obscuring race and regional bias in the regulation of women athletes. *Feminist Formations, Summer,* 1–39.

Longman, J., & Macur, J. (2019, May 1). Caster Semenya Loses Case to Compete as a Woman in All Races. Retrieved from *The New York Times:* www.nytimes.com/2019/05/01/sports/caster-semenya-loses.html

Lucas-Carr, C. B., & Krane, V. (2011). What is the T in LGBT? Supporting transgender athletes through sport psychology. *The Sport Psychologist,* 532–548.

McCombs, M. E., & Shaw, D. L. (1972, Summer). The agenda-setting function of the mass media. *The Public Opinion Quarterly, 36*(2), 176–187.

Morse, B. (2023, March 24). *World Athletics tightens rules on transgender women athletes.* Retrieved from CNN: www.cnn.com/2023/03/23/sport/world-athletics-transgender-ruling-spt-intl/index.html

Namibia National Olympic Committee (2021, July 2). *Namibia National Olympic Committee.* Retrieved from Facebook: www.facebook.com/NamOlympic/photos/a.828366073847470/4770073503010021/

Nicely, S. (2007). *Media framing of female athletes and women's sports in selected sports magazines.* Georgia State University, Department of Communication. Atlanta: ScholarWorks.

Nordqvist, C. (2015, October 29). What is the difference between sex and gender? Retrieved from *Medical News Today:* www.medicalnewstoday.com/articles/232363.php

Oral History Association (2018, October). *OHA Principles and Best Practices.* Retrieved from Oral History Association: www.oralhistory.org/principles-and-best-practices-revised-2018/

Ortega, R. P. (2023, April 4). World Athletics banned transgender women from competing. Does science support the rule? Retrieved from Science: www.science.org/content/article/world-athletics-banned-transgender-women-competing-does-science-support-rule#:~:text=How%20will%20WA's%20decision%20affect,has%20already%20adopted%20WA's%20rule

Paechter, C. (2021). The rights and interests of trans and intersex children: considerations, conflicts and implications in relation to the UNCRC. *Journal of Gender Studies, 30*(7), 844–854.

Puar, J. (2007). *Terrorist assemblages: Homonationalism in queer times.* Durham, NC: Duke University Press.

Puar, J. (2015). Bodies with new organs: Becoming trans, becoming disabled. *Social Text, 3*(124), 45–73.

Rabinow, P. (ed.). (1984). *The Foucault reader.* New York: Pantheon Books.

Rada, J. A., & Wulfemeyer, K. T. (2005). Color coded: Racial descriptors in television coverage of intercollegiate sports. *Journal of Broadcasting & Electronic Media, 49*(1), 65–85.

Reporters Without Borders. (2023, January 29). *Namibia.* Retrieved from Reporters Without Borders: https://rsf.org/en/index

Rifkin, M. (2011). The erotics of sovereignty. In Q.-L. Driskill, C. Finley, B. J. Gilley, & S. L. Morgensen (eds), *Queer indigenous studies: Critical interventions in theory, politics, and literature* (pp. 172–189). Tucson, Arizona: The University of Arizona Press.

Rodríguez, J. M. (2014). *Sexual futures, queer gestures, and other latina longings.* New York: NYU Press.

Ryan, K. M. (2020). *Pin Up! The subculture: Negotiating agency, representation, and sexuality with vintage style.* New York: Peter Lang.

Sandberg, K. (2015). The rights of LGBTI children under the convention of the rights of the child. *Nordic Journal of Human Rights, 33*(4), 337–352.

Saussure, F. (1916). *Course in general linguistics (Cours de linguistique générale).* (C. Bally, & A. Sechehaye, eds)

Scheufele, D. A. (2000). Agenda-setting, priming, and framing revisited: Another look at cognitive effects of political communication. *Mass Communication and Society, 2*(2/3), 297–316.

Shapiro, M. (2021, July 2). Namibia Sprinters Banned from Events Due to Elevated Testosterone. Retrieved from *Sports Illustrated*: www.si.com/olympics/2021/07/02/namibia-sprinters-banned-olympic-events-elevated-testosterone

Shipley, J. W. (2010, Summer). Africa in Theory: A Conversation Between Jean Comaroff and Achille Mbembe. *Anthropological Quarterly, 83*(3), 653–678.

Squire, L. R., Knowlton, B., & Musen, G. (1993). The structure and organization of memory. *Annual Review of Psychology, 44*, 453–495.

Travers, A. (2014). Sports. *TSQ: Transgender Studies, 1*, 194–196. Durham, NC: Duke University Press.

West, C., & Zimmerman, D. H. (1987). Doing gender. *Gender and Society, 1*(2), 125–151.

World Athletics. (2023, March 23). World Athletics Council decides on Russia, Belarus and female eligibility. Retrieved from World Athletics: https://worldathletics.org/news/press-releases/council-meeting-march-2023-russia-belarus-female-eligibility

Index

For Product Safety Concerns and Information please contact our EU
representative GPSR@taylorandfrancis.com Taylor & Francis Verlag GmbH,
Kaufingerstraße 24, 80331 München, Germany

Printed and bound by CPI Group (UK) Ltd, Croydon, CR0 4YY
01/05/2025
01858371-0001